FREUD
Appraisals and Reappraisals

Contributions to Freud Studies
Volume 1

Anna von Lieben, circa 1883
(Collection of Peter J. Swales)

FREUD

Appraisals and Reappraisals

Contributions to Freud Studies
Volume 1

EDITED BY
PAUL E. STEPANSKY

THE ANALYTIC PRESS

The Analytic Press

Distributed solely by

Lawrence Erlbaum Associates, Inc., Publishers
365 Broadway
Hillsdale, New Jersey 07642

Library of Congress Cataloging in Publication Data
Main entry under title:

Freud, appraisals and reappraisals.

Bibliography: p.
Includes index.
1. Freud, Sigmund, 1856–1939. 2. Psychoanalysis.
I. Stepansky, Paul E.
BF173.F85F727 1986   150.19′52   85-22814
ISBN 0-88163-038-1 (v. 1)

Printed in the United States of America
10   9   8   7   6   5   4   3   2   1

Contents

Acknowledgments

Nick Cariello did his usual superb job of line editing the manuscripts comprising this volume, and I echo the sentiments of all the contributors in thanking him for his clarifying input and finely honed red pencil. Two of the major essays in this volume, those of Peter Swales and Barry Silverstein, are outgrowths of papers first presented to the Section of Psychiatric History of the Department of Psychiatry, Cornell University Medical College; it is fitting, therefore, that I take this opportunity to thank the Section, and especially its director, Dr. Eric T. Carlson, not only for providing a forum for recent contributions to Freud Studies, but for warmly supportive interest in the work of younger scholars whose subject matter includes psychoanalytic history, to be sure, but traverses applied analysis, history of psychiatry, and history of medicine as well. Lastly, a special word of thanks to my wife, Deane Rand Stepansky, and my sons, Michael David Stepansky and Jonathan Peter Stepansky. Their unwavering support of both my scholarship and my editorial work goes without saying. Here I thank them more especially for collectively providing a milieu in which the demands of both endeavors, however great, always seem eminently tolerable and well worth the yield.

Contributors

JOHN E. GEDO, M.D., Training and Supervising Analyst at the Chicago Institute for Psychoanalysis, is coeditor (with George Pollock) of *Freud: The Fusion of Science and Humanism* (1976). Previous contributions to the theory and practice of psychoanalysis include *Beyond Interpretation: Toward a Revised Theory for Psychoanalysis* (1979); *Advances in Clinical Psychoanalysis* (1981); *Portraits of the Artist: Psychoanalysis of Creativity and Its Vicissitudes* (1983); and *Psychoanalysis and Its Discontents* (1984). His forthcoming volume, *Conceptual Issues in Psychoanalysis: Essays in History and Method,* will be published by The Analytic Press in 1986. Dr. Gedo is Clinical Professor of Psychiatry, Abraham Lincoln School of Medicine, University of Illinois.

PATRICK J. MAHONY, Ph.D. is Professor of English Literature at the University of Montreal and a member of the Canadian, American, and International Psychoanalytic Associations. Following publication of *Freud as Writer* (1982), he turned his attention to Freud's major case studies, offering commentaries that combine historical, psychoanalytic, and textual analyses (of the German) of Freud's presentations. The initial products of this integrative approach are *Cries of the Wolfman* (1984) and *The Catch Between Freud and the Ratman,* to be published in 1986.

BARRY SILVERSTEIN, M.A. is Professor of Psychology at William Patterson College and coauthor (with Ronald Krate) of *Children of the Dark Ghetto: A Developmental Psychology* (1975). A developmental psychologist by training, Professor Silverstein has pursued scholarly work in Freud studies in recent years. He is currently exploring two topics in the early history of psychoanalysis:

the role of personal and extratheoretical factors in Freud's theory formation, of which his contribution to this volume is an example; and the relationship between the psychological and the organic in Freud's early work, as represented in his recent article, "Freud's Psychology and Its Organic Foundation: Sexuality and Mind-Body Interactionism" (1985).

PAUL E. STEPANSKY, Ph.D. is Editor-in-Chief, The Analytic Press, and Research Associate, Department of Psychiatry, Cornell University Medical College. He also works as a private consulting editor for psychoanalysts throughout the country. He is the author of *A History of Aggression in Freud* (1977) and *In Freud's Shadow: Adler in Context* (1983), and coeditor (with Arnold Goldberg) of *Kohut's Legacy: Contributions to Self Psychology* (1984). He collaborated with Dr. Goldberg in the editorial preparation of the late Heinz Kohut's final book, *How Does Analysis Cure?* (1984).

PETER J. SWALES has pursued archival research of the early life and work of Freud and the origins of psychoanalysis for the past 11 years. He lectures extensively and has written numerous articles exploring the personal, familial, and historical circumstances attending the birth of analysis. His comprehensive biography of Wilhelm Fliess, *Wilhelm Fliess: Freud's OTHER—A Biography,* will be published in 1986. He is currently a Ph.D. Candidate and Teaching Assistant, Department of Philosophy, Rutgers University.

EDWIN R. WALLACE, IV, M.D., a psychiatrist and historian of medicine, has major contributions in the areas of psychiatric education (*Dynamic Psychiatry in Theory and Practice* [1983]), Freud Studies (*Freud and Anthropology: A History and Reappraisal* [1983]), and psychoanalytic epistemology (*Historiography and Causation in Psychoanalysis* [1985]). His editorial projects include *Essays in the History of Psychiatry* (with Lucius Pressley) (1983) and the forthcoming *Handbook of the History of Psychiatry* (with John Gach). Dr. Wallace is Director of Psychotherapy Education and Associate Professor of Psychiatry, the Medical College of Georgia.

Series Introduction

The era of "Freud studies" was upon us even before Freud's death. As early as 1923, Freud chided his sometime follower, Fritz Wittels, for an early examination of "Freud: His Personality, His Teaching, and His School" that fell considerably wide of the mark. "It seems to me that the world has no claim on my person," he wrote Wittels, "and that it will learn nothing from me so long as my case (for manifold reasons) cannot be made fully transparent" (18 December 1923, in E. Freud, 1960, p. 346). It was in obvious recognition of this fact that Arnold Zweig, admiring correspondent of Freud's later years, confessed to his "Dear Father Freud" several months before the latter's death that he knew "of no one adequate to deal with the material of your life except you yourself." For Zweig, it was sufficient to suggest that Freud leave certain "postscripts, etc. . . . to us, the reviewers of your memoirs" (25 March 1939, in E. Freud, 1970, p. 179).

In the years following Freud's death, scholars have boldly departed from the modest agenda envisioned by Zweig: They have proven resolutely unwilling to content themselves with the task of appending "postscripts" to Freud's shared reminiscences. Yet, owing to the complexity of the man, the range of his professional activities, the multiplicity and depth of his personal involvements, and the slow and selective release of documents bearing on his life and career, the lack of transparency persists; more than 60 years after Freud's admonitory aside to Wittels, his "case" continues to baffle analyst and historian alike. It is for this reason, no doubt, that Freud studies continues to be an arena for all manner of scholarly controversy, dialogue, and debate.

Why devote a new annual publication to Freud studies, and, perhaps more germanely, why initiate such a publication in 1985?

Inquiries into Freud's person, his psychology, his creativity, his scientific discoveries, his philosophy, and the movement spawned by
his work—these familiar topics have been joined from a variety of
disciplines. But it is this very disciplinary inclusiveness that has
tended to leave the student of Freud at sea. Major contributions to
the aforementioned topics are scattered among the journal and book
literature of all the disciplines that participate in the Freudian
heritage. For that reason alone, it is appropriate to offer a new forum
for original contributions to the field, contributions that would otherwise have to be ferreted out of an increasingly unwieldy multi-
disciplinary journal literature. Psychoanalysts, psychologists, historians, sociologists, and others inevitably will be at loggerheads in
these pages, but that is all for the best. Our assumption is that
"progress" in Freud studies not only grows out of new historical
findings, but out of the clash of disciplinary sensibilities brought to
bear on these findings. Accordingly, we appeal to readers who approach Freud from the standpoint of particular disciplines, to be
sure, but who willingly acknowledge that the study of Freud cannot
hope to be the exclusive preserve of any single scholarly domain—
even their own.

A second and related rationale for the undertaking concerns the
heightened scholarly activity in this field that marks the present
decade. The student of Freud of even ten years ago had a relatively
manageable compendium of secondary sources at his disposal. Ernest Jones's classic biography of Freud (1953–1957) had only recently been supplemented by Max Schur's *Freud: Living and Dying*
(1972). Likewise, Philip Rieff's benchmark studies of the Freudian
enterprise, *Freud: The Mind of the Moralist* (1959) and *The Triumph of the Therapeutic* (1966), had only recently been enlarged by
Paul Ricoeur's influential *Freud and Philosophy* (1970). In a more
polemical vein, Paul Roazen's *Brother Animal: The Story of Freud
and Tausk* (1969) had imparted momentum to a reassessment of
Freud's character, engendering, in its turn, Kurt Eissler's spirited
rejoinder, *Talent and Genius: The Fictitious Case of Tausk contra
Freud* (1971).

In 1975, students of Freud's early intellectual development, including the fateful "prehistory" of psychoanalysis, had to make do
with the published extracts of the Fliess correspondence (Bonaparte, A. Freud, and Kris, 1954), the pioneering articles of
Siegfried Bernfeld (1944, 1949, 1951), Didier Anzieu's *L'Auto-

Analyse (1959), the dated historical expositions of Marie Dorer (1932) and Rainer Spehlmann (1953), and the more recent, albeit circumscribed, textual analyses of Ola Andersson (1962), Peter Amacher (1965), and Walter Stewart (1967). A fitting culmination to the "era" of prearchival work in this area was the 1976 volume edited by John Gedo and George Pollock, *Freud: The Fusion of Science and Humanism,* with its illuminating studies of Freud's early mentors (Charcot, Breuer) and enlightening commentaries on Freud's early working methods, all deriving from the published record as it existed in the mid-1970s. Students of the history of the psychoanalytic movement, for their part, contented themselves with Freud's writings, his published correspondence with Abraham (H. Abraham and E. Freud, 1965), the four volumes of the *Minutes of the Vienna Psycho-Analytic Society* (Nunberg and Federn, 1962–1975), the reminiscences of various first- and second-generation analysts, and the formal histories of psychoanalysis in America by John Burnham (1967) and Nathan Hale (1971).

A decade later, the floodgates have seemingly burst. A new generation of historians has turned to the archives—understood in the broadest sense—and in so doing has both enlarged and altered our understanding of Freud, the man and scientist. The new archival rigor typifying the search for the early Freud can be found in works like Stephen Kern's *The Discovery of Child Sexuality: Freud and the Emergence of Child Psychology* (1970) and Kenneth Levin's *Freud's Early Psychology of the Neuroses* (1978), but the revisionist thrust of the "new" Freud studies only came to fruition with Frank Sulloway's monumental *Freud: Biologist of the Mind* (1979), a pathbreaking reassessment of Freud's relationship to 19th-century science as noteworthy for the questions it raised as for the answers it supplied.

Sulloway's work provides the scholarly backdrop for a spate of works that have appeared in recent years. I cannot undertake a comprehensive cataloguing of this literature here, but let me touch briefly on its high points. Scholars from several disciplines have continued to probe the epistemological status and historical meaning of psychoanalysis, whether conceptualized in terms of Freud's dialectical "odyssey" (Draenos, 1982), the Cartesian "structure" of his thought (Feffer, 1982), or the Derridean decoding of his "legend" (Weber, 1982). Historians of the past decade have provided detailed explorations of select topics within Freud's corpus and select facets of Freud's creative sensibility. Edwin Wallace's *Freud and Anthropology* (1983) and my own *A History of Aggression in Freud* (1977) typify the former category; Patrick Mahony's *Freud as a Writer* (1982) is an outstanding example of the latter. Our under-standing of the early reception of psychoanalysis has been greatly enriched by Hannah Decker's *Freud in Germany* (1977), whereas our understanding of the institutional history of psychoanalysis—including its political dimension—has profited from Russell Jac-oby's *The Repression of Psychoanalysis* (1983) and my own *In Freud's Shadow: Adler in Context* (1983).

Renewed scholarly interest in Freud the man has ineluctably shaded over into renewed interest in the origins of psychoanalysis. Recent inquiries in this area have taken a topical turn, using new historical findings as the basis for reconstructive hypotheses about Freud's personal and professional predicament at the dawn of the psychoanalytic era. Three studies offer provocative reassessments of Freud's reasons for repudiating the seduction hypothesis, Marianne Krüll's *Freud und sein Vater: Die Entstehung der Psychoanalyse und Freuds ungelöste Vaterbindung* (1979), Marie Balmary's *L'Homme aux Statues: Freud et la Faute Cahée du Père,* (1979), and Jeffrey Masson's *The Assault on Truth: Freud's Suppression of the Seduc-tion Theory* (1984). Dennis Klein's *Jewish Origins of the Psycho-analytic Movement* (1981) and Paul Vitz's "Sigmund Freud's At-traction to Christianity: Biographical Evidence" (1983) are fresh and historically revealing additions to a literature that, in the past, has been rich but uneven, ranging from the speculative forays of David Bakan (1958) and John Cuddihy (1974) to the more sober assessment of Marthe Robert (1974).

The pinnacle of revisionist Freud scholarship focusing on the origins of psychoanalysis is found in the work of Peter Swales, whose provocative historical excavations have unearthed a wealth of information on the formative influences—both intellectual and personal—of the early Freud. I cannot here summarize, much less comment critically on, his ranging contributions to the field, but I would single out his reassessment of the impact of Freud's experi-mentation with cocaine (1983b), his interpretive commentary on the Freud-Fliess relationship (1982a, in preparation), and his fas-cinating reconstruction of the familial circumstances surrounding the birth of psychoanalysis—including Freud's putative involve-ment with his sister-in-law Minna Bernays (1982b, 1983a)—as high points of his work and touchstones of controversy for many years to come.

At a more theoretical level, scholars continue to refract the "mind–body" problem and derivative issue of mentation as it emerges out of Freud's preanalytic and early analytic writings. The topical contributions of analytic scholars Mark Kanzer (1973, 1981) and Michael Basch (1975, 1976) are worthy of special mention, as are the more ambitious and ranging exegeses of Barnaby Barratt (1984) and J. Gordon Maguire (in press). This body of material, teamed with a recent study on Freud's early mind–body interac' tionism by Barry Silverstein (1985) and heretofore unpublished work by David Joseph, offer a deepened apprehension of Freud as a prototypical "psychologist of the mind," transcending the helpful, if formulaic studies of the preceding decade, notably, Andersson (1962) and Stewart (1967). It likewise transcends scholarship that, looking to the *Project for a Scientific Psychology,* sought to expose Freud's early psychology as a reified neurology. This latter literature takes the work of Amacher (1965) and Holt (1965) as hallmarks; it culminates in the "neurologizing" propositions of Pribram and Gill (1976).

The study of Freud's early disciples, both as theorists of stature and as members of the supporting cast in the history of psychoanalysis, is yet another area of Freud studies to undergo rejuvenation in the past decade. In addition to Paul Roazen's (1975) rich overview and Fran' çois Roustang's (1976) interesting Lacanian reading of the prob' lematic of discipleship, we now have a substantive reworking of Freud's involvement with his first highly invested disciple, Adler (Stepansky, 1983). The plethora of literature on the Freud–Jung relationship growing out of the publication of the Freud–Jung corre' spondence (McGuire, 1974) is highlighted by the full'scale reassess' ments of Steele (1982) and Hogenson (1983) and the thoughtful psychoanalytic commentary of Gedo (1983). Recent biographies of Ernest Jones (Brome , 1983), Otto Rank (Menaker, 1982), and Marie Bonaparte (Bertin, 1982) are welcome additions to the literature and valuable tools for the student of the history of psychoanalysis. Peter Swales's long'awaited biography of Wilhelm Fliess (in preparation), whom he casts in the guise of Freud's "Other," will be published in the near future.

All the foregoing testifies to a veritable renaissance in Freud studies. This volume, and the series it inaugurates, are a response to

this renaissance. We seek to provide both the scholars who contribute to Freud studies, and the clinicians and informed lay readers
who follow it, with a convenient sourcebook of current work in the
field. Series editors are prone to indulge in superlatives in characterizing the material they seek to amass, collate, and present to their
readers. I would be guilty of false modesty if I disclaimed any intention of amassing, collating, and presenting to my readers the "best"
article-length contributions to Freud studies in this series. But such
a wish is grandiose in a field that attracts so many able and original
minds from so many disciplines. It will be enough to present readers
with original articles that embody high scholarship and a thought-
provoking and imaginative use of the fruits of this scholarship. I will
consider original contributions to the literature irrespective of the
disciplinary affinities and personal *Weltanschauungen* of their authors—irrespective, that is, of whose feathers may be ruffled by
publication of their work. To provide an open forum for all who
participate in Freud's legacy is to be true to Freud in a most inspirit-
ing way. Freud himself could have wanted no more and presumably
would have tolerated no less.

PAUL E. STEPANSKY

References

Abraham, H. C., & Freud, E. L., Eds. (1965), A Psycho-Analytic Dialogue: The
    Letters of Sigmund Freud and Karl Abraham, 1907–1926,trans. B. Marsh & H.
    C. Abraham. New York: Basic Books.
Amacher, P. (1965), Freud's Neurological Education and Its Influence on Psycho-
    analytic Theory. [Psychological Issues, Monogr. 16.] New York: International
    Universities Press.
Andersson, O. (1962), Studies in the Prehistory of Psychoanalysis. Sweden:
    Bokforlaget/Norstedts.
Anzieu, D. (1959), L'Auto-Analyse—Son Rôle dans la Découverte de la Psycha-
    nalyse par Freud; Sa Fonction en Psychanalyse. Paris: Presses Universitaires de
    France.
Bakan, D. (1958), Sigmund Freud and the Jewish Mystical Tradition. Boston:
    Beacon Press, 1975.
Balmary, M. (1979), L'Homme aux Statues: Freud et la Faute Cahée du Père. Paris:
    Grasset.

Barratt, B. (1984), *Psychic Reality and Psychoanalytic Knowing*. Hillsdale, N.J.: Analytic Press.

Basch, M. F. (1975), Perception, consciousness, and Freud's "Project." *The Annual of Psychoanalysis*, 3:3–19. New York: International Universities Press.

———— (1976), Theory formation in Chapter VII: A critique. *J. Amer. Psychoanal. Assn.*, 24:61–100.

Bernfeld, S. (1944), Freud's earliest theories and the school of Helmholtz. *Psychoanal. Quart.*, 13:341–362.

———— (1949), Freud's scientific beginnings. *Amer. Imago*, 6:163–196.

———— (1951), Sigmund Freud, M.D., 1882–1885. *Internat. J. Psycho-Anal.*, 32:204–217.

Bertin, C. (1982), *Marie Bonaparte: A Life*. New York: Harcourt Brace Jovanovich.

Bonaparte, M., Freud, A., & Kris, E., Eds. (1954), *The Origins of Psycho-Analysis: Letters to Wilhelm Fliess, Drafts and Notes, 1887–1902*, trans. E. Mosbacher & J. Strachey. New York: Basic Books.

Brome, V. (1983), *Ernest Jones: A Biography*. New York: Norton.

Burnham, J. C. (1967), *Psychoanalysis and American Medicine, 1894–1918: Medicine, Science, and Culture*. [*Psychological Issues*, Monogr. 20.] New York: International Universities Press.

Cuddihy, J. M. (1974), *The Ordeal of Civility: Freud, Marx, Levi-Strauss, and the Jewish Struggle with Modernity*. New York: Basic Books.

Decker, H. S. (1977), *Freud in Germany: Revolution and Reaction in Science, 1893–1907*. [*Psychological Issues*, Monogr. 41.] New York: International Universities Press.

Dorer, M. (1932), *Historische Grundlagen der Psychoanalyse*. Leipzig: Meiner.

Draenos, S. (1982), *Freud's Odyssey: Psychoanalysis and the End of Metaphysics*. New Haven: Yale University Press.

Eissler, K. R. (1971), *Talent and Genius: The Fictitious Case of Tausk contra Freud*. New York: Quadrangle.

Feffer, M. (1982), *The Structure of Freudian Thought: The Problem of Immutability and Discontinuity in Developmental Theory*. New York: International Universities Press.

Freud, E. L., Ed. (1960), *Letters of Sigmund Freud*, trans. T. Stern & J. Stern. New York: Basic Books.

———— (1970), *The Letters of Sigmund Freud and Arnold Zweig*, trans. E. Robson-Scott & W. Robson-Scott. New York: Harcourt, Brace & World.

Gedo, J. E. (1983), *Portraits of the Artist: Psychoanalysis of Creativity and Its Vicissitudes*. New York: Guilford.

———— & Pollock, G. H., Eds. (1976), *Freud: The Fusion of Science and Humanism*. [*Psychological Issues*, Monogr. 34/35.] New York: International Universities Press.

Hale, N. (1971), *Freud and the Americans: The Beginnings of Psychoanalysis in the United States, 1876–1917*. New York: Oxford University Press.

Hogenson, G. B. (1983), *Jung's Struggle with Freud*. Notre Dame: Notre Dame Press.

Holt, R. R. (1965), A review of some of Freud's biological assumptions and their influence on his theories. In: *Psychoanalysis and Current Biological Thought,* ed. N. S. Greenfield & W. C. Lewis. Madison: University of Wisconsin Press, pp. 93–124.

Jacoby, R. (1983), *The Repression of Psychoanalysis: Otto Fenichel and the Political Freudians.* New York: Basic Books.

Jones, E. (1953–1957), *The Life and Work of Sigmund Freud,* 3 vols. New York: Basic Books.

Kanzer, M. (1973), Two prevalent misconceptions about Freud's "Project" (1895). *The Annual of Psychoanalysis,* 1:88–103. New York: Quadrangle.

––––––– (1981), Freud, Theodor Lipps, and "Scientific Psychology." *Psychoanal. Quart.,* 50:393–410.

Kern, S. (1970), *The Discovery of Child Sexuality: Freud and the Emergence of Child Psychology, 1880–1910.* Unpublished doctoral dissertation, Department of History, Columbia University.

Klein, D. B. (1981), *Jewish Origins of the Psychoanalytic Movement.* New York: Praeger.

Krüll, M. (1979), *Freud und sein Vater: Die Entstehung der Psychoanalyse und Freuds ungelöste Vaterbindung.* München: Beck.

Levin, K. (1978), *Freud's Early Psychology of the Neuroses.* Pittsburgh: University of Pittsburgh Press.

Mahony, P. (1982), *Freud as a Writer.* New York: International Universities Press.

Maguire, J. G. (in press), *Where Commonsense Fails: Toward a Resolution of the Paradoxes of Psychoanalytic Knowledge.* Hillsdale, N.J.: Analytic Press.

Masson, J. (1984), *The Assault on Truth: Freud's Suppression of the Seduction Theory.* New York: Farrar, Straus & Giroux.

McGuire, W., Ed. (1974), *The Freud/Jung Letters,* trans. R. Manheim & R. F. C. Hull. Princeton: Princeton University Press.

Menaker, E. (1982), *Otto Rank: A Rediscovered Legacy.* New York: Columbia University Press.

Nunberg, H., & Federn, E., Eds. (1962–1975), *Minutes of the Vienna Psycho-Analytic Society,* 4 vols., trans. H. Nunberg, E. Federn, & M. Nunberg. New York: International Universities Press.

Pribram , K., & Gill, M. M. (1976), *Freud's Project Reassessed.* New York: Basic Books.

Ricoeur, P. (1970), *Freud and Philosophy,* trans. D. Savage. New Haven: Yale University Press.

Rieff, P. (1959), *Freud: The Mind of the Moralist.* Garden City, N.Y.: Doubleday.

––––––– (1966), *The Triumph of the Therapeutic: Uses of Faith after Freud.* New York: Harper & Row.

Roazen, P. (1969), *Brother Animal: The Story of Freud and Tausk.* New York: Random House.

––––––– (1975), *Freud and His Followers.* New York: Knopf.

Robert, M. (1974), *From Oedipus to Moses: Freud's Jewish Identity,* trans. R. Manheim. Garden City, N.Y.: Doubleday, 1976.

Roustang, F. (1976), *Dire Mastery: Discipleship from Freud to Lacan,* trans. N. Lukacher. Baltimore: Johns Hopkins University Press, 1982.

Schur, M. (1972), *Freud: Living and Dying.* New York: International Universities Press.

Silverstein, B. (1985), Freud's psychology and its organic foundation: Sexuality and mind-body interactionism. *Psychoanal. Rev.,* 72:203–228.

Spehlmann, R. (1953), *Sigmund Freuds Neurologische Schriften: Eine Untersuchung zur Vorgeschichte der Psychoanalyse.* Berlin: Springer.

Steele, R. S. (1982), *Freud & Jung: Conflicts of Interpretation.* London: Routledge & Kegan Paul.

Stepansky, P. E. (1977), *A History of Aggression in Freud.* [*Psychological Issues,* Monogr. 39.] New York: International Universities Press.

———— (1983), *In Freud's Shadow: Adler in Context.* Hillsdale, N.J.: Analytic Press.

Stewart, W. (1967), *Psychoanalysis: The First Ten Years.* New York: Macmillan.

Sulloway, F. (1979), *Freud: Biologist of the Mind.* New York: Basic Books.

Swales, P. J. (1982a), Freud, Fliess, and fratricide: The role of Fliess in Freud's conception of paranoia. Privately printed.

———— (1982b), Freud, Minna Bernays, and the conquest of Rome: New light on the origins of psychoanalysis. *New American Review,* 1:1–23.

———— (1983a), Freud, Martha Bernays, and the language of flowers: Masturbation, cocaine, and the inflation of fantasy. Privately printed.

———— (1983b), Freud, cocaine, and sexual chemistry: The role of cocaine in Freud's conception of the libido. Privately printed.

———— (in preparation), *Wilhelm Fliess: Freud's OTHER—A Biography.* New York: Random House.

Vitz, P. (1983), Sigmund Freud's attraction to Christianity: Biographical evidence. *Psychoanal. & Contemp. Thought,* 6:73–183.

Wallace, E. (1983), *Freud and Anthropology: A History and Reappraisal.* [*Psychological Issues,* Monogr. 55.] New York: International Universities Press.

Weber, S. (1982), *The Legend of Freud.* Minneapolis: University of Minnesota Press.

Wittels, F. (1923), *Sigmund Freud: His Personality, His Teaching, and His School,* trans. E. Paul & C. Paul. New York: Dodd, Mead, 1924.

Major Essays

Anna von Todesco, circa 1861
(Collection of Peter J. Swales)

Peter J. Swales ————————————————————

Freud, His Teacher, and the Birth of Psychoanalysis

On June 20, 1885, Sigmund Freud was awarded a stipendium that would enable him to undertake postgraduate studies under the legendary French neurologist Jean-Martin Charcot—at that time a figure of considerable controversy on account of the deep skepticism which his current investigations into hysteria and hypnosis had evoked in many respected quarters. Filled with jubilation, Freud wrote to his fiancée predicting how he would "go to Paris and become a great scholar and then return to Vienna with a huge, enormous halo, and then we shall soon marry, and I will cure all the incurable nervous cases"—whereupon they would both live happily ever after (in E. Freud and L. Freud, 1968, p. 158). In the event, however, matters were to prove a little bit more complicated.

In late April 1886, following a five-month stay in the French capital, Freud set himself up in private practice in Vienna as a specialist in nervous diseases; and, in the September following, by then aged 30, he and his fiancée were married. Just a month afterwards, on October 15, 1886, he delivered an important lecture. Writing many years later, the psychiatrist Julius Wagner-Jauregg, one of Freud's student friends, would recall that fateful occasion:

> [In 1885, Freud] went to Paris and became enthusiastic about Charcot, at whose clinic in the [Hôpital de la] Salpêtrière he attended

This paper represents an expanded version of a lecture first presented on January 11, 1984 to the Section on Psychiatric History, Cornell Medical Center-New York Hospital. It is dedicated to Mrs. Janet Malcolm—*anch' io son pittore.*

3

lectures throughout his sojourn. After returning to Vienna, he gave a lecture [on hysteria] before the Society of Physicians in which he spoke only of Charcot and praised him in the highest terms. But the Viennese authorities reacted badly to this. In the discussion which followed, [the internist Heinrich von] Bamberger and [the psychiatrist Theodor] Meynert harshly rejected Freud; and, with that, he fell into disgrace, as it were, with the faculty. Thus, he was a practitioner in neurology but without any patients [Krankenmaterial]. But now there took pity on him a man whom I myself esteemed more than any other colleague with whom I came into contact: Josef Breuer. . . . He now kept Freud in work by referring hysterical patients to him for treatment. Out of this circumstance, psychoanalysis resulted. . . . The first case in which . . . psychoanalysis [was used] . . . was a patient of Breuer [Wagner-Jauregg, 1950, p. 72].

Here, of course, Wagner-Jauregg is alluding to the case of "Frl. Anna O . . ."—namely, Bertha Pappenheim—whom Breuer had actually treated not with analysis, as such, but with his novel cathartic technique, the so-called "talking cure," out of which Freud would subsequently evolve his psychoanalytic method.

Breuer's patient had exhibited a variety of psychological and somatic symptoms which he had construed to be hysterical in nature; and, under his guidance yet on her own instigation, she had succeeded during spontaneous autohypnoses in talking them away by actively tracing back their history to particular traumatic circumstances associated in her memory with their first occurrence. Breuer undertook this cathartic treatment during the years 1881–1882 (Breuer and Freud, 1893–1895, pp. 21–47); and it was in November 1882, then through the year 1883, that he described the circumstances in detail for the benefit of his young protégé (Jones, 1953, p. 226; Freud to Martha Bernays, 13 July 1883, in E. Freud and L. Freud, 1968, p. 47).

Freud was enthralled by all he was told and—given what he was then to witness at first hand in those domains while studying under Charcot in Paris (cf. Freud, 1886, pp. 9–13)—it was hysteria and hypnotism which gripped his imagination more than anything else when, in spring 1886, he established himself in neurological practice. At that time, Freud was translating for German-language publication a collection of Charcot's lectures; and, on their appearance in print later that year, he would present a copy of the book to Breuer with the handwritten inscription: "To his, before all others, most highly esteemed friend, Dr. Josef Breuer, secret master of hysteria and other complicated problems, in silent dedication, the translator" (in Swales, 1983a, p. 13n).

In his autobiographical sketch, written nearly 40 years later, Freud would recall the situation by which he had been confronted in respect of the phenomenon of hysteria during his earliest years in medical practice:

> The immediate question . . . was whether it was possible to generalize from what [Breuer] had found in a single case [viz., that of "Frl. Anna O . . ."]. The state of things which he had discovered seemed to me to be of so fundamental a nature that I could not believe it could fail to be present in any case of hysteria if it had been proved to occur in a single one. But the question could only be decided by experience [1925, p. 21].

And here it must be noted that Breuer was not himself prepared to seek such experience as, owing to the huge amount of time and energy which employment of the "talking cure" involved, his commitment to administering psychotherapy to Bertha Pappenheim had played such havoc with his life as a general practitioner that he had vowed never again to subject himself to such an ordeal (Ackerknecht, 1957, p. 170). And so, as Freud then goes on to explain:

> I therefore began to repeat Breuer's [cathartic] investigations with my own patients and eventually, especially after my visit to [the hypnotherapist] Bernheim [in Nancy] in 1889 had taught me the limitations of hypnotic suggestion, I worked at nothing else [1925, p. 21].

As a contemporary document attests, Freud was still using hypnotism therapeutically in 1894, and probably as late as 1896, in treating certain neuropathic conditions (Kann, 1974, p. 251; Freud, 1905, p. 260). Certainly by May 1889, however, he had begun experimenting with the cathartic method in the case of at least one of his patients—namely, "Frau Emmy v. N . . .," featured in the *Studies on Hysteria* of 1895 (Breuer and Freud, 1893–1895, pp. 48–105; cf. Ellenberger, 1977, p. 526). In that book, in the interests of advancing an essentially psychological theory of hysterical phenomena, Freud and Breuer detailed the results of their investigations with catharsis. And, to that end, they presented five complete case histories—beginning with Breuer's original case of "Anna O . . .," dating from more than a decade previously, followed by four cases of Freud deriving from the years 1889–1893. In the course of the book, however, the two authors also saw fit to include fragments of a number of other case histories; and by far the most notable of these is that of "Frau Cäcilie M . . .," a woman referred to by both Freud and Breuer in several different connections.

It is with this very woman that we shall here be concerned. Excepting what is to be learned of her life and illness from the *Studies on Hysteria,* virtually nothing is known about her. And yet—as I am in a position to assert on the basis of all that is here to follow—she was, so to speak, Freud's *own* "Anna O . . ." in the sense that she was a woman with whose cooperation he was able not only to duplicate Breuer's earlier experience but also to explore yet further unknown domains. Indeed, as we shall learn, Freud would subsequently accord this woman the distinction of having been his "teacher"—thereby automatically elevating her to the same rank as his celebrated mentors Ernst von Brücke, Josef Breuer, Jean-Martin Charcot, and Wilhelm Fliess. Let me then proceed to introduce this mysterious woman—beginning, first of all, with a summary of her case history to the extent that this can be partially reconstructed by reference to all of the fragments of it found scattered throughout the *Studies on Hysteria* (Breuer and Freud, 1893–1895, pp. 5n, 69n–70n, 76n, 103, 112, 175–181n, 208, 231–232, 238).

For no less than 30 years, Frau Cäcilie M. had been afflicted with a "chronic hysteria" featuring numerous psychic and somatic symptoms. The latter included a severe facial neuralgia; pains in the feet such as made walking impossible; and a penetrating pain in the forehead between her eyes. Her psychological symptoms included lapsing into *absences* for periods of time; she would complain of gaps in her memory; and, for nearly three years during the course of her treatment, she was beset by what would seem to have been an overwhelmingly moral dilemma—specifically, fears of her own "worthlessness" based largely on an accumulation of self-reproaches from bygone times. The latter Freud presented as a novel syndrome—viz., as "an hysterical psychosis for the payment of old debts."

Influenced by the ideas of Breuer and Charcot, Freud understood all of Frau Cäcilie's states and symptoms to be products of psychic traumas dating from far back in her past. And, for nearly three years, she relived, under his guidance, *all* of the many traumas of her past life—all of them involving events long-forgotten but now vividly reawakened and reexperienced with the most intense suffering. While recapitulating her whole life in this manner, apparently in reverse sequence (cf. Ackerknecht, 1957, p. 170), she exhibited one by one all of the physical symptoms which, according to her testimony, had accompanied each trauma when, long before, they had first been experienced.

Interestingly, as Freud mentions, when sometimes he was unable to attend, Frau Cäcilie would recollect these traumas for some or other deputizing physician. But, in that event, she would describe them *without* all of the associated emotions and their physical expression—such as might assume the form of tears, cries of despair, and so on—which she would reserve, and then enact, only for Freud. During nearly three years of this reliving of all her former traumas, the woman "repaid" 33 years' worth of "accumulated debts." This "purgation," then, was indeed a veritable "catharsis."

From all of the references to Frau Cäcilie M. as found throughout the *Studies on Hysteria,* one can reconstruct a picture of the illness and treatment as these might present themselves daily: For some hours the patient would lapse into a pathological state of moodiness—involving anxiety, irritation, or despair—which she would regularly attribute to some more or less trivial recent event. Alternatively, or perhaps additionally, an obsessive and tormenting hallucination, a neuralgia, or some other physical symptom, would begin seizing all her attention. And her mental capacity—that is to say, her alacrity, her capacity for reason, and her general mental "togetherness" (*Beisammenheit*)—would diminish in inverse proportion, to the extent that eventually her consciousness would become completely cloudy and she was dominated by her symptom to a point of total incapacitation, even "imbecility."

Then would regularly follow a hysterical crisis involving pains, spasms, hallucinations, long declamatory speeches, and the like. Immediately Freud would be sent for and, on arrival, he would rapidly induce a state of hypnosis and endeavor to abolish her symptoms by suggesting them away. After some time, however—and, thenceforth, for some three years following—he systematically made use of the cathartic method in seeking to dissolve these attacks. To invoke and thereby "abreact" the particular traumatic memory supposedly buried in the "unconscious" and directly responsible for the current symptom, Freud set himself to unravel many highly intricate and complex trains of thought—Frau Cäcilie's associations often involving pictures, symbols, and puns.

With the eventual reproduction of the sought-for traumatic memory, improvement followed very shortly afterwards—however, as Freud mentions, it was his regular custom to *hasten* the end of each attack by the use of some unspecified "artificial means." Frau Cäcilie's troubles having then disappeared "as if by magic," her mental lucidity and emotional stability were soon restored—until, that is, her *next* attack, just half a day later. Thus, Freud would be called upon twice a day; and, over a period of three or four years, he participated in "several hundred" such cycles. Thereby, as he asserts, he was able to gain the most instructive information on "the way in which hysterical symptoms are determined."

Particularly important for Freud, and especially significant about this particular patient, was her liability to that phenomenon named "hysterical conversion" by Freud, and which in her case involved an often almost comic mode of "symbolization." Sometimes some idea of hers would provoke a physical sensation while, at other times, a physical sensation might produce a related idea. Thus, once upon a time when she had been a girl of 15, a grandmother had been viewing her with suspicion and had given her a "piercing look"— supposedly provoking a penetrating pain between her eyes that would then, 30 years later, be reproduced in treatment with Freud. Another time, at a stay in a sanatorium in a foreign country where she had been confined to bed for a time with pains in her feet, her pains were suddenly exacerbated by the idea that she might not "find herself on a right footing" with all the strangers in the place.[1] A recurrent facial neuralgia was traced to a time long before when her husband had insulted her—it was "like a slap in the face." A piercing sensation in the region of the heart was associated with a time when she had felt she had been "stabbed in the heart." Pains in her head like nails being driven in—"oh, something's come into my head." Once she had had to "swallow an insult"—and so on, then. And one more example of this symbolic "conversion": Breuer had refused her request for a certain unspecified drug and so she had set her hopes on Freud, only to find him equally as intransigent. So she had gotten furious—whereupon she hallucinated Breuer and Freud hanging together on a tree in the garden. The meaning: "There's nothing to choose between the two of them; one's the *pendant*"—in French, a pun meaning both "counterpart" and "hanging"—"of the other."

Freud states in the *Studies on Hysteria* that Frau Cäcilie M. was a "highly intelligent woman, to whom I am indebted for much help in gaining an understanding of hysterical symptoms"—"indebted," *nota bene,* almost as if to imply, then, that she had played a very active role in elucidating their mysteries. And there are several other instances in the book where both Freud and Breuer express their remarkably high esteem for this woman. Towards contradict-ing the French view that hysteria is a product of "degeneration" or "psychical insufficiency," Freud asserts that, early on, he and Breuer had learned from their observations of Frau Cäcilie M. "that hysteria of the severest type can exist in conjunction with gifts of the richest and most original kind." Frau Cäcilie was particularly gifted artistically, it is said, and her "highly developed sense of form was revealed in some poems of great perfection." But she was also very capable of rational thinking—she played chess so excellently she enjoyed playing two games at once.

Freud states: ". . . I got to know [Frau Cäcilie M.] far more thoroughly than any other of the patients mentioned in these stud-ies." And he asserts: "Indeed, it was the study of this remarkable case, jointly with Breuer, that led directly to the publication of our 'Preliminary Communication' "—an 1893 paper that had preceded and heralded the *Studies on Hysteria.* No doubt Freud would have liked to tell the whole story—however: "Personal considerations unfortunately make it impossible for me to give a detailed case history of this patient, though I shall have occasion to refer to it from time to time." So, then, just who was this exceptional woman?

Extracting from the published fragments of the case of "Frau Cäcilie M . . ." those items of history that, hypothetically, would lie at the interface with the public record, one can easily enough infer from various statements that the woman must have been approx-imately 43 or 44 years old circa 1890–1891, and therefore would have been born circa 1846–1848. As Freud mentions, she had un-dergone a "first" pregnancy "more than fifteen years earlier"—

thus, she had probably given birth to more than one child, the first circa 1873–1875; and her marriage might well have taken place, therefore, circa 1871–1873. The woman must have lived in Vienna for Freud to have been in such constant attendance over such an extended period of time; and the likelihood is that she must have been rather rich in order to be able to pay her medical fees—also, perhaps, to have lived in a house with a garden if indeed that was the case. Note also how Freud would be "sent for"—another time, by the way, he states: "She got me to give her hypnotic treatment." Generally speaking, in the interests of gaining that authority on which all suggestive therapy depends, Freud would have preferred to dictate the terms of his treatment. So maybe—just maybe—this woman was not only rich but was also a person of some standing for her to have had Freud "run" for her like that.

Thus we are in possession of certain eligibility criteria. These do not of themselves assist us very far, however, towards identifying the woman concerned. Also we are informed, though, that "Frau Cäcilie M . . ." wrote poetry. Could it have happened, then, that some of it was published? But, assuming that that was so, how would one set about finding and identifying it? There has been much writing of poetry over the course of time; and libraries are not in a habit of cataloguing it separately. But then, let us ask ourselves: If some of her poetry was indeed published as a volume, then *who* would be the one person in the world who, it can be hoped, *might* have had a copy in his personal library? We need no ghost to come from the grave and tell us this. So we must inspect the surviving portions of Freud's library (Lewis and Landis, 1957; Trosman and Simmons, 1973; Bakan, 1975; Lobner, 1975; Eissler, 1979); and indeed—confining ourselves just to books from around the fin-de-siècle period—we find there is only *one* volume of poetry by a woman among all the many hundreds of Freud's books (Trosman and Simmons, 1973, p. 676, #481). Entitled *Gedichte*, meaning "Poems," and published in the year 1901, the poetess is one Anna von Lieben. And, very significantly—as one learns adventitiously from that same scrutiny of all those books—it does so happen that there is yet another book in Freud's library bearing the name Anna Lieben (Trosman and Simmons, 1973, p. 665, #250). It is a book by another author but it is inscribed with her name—suggesting rather strongly, then, some personal contact between this woman and Freud.

Now an inspection of Anna von Lieben's *Gedichte* reveals that the book was published *in memoriam*. And a reading of the actual poems informs us that, indeed, for many years this woman was severely ill in a manner entirely consistent with "Frau Cäcilie M . . ." in the *Studies on Hysteria*. Also, very significantly, one of the poems indicates that a certain "Breuer" was her physician. And then, from library and archival research, one can learn easily enough that Anna von Lieben was born in 1847 as the Baroness Anna von Todesco; that in 1871 she married the Viennese banker Leopold von Lieben; that she was a niece of the famous classical philologist Theodor Gomperz whose wife Elise—as recorded in the biographi-cal literature on both Freud and Gomperz (Jones, 1953, p. 340; Kann, 1974, pp. 170, 234–236, 251)—was a patient of Freud dur-ing his first decade in medical practice; and that she died of a heart attack in 1900.

It was in late 1979, having proceeded more or less this far with my research into "Frau Cäcilie M . . .," that Dr. Albrecht Hirschmüller of Tübingen—whose excellent book on Josef Breuer was published in Germany in 1978, and with whom I had already collaborated on research into certain of Freud's early patients—made a crucial contribution to this project. In the hope of finding out more about Anna von Lieben, he obtained through a library a copy of an obscure book entitled *Fifty Years of a Viennese House* (Winter, 1927) which documents in some detail the late-19th-cen-tury history of the von Lieben, Gomperz, Auspitz, von Todesco, and von Wertheimstein families, all of them interrelated. And from this book one can learn that Anna von Lieben was a mother of five children; that for many years she suffered from nervous illness; that Josef Breuer, the doctor of all the families, arranged for several "nerve specialists" to treat her over the course of time; that she painted and wrote poems; that she loved to play chess; also that her family owned a summer villa with a garden in a resort just a few miles to the south of Vienna named Hinterbrühl (Winter, 1927, pp. 18, 20, 42).

Well, that as good as clinched it. In an archive in Jerusalem I had been fortunate to encounter some unknown letters of Freud to Wilhelm Fliess. And in one of them, dated July 12, 1892, Freud tells his friend that he expects to be able to visit the summer villa of Fliess's fiancée's family, located in the Brühl, rather frequently, "as my prima donna has just moved into the Brühl"[2]—Hinterbrühl being a part of the Brühl. Then in 1981, a letter written by Freud during the penultimate year of his life was published in the *Sigmund Freud House Bulletin* in Vienna. Writing to Prince Hubertus zu Löwenstein on July 23, 1938, Freud states: "Your person was sur-rounded for me with an atmosphere of familiarity since I had dis-covered that you are a great-nephew of Anna Lieben, my former patient and teacher" (in Lingens, 1981, p. 28)—his former patient and "*Lehrmeisterin*," i.e., his teacher.[3] Moreover—as I have since been fortunate to learn—41 years earlier Freud had used that very same term, *Lehrmeisterin*, in referring to his patient in a letter to Fliess dated February 8, 1897, written just a few years after his treatment of the woman had ended.[4]

So let me now proceed to present a portrait of Anna von Lieben in the form of a description of her life, her illness, and her treatment by several physicians including Freud—all of this leading into a rather different scenario in respect of the prehistory of psycho-analysis than the standard version. What follows amounts to a jigsaw which, assisted by my wife Julia, I have had to compose out of innumerable pieces of data derived from diverse sources—records of births, marriages, and deaths found mainly in Vienna; a variety of historical documents, such as letters surviving in archives and cure lists preserved at spas; interviews and correspondence with descen-dants of the families concerned (again I owe thanks to Alex Hirschmüller who obtained for me the name and address of a grand-daughter of Anna von Lieben); published and unpublished memoirs; Anna von Lieben's poetry; and of course the *Studies on Hysteria* and other pertinent documentation relating to the early life and work of Freud.[5]

Anna von Lieben was born in Vienna in 1847 as the Baroness Anna von Todesco, the second of four children born to the banker Baron Eduard von Todesco and his wife Sophie, born Gomperz. Anna's great-grandfather, Ahron Hirsch Todesco, had been a silks and haberdashery merchant in the ghetto of Pressburg (now Bra-tislava) during the late 18th century, had made himself a fortune, and moved on to Vienna. There his son Hermann—then, in turn, the latter's three sons, Max, Eduard, and Moritz—became indus-trialists and bankers. It was Anna's grandfather Hermann who was ennobled von Todesco after he donated a sum of money for chil-dren's schooling.

As for Anna's mother's side of the family: Towards the late 18th century, Leopold Benedict Gomperz, descended from a long line of financiers, had been granted a monopoly on tobacco in the city of Brünn (now Brno), the capital of Moravia, 60 miles north of Vienna, where he then amassed a fortune and established his own bank. Early the next century, a son Philipp Gomperz married Henriette Auspitz, daughter of Lazar Auspitz—a cloth manufacturer who, with increasing industrialization, had come to dominate the Moravian textile industry. Like the von Todescos, both the Gomperzes and Auspitzes were Jewish. Reportedly, however, it was in the face of some opposition that, in 1845, Sophie Gomperz, a daughter of Philipp and Henriette, married Baron Eduard von Todesco—since the Gomperz family regarded the von Todescos as *nouveau riche.*

Over the course of the following decade, four children were born to the couple—Franziska, called Fanny, on April 14, 1846; Anna on September 27, 1847; then a son Hermann on September 5, 1849; and a third daughter Gabriella, called Jella, on August 19, 1854. It is probable that the children spent much of their early childhood in a city residence in Vienna; but they also spent a great deal of time at the Villa Todesco in the Brühl, near the town of Mödling just to the south of the city, where numerous other villas owned by members of the Viennese well-to-do were situated.

Surrounded by huge grounds, the Villa Todesco had been designed by an Italian architect. It had many rooms, all fabulously decorated, and there were uniformed servants in constant attendance. The children had nurses, a governess, and tutors. They were taught English and French, also painting and music. Anna painted what are said to have been remarkably true-to-life pictures, many of them portraits. She is also said to have played music and, from an early age, she began writing poetry. However, of utmost significance is the extraordinary social milieu in which Anna and her siblings grew up.

Their mother Sophie Todesco was an exceptionally gifted hostess; and constantly the villa was frequented by politicians and statesmen, bankers and industrialists, businessmen and soldiers, scientists and writers, actors and actresses, artists and musicians— among them many celebrated names. In a letter of 1857, Sophie's brother, Theodor Gomperz, complained about the lack of elbowroom in the villa and observed: ". . . as one turns around one encounters—not other people, but calibans, centaurs, monsters, who speak French and quote Victor Hugo when one would like to talk peacefully or even sleep" (Holzer, 1960, p. 50).

And then, around 1862–1863, when Anna was 15 or 16 years old, although keeping on the villa the family moved into a palace which they had had built in the very center of Vienna. Located at Kärntnerstrasse 51, it was situated directly opposite the new opera house, just off the newly constructed Ringstrasse which encircles the inner city. Built in the style of a Medici, the Palais Todesco had unbelievably lavish décor. And it was here that Sophie Todesco now began to stage feasts, balls, recitals, and the like, sometimes inviting hundreds of guests. Regular visitors included men such as Brahms, Liszt, Makart, von Lenbach, von Schwind, Tilgener, and Billroth—it was here that Johann Strauss, the waltz king, met his wife Jetty Treffz, formerly a mistress of an uncle of Anna.

In May 1864 the palace was symbolically inaugurated with the wedding of Fanny von Todesco and Baron Henry de Worms of England. One year older than Anna, and only just turned 18, it was not as if Fanny wanted to marry the man. Rather, her parents pushed her into it because they considered her suitor, a Rothschild descendant, to be very well placed; moreover, he threatened suicide if Fanny, reputedly the most beautiful girl in all Vienna, turned him down. Following their wedding the couple set up home near Egham, a town on the River Thames 25 miles to the southwest of London, where a daughter was born a year later.

Now by this time—more precisely, beginning circa 1862, when she was about 15 years old—Anna had fallen quite seriously ill, reportedly after catching a cold. There are two versions of the story—according to one, she caught it while lying on a stone bench in the garden of the Villa Todesco in the Brühl; according to another, she caught it on entering a cellar under the villa where ice was stored during summer. In any event, her cold is said to have developed into an illness of the womb and/or the ovaries; and, soon enough, she began to display psychological symptoms of a distinctly pathological nature.[6]

From the *Studies on Hysteria* we learn that, during this time, Anna was nursed by a grandmother—this is likely to have been Henriette Gomperz, born in 1792, a veritable matriarch remembered for her calm, clear gaze and who is said to have frowned upon all excesses of emotion. But, from Anna's poems, it is clear that she was also cared for during these years by her aunt Josephine von

Wertheimstein, called Aunt Pepi—the oldest child of Philipp and Henriette Gomperz and of course a sister of Anna's mother. Married to Baron Leopold von Wertheimstein, a man employed as a financial expert by the Bank of Rothschild, Josephine had two children of her own—Franziska, called Franzi, three years older than Anna; and a son Carl, the same age as Anna.

Apart from the reported illness of the female organs, we know nothing about the physical symptoms of Anna's illness during its earliest stages. And, as regards its psychic aspect, we have available only scraps of information that are to be gleaned from a series of poems which she wrote during her youth. As a rule, her poetry is deeply subjective, documenting her thoughts and imaginings, her whims and fancies, her mental states and her sufferings; and it is therefore capable of serving as an autobiographical record of the periods when it was written.

Anna asks in one poem whether it was "youthful love" or "passion"—or, again, "was it a plague?"—that had caused her illness (Lieben, 1901, p. 19). And other of her poems, allowing for their heavily veiled symbolism, would seem to intimate that, during her early youth, she had experienced passionate feelings, probably most often in secret, toward various men (pp. 25, 29, 35, 77, 115, 156).

In other of her poems, there are strong hints that Anna was unhappy at home (pp. 85, 87, 104–105; cf. p. 15); also that her parents, and perhaps even most of her family, did not really take her illness very seriously, believing instead that she was responsible— whether through fault or default—for perpetuating her condition (p. 85). Certainly in later years, her sister Fanny would speak slightingly of Anna's illness, saying she had had far too much luxury for her own good and had had things far too easy.

One of Anna's poems suggests that her parents felt she should be able to see it was only a "madness" that was possessing her—as if they supposed her mere acceptance of that notion would, of itself, be sufficient to set matters right (p. 85). And in a slightly later poem, explicitly dedicated to her Aunt Pepi (pp. 104–105), Anna writes:

> When I think of you I feel as though I should pray!
> You were always a divine being for me,
> I could recognize the most noble in your eyes. . . .

You called me your child; with sweet kisses
Drawing me toward you, you taught me feeling. . . .

You were the only one to completely understand me,
In your nearness I felt so secure,
And all of my heart's warm glow
Was at first directed toward you alone.

And when I was ill I heard only your step,
Then saw your head tenderly leaning over me,
Then my pains wanted to be silent—
Only when you were gone did I feel I was suffering.

It was also from you that I learned to bear suffering,
The most bitter, the most severe, without complaint,
Otherwise, my dearest, I would have to completely despair. . . .

But in considering these sentiments of Anna in respect of her aunt, Josephine von Wertheimstein, we find ourselves instantly confronted by a vast realm of history that is as fascinating as it is worthy of discussion—yet it is a realm which, simply in virtue of its immensity, it would be impossible to discuss in any depth within the scope of a paper such as this. For the truth of the matter is that Anna von Lieben had been born into what it is certainly not unfair to characterize as a pathogenic milieu *par excellence*. And any adequate description and discussion of that milieu would require a long paper on its own.

Suffice it to say here, then, that the von Wertheimstein family, their relatives, and their social and cultural environment have been extensively portrayed and discussed in a great many books before now—most of them available, however, only in German.[7] For Josephine and her daughter Franzi are famous for having presided over one of Vienna's most celebrated intellectual salons of the 1870s and 1880s. One might almost go so far as to say, though, that the mother and daughter—also certain of their relatives—are nearly as well remembered for the nervous and mental illnesses by which they would seem to have been almost constantly afflicted.

Traits for which they are notorious are obsessive brooding, doubting mania, hypersensitivity, and hypernervosity. Absorbed in matters of culture, in art and in ideas, the women of these aristocratic families lacked any firm contact with the hardships of everyday existence, certainly as we would know these, and are said to have inhabited an almost dreamlike realm. With the result—here to quote from a memoir by a friend of the von Wertheimsteins—"the mere contact with sickness or with misery caused them psychological and physical pain" (Ewart, 1907, p. 78). In effect, then, they were liable, to an extreme, to the phenomenon of "hysterical conversion."

But psychopathological traits also extended to certain men of the families—to Theodor Gomperz, for example, the brother of Josephine von Wertheimstein and Sophie Todesco and an uncle with whom Anna was very close despite the 15 years which separated them (cf. Lieben, 1901, p. 106). Subject to acute depressions punctuated with bouts of wild behavior, Gomperz was of the almost superstitious belief that the family was cursed with the psychopathic inheritance of a grandmother, Rosa Auspitz. Late in the 18th century, in a fit of religious zeal in reaction to her family's increasing liberalism, the wife of Lazar Auspitz had set about sacrificing their children to the Lord with a knife. She was stopped just in time, however, then placed in confinement till the end of her life.

While, for the reasons stated, we are unable here to pursue this broader aspect of the pathology-precipitating nature of the social and family milieu of which Anna von Lieben was a product, we should nevertheless allow in proceeding that, at the very least, the girl may have learned from her Aunt Pepi not simply how to "bear suffering" but perhaps also—given what would appear to have been a very powerful identification with her aunt—how to suffer in the first place. And in 1866, let it be noted, Josephine von Wertheimstein plunged into a severe mental illness following the sudden and tragic death of Carl, her only son—with which she was confined to a sanatorium in the north of Vienna where she would remain in isolation for some years to come.

In the summer of 1866, just a few months following her beloved aunt's breakdown, 18-year-old Anna travelled to England where she would remain for two years. By this time she had begun to transcribe her finished poems into a leatherbound volume that had a photographic portrait of herself set into the outside front cover. And it is to those of the poems in this book that would later be selected for publication that we owe most of our knowledge of her illness, also much of our knowledge of her movements, over the subsequent seven years.

After visiting Brighton and London for a period of time, in 1867 Anna retreated to the town of Egham where her sister Fanny was living. And there she underwent a period of severe nervous illness during which, it would appear, she must have spent a year or more largely confined to bed (Lieben, 1901, pp. 20, 54; cf. pp. 18, 35, 91, 97, 104).[8]

In her poems from that time, Anna wonders whether her existence was intended only for her to have to suffer (p. 15). She supposes that nobody on earth has to suffer like someone "nervously ill" (p. 20). Because she is always preoccupied with a struggle to exercise self-control, the simple joys of life are closed to her (pp. 15, 20). On occasion—possibly even under the influence of morphine, given a reference to that drug in one particular poem (p. 54)—she suffers feverish dreams and nightmares (pp. 34–35). Constantly she seeks refuge and consolation in fantasies—although confined to a sickroom, "my fantasy carries me outside/then for hours I depart/how much I have to thank it [the fantasy] for this liberation" (p. 99).

In most of her imaginings she seems to have constructed a glorious future—yet she felt powerless to make this future a reality (pp. 23, 97, 99). She is desperate that her plight should be resolved quickly rather than being drawn out endlessly (pp. 15, 18, 19). In one poem she pleads: "Lord, I beg with all my heart, make an end to my dilemma, give me life or death" (p. 18). And, were it not for the example set by her Aunt Pepi, she would have given up hope long ago (pp. 104–105).

Other poems indicate that, while she apparently cherished her father and mother (pp. 97–99), their relations had not been at all good (pp. 85, 87, cf. p. 15). Her parents were presently trying to pressure her into returning to Vienna and they held out the promise of everything she could possibly wish for toward making her life more comfortable (p. 85, cf. p. 15). In a poem she quotes them: "The whole house will do as you wish / two carriages await you should you wish to go out . . ." (p. 85). But Anna scorns their flagrant materialism, mocking them with their own words: "When finally you see you are lacking nothing, then finally you will realize it was only a madness that was plaguing you!" (p. 85).

One line of that same poem—a line likewise imputed to her parents—suggests a great deal about the specific nature of her current dilemma: "Nobody holds it against you, even though you refuse him ten times" (p. 85). From this, taken in conjunction with the testimony of a descendant of the family, it is virtually certain that Anna's parents wished to marry her off to someone noble and rich, as indeed had been the case with Fanny. But Anna had no wish to oblige.

Clearly, as some of her poems testify, there were men whom she had loved (pp. 19, 25, 29, 34–35, 115–156). But presumably either they, or she, were ineligible as suitors by virtue of social standing, money, age, or perhaps even illness or marital status. Her one great regret, as expressed in another poem, was that she felt doomed to die so young of a "tired heart" (p. 19).

Anna stayed in Egham until the spring of 1868 when she took a boat from Dover back to the Continent. The day before her departure, June 7, 1868—possibly even in the spirit of turning over a new leaf—she began a new notebook. This was a journal in which she sometimes set down poetry but, more often, her innermost thoughts and ponderings. The book opens with an account of a dream of hers about a sea voyage; and another of its pages is headed "*Traumesdeutung*"—the interpretation of dreams.[9]

Anna spent that summer in the spas of Baden Baden in Germany and Franzensbad in Bohemia. Baden Baden was famous for treatment of a wide variety of diseases but perhaps especially neuralgic, respiratory, and cardiac conditions. Franzensbad specialized, on the other hand, in female disorders. But, in those days, young women in wealthy families were fed very extravagantly and lacked normal exercise so there was constantly a risk of their getting fat, thus necessitating slimming cures at spas every summer. And indeed, we shall learn how, in the years to come, Anna would develop a severe weight problem—a condition that may already by now have been in its earliest stages (cf. Lieben, 1901, p. 92).

In a poem written on her 21st birthday, September 27, 1868, Anna reflects on her youth with tears: "Not one of the years was a joy to me, . . . fearfully I look toward the future" (p. 36). Then, on returning to her family in Vienna, she was expected to participate in social life, to attend balls, soirées, and the like, presumably with a view to meeting a future husband; but she did not want to have to face people, not even the members of her family, and longed just for peace and quiet (p. 87, cf. p. 84). In June 1869 she returned to Franzensbad—this time apparently in the company of her friend and future aunt Elise von Sichrovsky, one year younger, who, that August, would marry Theodor Gomperz (cf. Lieben, 1901, p. 107; Kann, 1974, pp. 52–55).

Anna spent all the following winter at the Swiss spa of Rigi, also at Montreux, before she then returned to Vienna and the Brühl in 1870. That same year her aunt Josephine von Wertheimstein made what appeared to be a truly miraculous recovery from her mental illness—a cure credited to the psychiatrist Theodor Meynert with

whom the aunt would thenceforth remain on close terms of friendship (Holzer, 1960, pp. 72, 79; Ewart, 1907, p. 76). The woman
would always remain melancholic (Holzer, 1960, pp. 79, 125). But
it was during the subsequent two decades that she and her daughter
Franzi would preside over their legendary salon—"the house of
geniuses and demons," as it has been called (cf. Holzer, 1960).
Regular guests at these intellectual gatherings included the philologist Theodor Gomperz; the philosopher Franz Brentano; the psychiatrist Theodor Meynert; the physiologists Ernst von Fleischl and
Sigmund Exner; and Dr. Josef Breuer, the family's devoted
physician.

Now one other guest at these regular evening gatherings was
Leopold von Lieben. Born in 1835, the son of a rich Jewish banker,
by about 1870 he had amassed for himself a considerable fortune out
of banking. A highly educated man, he was quiet, reserved, yet
confident; he loved to paint as a hobby and he collected art. On
December 31, 1870, he formally proposed marriage to 23-year-old
Anna von Todesco, and she accepted (cf. Lieben, 1901, p. 126).
During the winter and spring following, Anna travelled in Italy
visiting Florence, Rome, and perhaps Naples—part of the time, it
seems probable, in the company of Theodor and Elise Gomperz (cf.
Kann, pp. 58, 62–63). Sometime later in 1871, she visited the spa of
Bad Ischl in Austria's Salzkammergut. Then, on December 3, 1871,
almost a year after their engagement, she and Leopold were married
and they set off for southern Italy for a three-month honeymoon.
    In a New Year's Eve poem, Anna reflected on her newfound
happiness; and another poem from the time may even hint at some
relief about having solved at last the problem of marriage (Lieben,
1901, pp. 111, 126). On January 16, 1872, still on honeymoon,
Leopold von Lieben wrote from Naples to a friend in Vienna:

> . . . As you had anticipated, marriage agrees very well with my wife,
> and up till now our married life has proceeded as normally and as
> pleasurably as possible. [Nervous] states and complaints which have
> been going on for so many years cannot be wiped out overnight and
> can improve only slowly—as far as I can judge everything is running
> smoothly. Probably the relaxing sojourn here [in the south] has con-
> tributed much to that.[10]

On returning to Vienna, Leopold and Anna made their home in
an apartment in the Palais Todesco. However, they would also

spend a great deal of time, including their summers, at the Villa Todesco in Hinterbrühl; and presumably on occasion they also visited an estate, the Hirschbrunft at Vaszony near Veszprem in Hungary, some 120 miles from Vienna, which Anna acquired for herself around this time. Between 1873 and 1875, two daughters and a son, Ilse, Valerie, and Ernst, were born to the couple; then, in 1878, there followed another son, Robert.

But Leopold's hopes that marriage would lead to a permanent respite in his wife's condition were not to be fulfilled. It would appear as if, with the birth of her first child Ilse in 1873, Anna might have felt she at last had something real and firm to hold on to—she had celebrated that birth with a series of poems (Lieben, 1901, pp. 100, 140–142), the last she would enter into the book begun when leaving England seven years before. But at least by 1874—that is to say, midway through her first three pregnancies—her condition had begun to deteriorate (cf. Lieben, 1901, p. 128). Interestingly, though, despite some apparent contradiction, it is said by a descendant that those times when Anna was actually pregnant were in fact the only times when she experienced anything resembling real remissions of her illness.

That year, 1874, Anna spent some time at the spa of Bad Ischl and, in a poem, described herself as afflicted with anxiety and existing week after week in a state of "eternal semi-sleep" (Lieben, 1901, p. 128). She was living in darkness and seldom saw daylight—probably on account of the very severe insomnia by which she came to be afflicted which caused her to turn day into night and night into day. Her poetry from these years tends to reflect sorrow and depression (cf. pp. 123–154). Just why that was the case is not really clear—reportedly, however, in an unpublished poem or diary entry, she bemoans the fate of her marriage and supposes she would not still be ill had she married the right man.[11]

Also, though, it would seem that she rebelled against her responsibilities as a mother. In one of her poems she complains of the "selfishness" of her family circle—supposedly her own wishes count for nothing; she does not want to have to nurse her babies and undertake other chores; she would prefer to be doing other things; but the family prevents her from doing so (p. 86). That is not to say, however, that Anna was expected to undertake the kind of chores which most mothers do. Not only were there any number of chambermaids and servants; there was also a faithful nurse, Meja Ruprecht, who looked after both Anna and the children and who supervised the running of the household. Of this woman all the children grew devotedly fond—she became as their mother.

It is said that the children did love and cherish their own mother—she was a good, tender, gentle woman who remained an impressive personality and, as far as possible, was well loved. But having Anna as their mother did cause the children many difficulties and considerable distress at times. Because of her increasingly frequent bouts of nocturnal existence, it was never certain whether she would appear for lunch. And it was a trying experience for the children, seated at the table at which their stern father forbade them from talking, waiting to see if their mother would arrive so lunch could proceed.

Then again, in the late afternoon or early evening, having been unable to make up her mind about going any earlier, Anna might suddenly decide to disappear in a carriage for the purpose of satisfying her passion for beautiful fabrics. This particular indulgence of hers sometimes became so much of a compulsion that, as descendants of the family tell it, stores were eventually forced to order her out—Anna having kept them specially open way past closing time. Whereupon she would arrive home late for the evening meal, having kept all the family waiting her return.

During these years, the 1870s and the 1880s, Anna also began to develop a number of other eccentricities. For long periods of time—possibly even with the idea in mind of combating her vastly increasing weight and size—she would exist solely on caviar and champagne. And then, while staying at the Brühl, she would sometimes arrange for a few weeks or so at a time to have a man travel down each day especially from Vienna with a delivery of lamb cutlets—something she had grown to love having for breakfast while staying in England. Stricken with insomnia, she would hire a professional chess player to literally wait outside her room all night so that she could then play chess—or, one would presume, two games of chess simultaneously—if and when the fancy took her. And the games might go on all night.

Because of this nighttime existence, it would also sometimes happen that the children would be suddenly summonsed from their beds late into the night—just then their mother happened to be feeling fresh and wanted one or another to share her company. At other times, though, she might go quietly and watch them asleep in their beds—in one of her poems, written after one such nocturnal visit, she expresses a wish always to be able to protect them (p. 137).

Occasionally it did happen that, for more or less protracted periods, Anna would leave her sickroom and live approximately normal hours. Sometimes she would even watch the children play and take some kind of an active interest in their education and upbringing. But, as often as not—and, in all probability, more often than not—the children would be kept away from her on account of her illness; and all they would ever hear of their mother would be the obtrusively audible sounds of her crying, screaming, and raving while she underwent her recurrent crises in another part of the house.[12]

In one of her poems, Anna expresses concern about the possibility of being separated from her children (p. 138). And it would probably not be unreasonable if we were to suppose that such a thought could betray certain fears she may have experienced from time to time about being permanently confined to a psychiatric institution. Anna's condition was so chronic and much of the time so acute, the threat must often if not constantly have existed that she would be dispatched to a sanatorium—perhaps never to return. This, of course, had been so for more than four years in the case of her aunt, Josephine von Wertheimstein; while the latter's unwed daughter Franzi, just three years older than her cousin Anna, had very possibly already been admitted to sanatoria for periods of time on account of her chronic hysteria. In 1880, furthermore, at the age of 42, Leopold von Lieben's sister Helene Auspitz—a very talented painter, singer, and pianist, but a woman stricken with melancholia—was confined by her family to an asylum where she would spend the next 16 years till her death, never again to set eyes on her two young children, both close companions of the von Lieben children.

Indeed, one can only wonder how it came to pass that, to our knowledge, Anna was never referred against her will to some or other institution. It cannot be doubted that she was in a chronically borderline state, forever on the brink of lapsing into psychosis.[13] And here I would like to venture three possible reasons why she was not hospitalized. First, despite her often extreme condition, Anna did remain an impressive and well-loved personality and would seem to have retained a somewhat royal respect and authority even at the worst of times. Second, it would seem probable that her condition, while erratic—being liable to sudden improvements and relapses during more than 30 years of illness—was nevertheless one of stable instability; and, on the basis of *my own intuition* about this woman, I am driven to speculate that the very threat of confine-ment may well, in and of itself, have precipitated her remissions. And then, third, I would offer a somewhat cynical but nonetheless eminently plausible socioeconomic speculation: Anna was of course the wife and the daughter of two of the richest men in all Vienna, both of them bankers—her husband had been appointed president of the Austrian Stock Exchange. Thus, her family could well afford to have physicians in constant attendance and, had she been institu-tionalized, her doctors would have forfeited huge earnings. The latter had a powerful vested interest, then, in keeping the woman out of confinement for so long as she remained credibly functional and some faint hope persisted that she might eventually recover.[14]

An undated poem indicates a definite cynicism on the part of Anna toward some or other physician who was treating her—as if his treatment was a mere pretense and he was impotent to really help her (Lieben, 1901, p. 71). Just who this physician was, we do not know; and, over the course of the years, she must have seen many doctors. At least by 1880, however, her physician was Josef Breuer, by then family doctor to all the Wertheimsteins, Todescos, Auspitzes, Gomperzes, and Liebens in addition to the whole Vien-nese Jewish aristocracy. Being a general practitioner, Breuer would have supervised Anna's treatment, enlisting various specialists as he saw fit who would then report to him (cf. Hirschmüller, 1979, p. 148). And one such specialist, a good friend of Breuer, was the gynecologist Rudolf Chrobak—a man whom Anna seems to have revered seeing as she once gave him a bearskin as a gift with an accompanying poem in which she glorified his command of the pharmacopoeia in the endeavor of "overcoming the wild powers of nature" (Lieben, 1901, p. 114). But how do we know that Breuer was appointed Anna's physician by the year 1880?

Once upon a time, while staying at the spa of Bad Nauheim a little to the north of Frankfurt am Main in Germany, Anna wrote a poem addressed to her husband. And there she complains of the strictness of the treatment, indeed of the "martyrdom," which she is having to undergo in accordance with the prescription of "your Breuer" (p. 132). Regrettably the poem is undated; but inspection of the surviving cure lists reveals that she visited this spa for nearly three months beginning late May 1880 and not, apparently, during the years subsequent.[15] Nauheim specialized, incidentally, in the treatment of heart diseases; and, given Anna's vastly increasing weight, possibly Breuer had grounds for concern in this respect, causing him to impose dietary regimens and the like. This particular spa, by the way, was little patronized by Viennese; and, that being so, conceivably Anna chose to go there precisely so as to avoid encountering persons who would recognize her.

In the year 1882, Anna gave birth to Henriette—a fifth and last child, surely named after Anna's grandmother Henriette Gomperz who had died the previous year. And one might be tempted to suppose that, for this birth to have occurred, Breuer must have been having some success in improving the general state of health of his patient. But, whether or not that was so, there was certainly no lasting improvement in Anna's condition; and there are certain indications that, by now, her relationship with her husband had become, if anything at all, more a source of mutual frustration than any kind of an edification (cf. Lieben, 1901, pp. 86–153).

In 1888 the family moved into a new home—a large first-floor apartment situated in a house just off the Ringstrasse, opposite the new Burgtheater, at Oppolzergasse 6. The house had been built in 1874 for some of the Auspitz family and some siblings of Leopold von Lieben. And certain members of these families were now occupying other apartments in the building—besides, in one of them, the philosopher Franz Brentano, remembered for his 1874 opus, *Psychology from an Empirical Standpoint.*

In the year 1880, Brentano had married Ida von Lieben, a younger sister of Leopold; and, with their newly born son Giovanni, called Lujo, the couple now lived in an apartment on the third floor. Brentano assisted in the education of all the children of his wife's relatives; and, although certain members of Ida's family had originally opposed her marriage to a non-Jew—a former Roman Catholic priest, at that—after a few years Brentano had become well loved by all.[16] It would appear that, shortly after the von Lieben family's arrival at Oppolzergasse 6, Ida Brentano began assisting in—perhaps she was even dragged into—the care of Anna. In an undated letter from around this time, she states: "On account of the illness of my sister-in-law Lieben . . . I rush back and forth like a pendulum and get nothing else done."[17] Although the von Lieben family occupied the first floor, Anna may have been confined in her illness to a room somewhere nearer the top of the five-story house. For it is said that, in view of the sluggishness in movement that resulted from her obesity, the family saw fit to get an elevator specially installed for her benefit.

It was here in this distinguished house, then, that the young Dr. Sigmund Freud, a neuropathologist in practice just five minutes' walk away at Maria Theresienstrasse 8, would begin treatment of the woman who would become his "prima donna" and "teacher"— namely, Frau Anna von Lieben, born a baroness and one of the wealthiest, not to say one of the most eccentric, women in all Vienna. From the later *Studies on Hysteria,* it is clear that Freud treated his patient in collaboration with Breuer—meaning under the latter's supervision. So it would be only natural to suppose it was Breuer, his mentor and benefactor,[18] who was responsible for assigning Freud to the case. A distinct possibility does exist, however, that the referral came instead directly from Anna's gynecologist, Rudolf Chrobak.

Siegfried Bernfeld, pioneering researcher into the origins and prehistory of psychoanalysis, was aware as long ago as 1950 that Anna von Lieben had been a patient of Freud, albeit not that she was the "Frau Cäcilie M . . ." of the *Studies,* because the analyst Heinz Hartmann informed him that year that his grandfather, Chrobak, had once referred this woman to Freud.[19] And, indeed, it is certainly so that Chrobak was unusually well disposed to the young Freud in that, like Breuer, he too sometimes referred him patients.[20] In a published letter of October 24, 1887, Freud mentions to his wife's mother and sister that he had recently been asked by Chrobak to attend a joint consultation "at Frau L.'s" (in E. Freud and L. Freud, 1968, p. 233)—possibly, then, Frau Lieben's.[21] So conceivably Freud's treatment of Anna commenced as early as 1887— presumably, in that case, some time following her return from a visit which she made that year to the cure resort of Abbazia on the Adriatic (cf. Lieben, 1901, pp. 157–158). At any rate, as we shall learn, Freud had certainly begun treating her by 1888.

Now, from certain points of view, to assign Freud to this case was a rather bold and adventurous step on the part of Breuer or Chrobak, or perhaps the two of them. Following his 1886 lecture on hysteria before the Society of Physicians—and even more so following autumn 1888 when he began openly espousing hypnotic therapy—Freud became a controversial and somewhat marginal figure vis-à-vis the Viennese medical establishment (Wagner-Jauregg, 1950, p. 72; cf. Freud, 1888b, p. 81; 1889, pp. 91–96; Strachey, 1966a, p. 64). And it could very easily have been alleged—as, indeed, it is said was the case on the part of certain cynics within the von Lieben family's circle—that Freud was just an ambitious young upstart, if not actually a charlatan, eager to line his pockets with the large income to be gained from treating such a rich woman.[22] And here it will be appropriate if we undertake a brief digression.

Many years later, in conversation with Princess Marie Bonaparte, Freud would represent that, during his early years in medical practice, he had treated "only poor people" (in Hartman, 1983, p. 567). But that is really not true. From an unpublished letter of Freud to his friend Carl Koller, sent from Teplitz in Bohemia on March 24, 1887, it is evident that, at Koller's father's wish, Freud was sent over 200 miles in order to give a second opinion on the severe neurological illness of a brother of the father who owned a large factory there.[23] In an unpublished letter dated April 14, 1888, the famous Viennese poetess Betty Paoli (Elisabeth Glück), a patient of Breuer, tells a friend she has just begun consulting Dr. Freud about her "nervous illness" and he has started her on a cure.[24] In June 1889, as a token of her gratitude and respect, Frl. Mathilde Schleicher made Freud the gift of a book (cf. Trosman and Simmons, 1973, p. 686, #688)—some 27 years old, she was a daughter of Cölestin Schleicher, an artist well known in Vienna.[25]

A month before, in May 1889, Freud had begun treating "Frau Emmy von N . . ." whom, from the researches of Andersson (1965) and Ellenberger (1977), we now know to have been Frau Fanny Moser, born von Sulzer-Wart, of Au near Zürich—the widow of a Russian-Swiss industrialist and reputedly the richest woman in Europe (Ellenberger, 1977, pp. 528–529). In truth, then, just three years after setting up in practice, Freud had in treatment in the persons of Fanny Moser and Anna von Lieben two of the richest women in the world. Moreover, as early as summer 1886, Elise Comperz, the friend and aunt of Anna and a woman who had plenty of money at her disposal, was projected to receive treatment from Freud under Chrobak's supervision. The attraction was, to cite a letter from the time of her husband Theodor, that Freud was "a pupil of Charcot" (in Kann, 1974, p. 170)—for Freud in those days a very prestigious association (cf. Freud to Fliess, 4 February 1888,

in Bonaparte, A. Freud, and Kris, 1954, p. 55) albeit a very controversial one to the extent that it automatically alienated him from a
large faction of the Viennese medical establishment.

Interestingly—and here just to alter the thrust of this digression
in the interests of attaining a general perspective—at that time,
Theodor Gomperz wrote a letter, a passage from which gives us
some valuable insight into the intrinsically pathological quality of
the families' milieu. By then for some time his wife had been suffering acutely from neuralgic and sciatic pains; moreover, given to
extremes of love and hate, she was greatly excitable and choleric
almost, it would seem, to the point of mental derangement (Kann,
1973, pp. 15, 84, 170, 234, 235, 236, 251; cf. H. Gomperz, manuscript, p. 1464; Holzapfel-Gomperz, 1980, pp. 13–14, 142).[26] On
August 23, 1886, Gomperz wrote to his sister Josephine and niece
Franzi:

> Elise . . . has suffered so much from her nerves lately that I got
> worried and the realization came to me that for her, too, something
> lasting has to be done. Thus, looking around our family circle, there
> are not too many bright points. Nearly everywhere, at the least,
> irritable and excited nerves—the inheritance of a very old civilized
> race and of the urban life. . . [in Kann, 1974, pp. 169–170].

So one would assume that, by now, the whole family must have been
pretty desperate and, in the interests of a cure, were ready to be
persuaded to try something quite novel and controversial, even
untested and unproven. And indeed, we have subsequent testimony
of Freud that his patient Anna von Lieben was handed over to him
for treatment "because no one knew what to do with her" (1925, p.
18; cf. below, p. 36)—as if to imply, then, that probably everything
had been tried during the 30 or so years of her illness but no one had
had any success in curing her.

This aspect of things could one day prove particularly relevant,
incidentally, if it were ever shown to have been the case that
Freud's former teacher, the psychiatrist Theodor Meynert, had once
treated Anna von Lieben. Although there is no direct evidence in
support of the idea, it is nevertheless virtually inconceivable that, at
some point, Meynert was not called in on the case. He was a close
friend of Anna's parents, also of members of the von Lieben family
(Stockert-Meynert, 1930, pp. 152–153); and of course he had become a close friend of Anna's revered aunt, Josephine von

Wertheimstein, who attributed her own cure to him (Holzer, 1960, p. 72; cf. Kann, 1974, p. 44). If, then, it was indeed the case that Meynert had once sought to cure Anna but had failed, and if we allow ourselves to suppose that all kinds of professional rivalries tend to go on behind the scenes, such a circumstance would surely not be without relevance in respect of the bitter contempt which Meynert manifested towards Freud after, in 1888, he had begun actively crusading the cause of suggestive therapy (cf. Freud to M. Bernays, 13 May 1886, in E. Freud and L. Freud, 1968, p. 225).[27]

Having supposed that it must have been Breuer or Chrobak, or perhaps the two of them, who assigned Freud to the treatment of Anna von Lieben, we are now confronted by the altogether remarkable fact that—in or shortly before 1888, and probably in 1889—the woman was treated by Jean-Martin Charcot, who may also therefore have been influential in Freud's assignment to the case. This fact of Charcot's treatment is communicated by descendants. Anna's son Ernst, born in 1875, accompanied his mother to Paris; regrettably, however, in later years he felt disposed to recall only how he had visited some of the very best restaurants in her company.

From a series of surviving letters of Charcot to Freud, it is also reportedly evident that Anna was treated by the Frenchman on several occasions.[28] The letters, however, have not been made available for scholarly inspection with the result that, assuming they may contain such information, it is not known whether or not Freud had already treated the woman before she sought help from Charcot—let alone whether in that event he may himself have played some role in arranging her treatment in Paris.[29] All that can be said is that, not so surprisingly, Freud and Charcot kept up an intermittent correspondence during these years—on January 23, 1888, incidentally, the Frenchman inscribed a set of his collected works for his German translator, presumably sent as a gift.[30]

Charcot, the fabled "Napoleon of the Neuroses," charged extremely high fees of his private patients with the result that his clientele was composed exclusively of the world's rich and royal. Regrettably, very little is known of his treatment of Anna von Lieben. It is said, though, that, after undergoing Charcot's hypnoses, during which French was spoken between them, for some time afterwards she spoke only in that tongue—which is to say, she suffered a hysterical aphasia in German. And indeed, there is a real possibility that, at some time or other, Freud was himself witness to this condition while undertaking Anna's treatment (cf. Freud, 1893a, pp. 161–164; Breuer and Freud, 1893–1895, p. 181).

Reportedly it was in October 1888 that Charcot wrote Freud a letter in which—as was perhaps the case in other of their letters—he devoted some discussion to their patient, Anna von Lieben:

> The delicate and complete analysis that you have made of the phys-iopsychical phenomena, which are so varied and so complex, shows well enough that you have attached yourself to this interesting per-son just as we ourselves got attached to her during her stay in Paris. . . . But—and I repeat what I have said—rather it is psychi-cally that one has to act, as you well understood; and it is in this manner that one can be effective in this case. I must tell you, besides, that the [Frau von Lieben] of today is in every respect far superior to what she was formerly. As a matter of fact, she is—and she herself acknowledges it—prepared to a certain extent for the struggles of life, which formerly she was not.[31]

Charcot's reference to the "physiopsychical phenomena" probably relates to those of her symptoms understood by Freud to be traumat-ic ideas transformed by "repression" and "conversion" into sym-bolically related somatic disturbances. And, while not altogether apropos, a curiosity might here be mentioned in this general respect. It is said that Anna was able to stick a knitting needle through her arm—possibly while she was in a state of trance; and presumably without any pain or blood—a phenomenon a little reminiscent, perhaps, of some of the tricks performed on Charcot's hypnotized patients at the Salpêtrière (cf. Owen, 1971, p. 79).

Whether or not Freud had indeed treated Anna von Lieben before she visited Paris, Charcot's statements do tend to suggest that it was only now, in autumn 1888, that Freud began to develop a rapport with this woman, nine years his senior. Moreover, state-ments found in the Studies on Hysteria indicate that Freud was initially called upon to treat Anna for a violent facial neuralgia that lasted "from five to ten days" which had erupted "two or three times a year" for the past "fifteen years"; that such treatments continued sporadically for perhaps a year or so; and that it was only then, at her request, that he first used hypnotic suggestion towards combating this condition (Breuer and Freud, 1893–1895, pp. 176–

177)—certainly the sense in which Charcot's reference to psycho-logical influence is to be understood (cf. Charcot, 1889, pp. 307–309).

And it is in light of all these pieces of information, taking them in conjunction with one another, that we now find ourselves in a position to be able to construct a tentative scenario with respect to the earliest phase of Anna's treatment by Freud. Probable is that, beginning in 1887, Freud was intermittently called upon in his capacity as neuropathologist in connection with Anna's facial neu-ralgias, and that his treatment of that condition proceeded under the supervision of Breuer and perhaps Chrobak. Probably it was a year or so later, following her return from Charcot, that Freud first treated Anna's attacks with hypnotic suggestion and possibly, by the time 1889 arrived, such psychic treatment had become a regular, perhaps even a daily, occurrence—given that, for reasons never explained, it would appear Freud found himself suddenly and unex-pectedly very busy during the final months of the year 1888 (Strachey, 1966b, p. 73), something of which Anna von Lieben may have been the cause (cf. Breuer and Freud, 1893–1895, p. 178).

Supposing this scenario to be essentially accurate, then in all probability Freud's therapy was interrupted for a time during 1889. For it would appear that, at some point that year, whether or not at his instigation, Anna returned to Paris to consult yet again with Charcot. This is to be supposed in virtue of the fact that there exists a poem of Anna dated "Paris, 1889" (Lieben, 1901, pp. 151–152). Conceivably, like Theodor Gomperz (Kann, 1974, pp. 209–211), she travelled to Paris that summer to visit the Universal Exhibition and to see the newly opened Eiffel Tower. Given her severe illness, however—and in the poem in question she writes of her mind as "ill" and her foot as "weak" (p. 152)—that is barely likely. And so it is altogether probable—assuming, that is, that the published poem has been properly attributed—that Anna sought help from Charcot once again that year.

Reasonably to be wondered, though, is whether this hypoth-esized 1889 visit would have taken place before or after Freud's visit that July to the clinic of the hypnotist Bernheim in Nancy, an event that had a critical impact on his thinking (Freud, 1925, p. 17; cf. Strachey, 1966a, p. 67). Although he would never endorse Bernheim's views unreservedly, Freud would take up a position against his former teacher in the bitter dispute then being waged between the Paris and Nancy schools over, respectively, the physiological versus the psychological bases of hypnosis and suggestion (Freud, 1893b, pp. 22–23; Roback, 1957, p. 25). One might consequently be tempted to suppose that—as someone with, by 1889, a say in Anna's treatment—Freud would hardly have approved of her returning to Paris following his visit to Nancy. However, it was not really until Charcot's death in summer 1893 that Freud made evident the switch in his theoretical position (Freud, 1893b, pp. 22–23; cf. Strachey, 1966a, pp. 67–68); and this eventual transfer of allegiance might then, for all we know, have been of comparatively recent occurrence.

To be allowed is that, aware of Freud's translation of a book by Bernheim in 1888, and after presumably getting to learn of his translator's visit to his opponent in summer 1889, Charcot may have communicated some feelings of disappointment, dissatisfaction, perhaps even distrust, to Freud. And, while all of this constitutes a speculative scenario, it may nevertheless provide an authentic explanation for the fact that—as attested by a surviving reply of the Frenchman[32]—in December 1889 Freud saw fit to notify Charcot he had named a newly born son Jean Martin in his honor, and was possibly therefore engaged in something of a reconciliatory gesture. But, in any case, while Freud's theoretical allegiance to Charcot may already have begun to waver during the summer of 1889, we see that matters are not so simple; and it would be hazardous, therefore, to venture any thesis on that basis as to the precise time in 1889 when, as would appear to be the case, Anna von Lieben returned to Paris in order to consult once again the celebrated Frenchman.[33]

Charcot was concerned with hypnosis primarily insofar as, in the interests of experiment and demonstration, it enabled him to simulate through suggestion in hysterical patients the same somatic symptoms as were characteristic of traumatic hysteria and which he supposed to originate during a kind of analogous yet spontaneous hypnoid state. Conditionally, he did also endorse the value of hypnotic suggestion in the treatment of hysterical conditions (Charcot, 1889, pp. 307–309; Moll, 1890, pp. 314–315; Owen, 1971, pp. 124–146). However, when Freud first began employing hypnosis therapeutically towards the end of 1887—by when he must have finally acquired some confidence in his abilities as a physician (cf. Freud, 1927, p. 253; Jones, 1953, pp. 27–28, 58, 64, 81, 171)—

certainly he did so under the influence of the 1886 book of Bernheim on the therapeutic applications of suggestion which, around that same time, he undertook to translate for publication in German (cf. Breuer and Freud, 1893–1895, p. 77; Freud to Fliess, 28 December 1887, in Bonaparte, A. Freud, and Kris, 1954, p. 53; Freud, 1925, p. 17; Macmillan, 1979, p. 301).

As stated, it was probably autumn 1888 when, at her request, Freud first administered hypnosis to Anna von Lieben; and, through suggestive influence, he obtained some immediate success (Breuer and Freud, 1893–1895, p. 177). As we learn from the *Studies on Hysteria,* it was "about a year" after this episode that an "old memory" suddenly returned to the patient—presumably some memory from long before that appeared to render intelligible the genesis of a particular symptom—whereupon "for nearly three years after this she once again lived through all the traumas of her life" under Freud's daily guidance (Breuer and Freud, 1893–1895, pp. 70, 177). We would therefore suppose, in other words, that, circa autumn 1889—about a year after he had apparently treated Anna with hypnotic suggestion—with her cooperation Freud began systematically employing the cathartic method.

Now in the *Studies on Hysteria,* using the pseudonym "Frau Emmy von N . . .," Freud presented the case of Fanny Moser—whom he had begun treating on May 1, 1889 (Breuer and Freud, 1893–1895, p. 48; cf. Ellenberger, 1977, p. 526)—as the first in which he had used Breuer's novel method, combining it at that time with straightforward hypnotic suggestion. But we must allow that, in writing up his case histories for that book, Freud was influenced in his presentation by didactic considerations (cf. Strachey, 1955, pp. xvi–xvii); also that he would later recall having used hypnotic suggestion "from the very first" in conjunction with Breuer's technique (1925, p. 19; cf. 1888a, pp. 56–57). A possibility does exist, then, certain chronological difficulties notwithstanding, that already before May 1889, perhaps more or less sporadically and spontaneously rather than methodically and with deliberation, Freud had begun experimenting with the cathartic method in a number of cases—including, as indeed James Strachey has considered (Strachey, 1955, p. xi), that of "Frau Cäcilie M . . . ."

At any rate, on Friday, July 19, 1889, presumably following a more than 18-hour train journey direct from Vienna, Freud visited Fanny Moser at her estate near Zürich following her return there from Vienna a month or so earlier after being successfully treated by him (Breuer and Freud, 1893–1895, p. 77; Ellenberger, 1977, p. 526). Freud was presently en route to Nancy to visit Prof. Hippolyte Bernheim and the latter's teacher in hypnotism, Ambroise Liébeault; and probably a major consideration in his decision to stop off in Zürich was a wish to visit the distinguished Swiss psychiatrist and neurologist Auguste Forel, a friend of Fanny Moser.[34] Freud had recently written an enthusiastic review of a short book by Forel on hypnosis, the first installment of which had been printed in a Viennese medical weekly just a few days earlier (Freud, 1889, p. 90). According to Ernest Jones, when Freud arrived in Nancy, he bore a letter of introduction from Forel (Jones, 1953, p. 236; cf. Freud, 1889, p. 90)—who had himself visited Bernheim's clinic two years before and been overwhelmed by all that he had seen (Forel, 1937, p. 167).

In his autobiographical sketch of 1925, Freud would offer the following recollection of his own visit:

> With the idea of perfecting my hypnotic technique, I made a journey to Nancy . . . and spent several weeks there. I witnessed the specta-cle of old Liébeault working among the poor women and children of the labouring classes. I was a spectator of Bernheim's astonishing experiments upon his hospital patients, and I received the profoun-dest impression of the possibility that there could be powerful mental processes which nevertheless remained hidden from the con-sciousness of men. Thinking it would be instructive, I had persuaded one of my patients to follow me to Nancy. This patient was a very highly gifted hysteric, a woman of good birth, who had been handed over to me because no one knew what to do with her. By hypnotic influence I had made it possible for her to lead a tolerable existence and I was always able to take her out of the misery of her condition. But she always relapsed again after a short time, and in my ignorance I attributed this to the fact that her hypnosis had never reached the stage of somnambulism with amnesia. Bernheim now attempted sev-eral times to bring this about, but he too failed. He frankly admitted to me that his great therapeutic successes by means of suggestion were only achieved in his hospital practice and not with his private patients. I had many stimulating conversations with him. . . . [pp. 17–18].

It has been speculated that the woman of "good birth" who "fol-lowed" Freud to Nancy was Fanny Moser (Strachey, 1966a, p.

65n). Such a notion is rendered untenable, however, by the fact that entries in a surviving guest book from her estate at Au show her to have had several visitors during the 12 days immediately following the occasion of Freud's signature, July 19, 1889.[35] Now it was inevitable that I should have wondered, once I had identified "Frau Cäcilie M . . ." as Anna von Lieben, whether in fact she may have been the woman concerned. But, despite some research that I instigated in France,[36] I was unable to find anything out; and it was only later, thanks to someone's indiscretion, that I was fortunate to obtain verification of the hypothesis.

It is a little-known fact that, during these years, Freud kept up a correspondence with his wife's younger sister, Minna Bernays—someone whom he characterized in an 1894 letter to Wilhelm Fliess as being, next to his wife, his closest confidante.[37] And, interestingly enough, in that correspondence he seems to have kept his sister-in-law informed not only about events in his family but also about important developments in his professional and intellectual lives. Now this I do not know from having inspected the correspondence, which is jealously withheld from scholarly scrutiny. But what I have stated can be inferred, reasonably enough, on the basis of those select fragments of it that have actually been published (E. Freud and L. Freud, 1968, pp. 44–46, 130–132, 191–193, 210–212, 232–234, 238–240; Simitis, 1978, pp. 131, 148; Blumenthal, 1984, p. 2).[38] Furthermore—as I can now go on to say, thanks to what I shall call "authoritative gossip"—in a letter to his sister-in-law sent from Nancy sometime in July 1889, Freud notes that he goes each day to the hotel where Frau von Lieben is staying—presumably, then, one of the city's fanciest, beyond his own means—in order to continue his treatment of her. And he advises Minna Bernays that, should she be at all curious as to what the actual experience of his treatment of this woman is like, then she should consult the novel *Dr. Heidenhoff's Process* by the American author Edward Bellamy.[39]

Now Bellamy would seem to have been a man possessed of a truly incredible, futuristic vision; and his novel *Dr. Heidenhoff's Process*, published in 1880 and today virtually forgotten, should, in my opinion, be hailed as a psychiatric classic. The story tells how, following moral transgressions of an implied sexual kind, a young provincial woman is driven by the traumatic power of her memories—or, at least, by their traumatic effect on her conscience—into a state of acute melancholia punctuated with bouts of hysterical excitement. Then desperate, driven by her memories into an almost suicidal state of despair, she goes as a last resort to a mysterious doctor—or is the man a charlatan?, we cannot be quite sure—named Gustav Heidenhoff, who practices in Boston. The man, who speaks with a German accent, specializes in what he calls "thought extirpation"; and his revolutionary, still experimental treatment, or "process," is a kind of hybrid version of catharsis and ECT. But now this in 1880, let us not forget!

So in order that the woman may gain liberation from her pathogenic memories, Heidenhoff gets her to tell him her story—that is, she has to plunge into her past and tell him what is troubling her so deeply.[40] Whereupon all of her traumatic memories are abolished during their narration through the action of an electric machine that Heidenhoff has himself invented which, although it does not induce any convulsions as such, does involve electrodes being attached to the patient's head that automatically wipe out all the troublesome reminiscences. The treatment, only one session,[41] is apparently successful; and the woman is as if restored miraculously to youth, innocence, and health.[42]

The underlying theme of Bellamy's extraordinary book is the medicalization—one might say, the "psychiatrization"—of morals and values.[43] And his grasp, in 1880, of some of the ethical ramifications of what was for him, of course, futuristic psychiatry is at once both profound and incredible. To what extent Freud was perhaps influenced by this book cannot be said. But—as far as we are concerned here—the only real basis that I can see for Freud's comparison as made in his letter to Minna Bernays between the "process" of Dr. Heidenhoff and his own treatment of Anna von Lieben is if, by the time of writing it, he had already begun to use the cathartic method to induce this woman to recall those memories from her past life that were supposedly responsible for her illness. Which is to say: it would appear that, even if somewhat irregularly, Freud had begun to use the "talking cure" with Anna von Lieben before his departure from Nancy in summer 1889—if, indeed, he had not already begun using it with her in Vienna during the preceding months.

Freud's later recollection (1925, p. 17) that he had spent "several weeks" in Nancy with Bernheim is hardly accurate. Given his visit to Frau Fanny Moser near Zürich on July 19, 1889, probably he would not have arrived in Nancy before the following day; and, according to Ernest Jones, in the company of Bernheim and Liébeault he then travelled on to Paris to attend the international congresses on psychology and hypnotism, arriving there on July 30 (Jones, 1953, p. 181). On that very day, however, Bernheim wrote to his friend Auguste Forel in Switzerland notifying him he would be in Paris beginning August 4 and saying he was glad to learn that Forel, too, would be there. He also noted that he was expecting the Munich psychiatrist Albert Freiherr von Schrenck-Notzing to join him in Nancy for the trip to Paris; and he remarked: "Dr. Freud is currently in Nancy and will go to the congress; he is a lovely lad" (in Walser, 1968, pp. 223–224).

There is a strong possibility, then, that it was not until August 4, 1889, or perhaps the day before, that Freud left Nancy in the company of his colleagues[44]—meaning that he would have spent two weeks in that city. According to Jones, Freud was "very bored" with the congresses and, after "ten days," spent mainly in sightseeing, he left Paris for Vienna on the evening of August 9 (Jones, 1953, p. 181). The congresses, however, took place at the Hôtel Dieu between August 6 and 12 (Ellenberger, 1970, p. 759). Thus, if it is indeed the case that Freud spent "ten days" in Paris, then it is probable that, however bored he may have been, he did not leave the French capital before the congresses had ended. Charcot, incidentally, was absent from Paris during this period (Jones, 1953, pp. 187–188; Ellenberger, 1970, p. 759; cf. Jones, 1957, p. 137). But those who attended the congresses included the American psychologist William James; the Italian alienist and anthropologist Cesare Lombroso; the Viennese neurologist Moritz Benedikt; the Belgian philosopher and psychologist Joseph Delboeuf; and a young French philosopher by the name of Pierre Janet.

On August 10, 1889, at the congress for hypnotism, two French physicians, H. Bourru and P. Burot, presented a joint paper in which they described how, some two years earlier, they had hypnotized a hysterical woman and thereby induced her to relive a traumatic experience from her past with the object of neutralizing its supposed pathogenic influence. Later, without hypnosis, under their guidance she had again recalled the episode with hallucinatory intensity, whereupon she recovered from her illness. The previous year, these two authors had published a book in which they reported similar cures obtained through the retrieval of traumatic memories and the reliving of associated emotions; and this work was influential in that it had prompted Janet to undertake similar investigations (Bourru and Burot, 1888, 1889; Chertok, 1961, pp. 284–287). Under hypnosis he had induced certain women to relive forgotten episodes associated with the onset of their illnesses and had sought to dissolve the traumatic power of their recollections by modifying them with suggestion (Chertok, 1961, p. 285).

Janet had presented the results of his research in a thesis published in spring 1889. By then, however, an almost identical method of psychotherapy had been anticipated by Delboeuf, as reported in installments of a paper published between November 1888 and March 1889 which, that spring, had also appeared as a book. Early in 1888 he had visited Bernheim's clinic in Nancy and, by means of hypnosis, had induced a woman there to relive a traumatic event that was tormenting her, thereby to render its memory innocuous through suggestive influence (Delboeuf, 1889; Janet, 1889; Macmillan, 1979, pp. 299–309). Moreover, it was during this same period that Benedikt—a longtime practitioner of hypnosis, who in 1885 had provided Freud with a letter of introduction to his friend Charcot (Jones, 1953, pp. 208, 251; Lesky, 1976, pp. 351–352)— was evolving a strikingly similar method of psychotherapy. It involved probing deeply into the mental lives of patients in search of what Benedikt termed "pathogenic secrets" (Ellenberger, 1970, pp. 46, 301, 486, 518, 536, 714, 762, 767).

Doubtless, then, talk about such matters was very much in the air during Freud's 1889 visit to Paris. And it is probable that, even if bored with the congress itself, he would nevertheless have spent some time conversing with his colleagues in social contexts (cf. Forel, 1937, p. 185). In addition to Forel and Schrenck-Notzing, Bernheim's circle of friends included Joseph Delboeuf, who had visited Charcot's institute during the same period as Freud (cf. Walser, 1968, pp. 225–226, 230–232; Ellenberger, 1970, pp. 96, 436, 753). In Forel's later recollection, Delboeuf was "as learned in the classical tongues as in mathematics, in philosophy as in hypnotism"; he was "also an admirable writer, a man of astonishing vivacity, and a brilliant wit" (Forel, 1937, p. 185). And that Freud himself made this man's acquaintance is strongly intimated by references to the Belgian professor found in his later works that, given the circumstances described, surely betray a firsthand impression (cf. Breuer and Freud, 1893–1895, p. 101; Freud, 1900, p. 60).[45]

In his later works, Freud would represent that he had begun employing the cathartic method under the influence of what he had learned from Josef Breuer about the treatment of Bertha Pappenheim during the period 1881–1882 (1910, pp. 9–22; 1914, pp. 7–12; 1925, pp. 19–27). Here we see, however, that, by the year 1889, such a mode of therapy was very much a product of the *Zeitgeist*—quite obviously it was an idea whose time had come, different persons having adopted similar methods more or less simultaneously although technically acting independently of one another. It had long been maintained by many that memories can be stored unconsciously and be liable to retrieval by artificial means. An instance of this—involving a woman who, afflicted with a fever, recalled words in a foreign language once spoken by a former employer—had been reported by Samuel Taylor Coleridge, cited by the English psychiatrist Henry Maudsley, and made famous by Franz Brentano in 1874 when, in his *Psychology from an Empirical Standpoint,* he quoted Maudsley in seeking to repudiate his thesis that there exist thought processes unconscious in nature (Brentano, 1874, pp. 59, 114; cf. Swales, in preparation). There was only a short step involved, then, in supposing that the medium of hypnosis might be used to retrieve long-lost memories.

During the late 1860s and the 1870s, demonstrations of hypnosis presented in cities all over Europe by the Danish hypnotist Carl Hansen excited a great deal of popular controversy but, also, considerable scientific interest (Sextus, 1893, pp. 28–30; cf. Ellenberger, 1970, pp. 750–751). It was after having witnessed one such demonstration that Charcot set about investigating the phenomenon (Sextus, 1893, p. 29); the same was true in the case of the Breslau physiologist Rudolf Heidenhain, who thereafter undertook to research the changes in reflex action produced by hypnosis (Heidenhain, 1880; Sextus, 1893, p. 30); and it was in all probability under Hansen's provocation that, early in 1880, Brentano visited Breslau for the purpose of observing the experiments of Heidenhain (cf. Hirschmüller, 1978, pp. 129–130).[46] Over the course of the next few years, Charcot would publicly contend that the symptoms of hysteria, widely considered to be mere imitation, were authentic physiological or "functional" phenomena produced by the influence of particular traumatic ideas engendered during a kind of hypnoid state—a state that he claimed to reproduce artificially, complete with the symptoms as required, through hypnotic suggestion.

Confronted with the case of Bertha Pappenheim, whose hysterical symptoms had frequently disappeared when the traumatic ideas associated with their original occurrence were recollected and talked away, Freud and Breuer looked upon Charcot's ideas as providing an essential explanation (cf. Freud, 1910, p. 21; 1914, p. 17). Despite the controversy then surrounding them, Charcot's ideas were also found cogent by many other scientists, neurologists and psychiatrists in particular. And the general notion that, indeed, hysterics suffered from traumatic ideas—reminiscences, even, liable to retrieval and extirpation—would have been granted considerable popular currency by a book such as the novel of Edward Bellamy, published in 1880. It is really not so surprising, then, that by 1889— under the cumulative influence of persons such as Hansen, Charcot, Bernheim, and perhaps even Bellamy—different investigators, working separately from one another, should have evolved strikingly similar modes of psychotherapy.[47]

In the particular case of Freud and Breuer, however, there was yet another powerful source of inspiration that would certainly have served to assure them that they were on to something big, also something very real. In his *Poetics*—wherein he conceives of drama, poetry, and music as being, fundamentally, modes of "imitation"— Aristotle interprets theatrical tragedy as a medium which, by invoking pity and fear, accomplishes a "catharsis of such emotions" among the audience (*De Poetica*, 6. 24–28). This passage was long understood to imply either a moral or an aesthetic purgation of the emotions; but, in 1857, the classical philologist Jacob Bernays had advanced a novel medical interpretation, arguing that Aristotle had conceived of tragedy as a catharsis of emotions which, if undischarged, would assume a noxious property (cf. Hirschmüller, 1978, pp. 206–207).

Bernays's work had been republished in 1880, a year before his death; and this, together with a series of obituaries which then appeared in popular newspapers, would appear to have been responsible for stimulating a surge of interest in "catharsis" to the extent that—as Dalma (1963) and Hirschmüller (1978, pp. 206–212) have

demonstrated—it then became a very fashionable topic of discussion among the fin-de-siècle Viennese *haute bourgeoisie*. To our
knowledge, it was not before 1892–1893 that Freud and Breuer
would first use the terms "catharsis" and "abreaction" (Breuer and
Freud, 1893–1895, p. 8; Hirschmüller, 1978, p. 209). However, as
the two mentioned historians have convincingly argued by means of
their reconstructions of the contemporary *Zeitgeist*, it is virtually
inconceivable that, when formulating their joint theory, Freud and
Breuer were not under the influence of Bernays's conception; and
the same basic argument can be extended to apply to the very
inception of Breuer's method while treating Bertha Pappenheim
during the years 1881–1882 (cf. Jensen, 1984, pp. 37–38).

One of those who participated in the catharsis discussion and had
written an obituary on the occasion of Bernays's death in 1881 was
the philologist Theodor Gomperz. Not only was he a friend and
patient of Breuer (Kann, 1974, p. 60), it is also reported that Bertha
Pappenheim was herself acquainted with his family and that she
maintained an active interest in matters concerning theater (Jensen,
1984, p. 37). Besides, Bertha's father was appointed the legal guard-
ian of Bernays's niece Martha, later the fiancée of Freud, following
the sudden death of her father in 1879, and she and Martha were
closely befriended (Jensen, 1984, p. 35). Between Gomperz and
Breuer there existed a close intellectual rapport (cf. Hirschmüller,
1978, pp. 285–293) and this would later extend to Freud. In 1892,
Gomperz considered it highly desirable that his older son Heinrich
should meet the young German experimental psychologist Hugo
Münsterberg, in part because of the high esteem for his work which
Freud must at some point have expressed in personal communication between the two of them.[48]

In light of this backdrop, then, it can be confidently asserted that,
by the late 1880s, "catharsis" would hardly have been an unfamiliar
notion for Anna von Lieben. That she would have been familiar
with the Bernays interpretation of Aristotle's "catharsis" is altogether probable—given, that is, the extent of her culture and her
close relationship with her uncle Theodor.[49] That by word of
mouth she may even have heard about the extraordinary illness and
treatment of Bertha Pappenheim is a distinct possibility—given,
that is, Bertha's acquaintance with the Gomperzes and Breuer's
treatment of both women during the same period.[50] Besides, it is
unlikely that Freud would have begun to treat Anna with Breuer's

novel method without first describing its nature and outlining his hopes and expectations in that regard (cf. Freud to Fliess, 28 April 1897, in Bonaparte, A. Freud, and Kris, 1954, pp. 195–196). Thus, insofar as the essential concept of a "catharsis" being systematically undertaken to effect a psychological "purgation" precedes Freud's actual use of the method, then probably his patient would have subscribed to the beauty of the idea, would more or less have known what was expected of her, and would probably not have wished to disappoint her expectant and eager young physician.

In a poem entitled "Case History" (Lieben, 1901, pp. 155–156), Anna describes the reliving of old memories; and although, because it is undated, it is not possible to say if it was written before or after the commencement of Freud's treatment, the poem is clearly of great significance in this latter respect:

I

My memory I have to loathe,
It will not let my heart be at peace.
Like a beast of prey lurking in wait,
Forever through pain and shuddering
It rattles at the horror of the graves
Of that which only seems to be dead.
Each pain, buried too early,
Is to return to life again,
Once again to gulp breath,
In order to sink away forever,
As Nature invents the curse—
The ghostly procession [of memories] begins.

II

First I see my youth,
All of it hidden deeply by veils;
Through the veil gazes the eye—
Dark, questioning, filled with pain.

In the distance, lovers [*Amoretten*] are waving;
The urges of hot yearning awaken,
But only heavy chains of suffering
She drags sighing, for years.

Finally, tired, it ceases,
She being powerless, it closes her eye,

But in the grave it still breathes flames,
Disturbing my life's peace.

*   *   *

Youth that was buried too early
Must have life once again,
Once again to gulp breath,
In order to sink away forever.[51]

Here the poetess professes to loathe her memories. Given, however, her fanciful bent, her cultured sensibility, and the monotony of her physical circumstances, the probability is that, nevertheless, she would have taken to abreacting them—that is, to "catharsis"—with a passion.

It was presumably, then, at some point during 1889—and possibly even some time prior to the trip to Nancy that July—that Freud began systematically employing the cathartic method in treating Anna von Lieben. As we learn from the *Studies on Hysteria,* an old memory of hers suddenly intruded into the full light of her consciousness—whereupon, for nearly three years, she lived through her "hysterical psychosis for the payment of old debts," involving the reproduction of all her many traumas and associated symptoms, accumulated over a 33-year period, during recurrent hysterical attacks (Breuer and Freud, 1893–1895, pp. 69–70). Thus, often twice a day over the course of the three years or so following, Freud would be called upon to minister to a mind diseased—to pluck from the woman's past some rooted sorrow; to erase troubled memories from her brain; and, with the aid of some unspecified "artificial means" that served to hasten the end of her attacks (Breuer and Freud, 1893–1895, p. 178), to soften the weight on her heart so that she might overcome those agencies keeping her from rest.

During the period in question, with Anna von Lieben's cooperation, Freud would modify his method of treatment in a manner fateful for the whole future of his work. But, to acquaint ourselves with this innovation, we have first to return to his visit to Nancy in July 1889 and inspect yet another version of that episode—this one featuring a sequel:

. . . Freud and Breuer continued to treat cases of hysteria . . . but they were soon confronted by . . . a great many people who

. . . could not be hypnotized. They were especially interested in a certain very intelligent woman whom they made every effort to hypnotize, but without success. Finally Freud took her to Bernheim in France, who was reputed to be able to hypnotize almost all of his patients, but he, too, could do nothing with her. What was to be done? Freud then thought of an experiment that he saw in Bernheim's clinic. . . .

After . . . a post-hypnotic suggestion Bernheim would ask the pa-tient to try and recall what happened while he was unconscious. The latter would say that he remembered nothing; he was urged on, however, to concentrate and think until at first some vague reminis-cence came to consciousness, and finally the very suggestion that was given during the hypnosis. Now Freud saw no reason why the same thing could not be done with his patient who could not be hypno-tized; if it was possible to recall a post-hypnotic suggestion, why should it be impossible to recall the episode associated with her symptom? He set about questioning the woman; at first she could recall nothing; he would insist upon her telling him what came to her mind, as she was concentrating her attention upon the symptom. She talked about many things that had no apparent connection with the particular situation; she went on and on and he noted very carefully everything she said. In this way, he finally reached the origin of the symptom. He then found not only that hypnotism was not necessary but that it was much better to treat a patient without it, for people, as a rule, have an almost instinctive dread of hypnosis. That is how he developed what he called the "continuous [= "free"] association method"; it was the most significant contribution to the psycho-analytic procedure [Brill, 1921, pp. 16–18].

Now what is to be made of this story? It goes so far as to attribute Freud's introduction of his "free association" method to his treat-ment of the same woman who visited Nancy with him—a sequel absent from Freud's own account of that episode as found in his autobiographical sketch of 1925. We might therefore be inclined to suppose this to be a mere corruption of Freud's own version—but not, however, when we take into account that the story as quoted is to be found in a book entitled *Fundamental Conceptions of Psycho-analysis* by Abraham A. Brill, Freud's American translator, that was published in 1921. Under the terms of his will, Brill's letters from Freud are restricted till the year 1998 (Jones, 1955, p. xiii). In the meantime, though—while in the hope of one day obtaining some positive confirmation—we are bound to assume that, in reporting the episode in question, Brill must have been basing himself directly on conversations or correspondence with Freud. For, in 1921, the fact that a woman patient had visited Nancy with Freud in 1889 in the hope of being more effectively hypnotized by Bernheim was not a matter of public knowledge.

It is of great significance that, as we would assume to be so, in personal communication with Brill, Freud attributed the very introduction of his "free association" method—and therefore the birth of psychoanalysis proper—specifically to his treatment of a woman whom we now know to have been Anna von Lieben. Up till now we have been concerned with Freud's introduction of the cathartic method, using it to replace straightforward hypnotic suggestion. But now, from Brill, we learn how Freud subsequently went on to dispense altogether with hypnosis, replacing it with the "association" technique. This method required the patient to lie on a sofa while Freud sat nearby. And the fact that Anna spent most of her time reclining on a *chaise longue* could well have been, therefore, a crucial factor in precipitating this development.

Like Freud himself (Breuer and Freud, 1893–1895, pp. 109–111; Freud, 1925, pp. 27–28), Brill connects Freud's innovation of the "association" method with his recollection of Bernheim's success in retrieving suggestions implanted during hypnosis. And, while it is possible that following the visit to Nancy Freud ceased altogether attempting to hypnotize Anna von Lieben, it may nevertheless have been the case that, in seeking to dissolve her hysterical attacks twice a day for some three years, it was only gradually that he relinquished hypnotism and, having to unravel the most intricate threads of her memory, allowed the "free association" technique more or less spontaneously to assert itself. And, presumably, in adopting this latter method, Freud employed it in combination with his so-called "pressure technique" whereby, on the model of what he had watched Bernheim do towards retrieving hypnotic suggestions, he would lay his hand on his patient's forehead, or take the patient's head between his hands, assuring the person that this would stimulate the particular memory requiring recollection (Breuer and Freud, 1893–1895, pp. 109–111; Freud, 1925, p. 28).[52]

Now there is an important detail absent from the fragments of the case history of "Frau Cäcilie M . . ." as found in the *Studies on Hysteria*—specifically the fact that Anna von Lieben was a severe morphine addict. If we are to give significance to a reference to the drug found in a poem written during her period of illness in England (Lieben, 1901, p. 54), then possibly her use of morphine had begun during her youth and had since continued more or less sporadically. We do not know when she became actually dependent on the drug—however, one would assume this must have occurred some time following 1882, the year when she gave birth to the last of her children. At any rate, Meja Ruprecht, the nurse and housekeeper, was put in charge of all of Anna's medicines—the morphine included. And now everyday Freud would visit the nursery to give Meja instructions and fetch morphine from her—the drug was certainly, then, the "artificial means," referred to by Freud in one of the fragments of case history, which he used to "hasten the end" of his patient's hysterical attacks (Breuer and Freud, 1893–1895, p. 178).

Now, in my opinion, the absence of any reference to the morphine addiction of "Frau Cäcilie M . . ." represents a serious omission from the *Studies on Hysteria*. From one fragment of her case history, we learn that Breuer and Freud once had occasion to refuse their patient "a drug she had asked for" (Breuer and Freud, 1893–1895, p. 181); and, elsewhere in the book, Breuer makes reference in passing to an "acute hysteria" that "arose in association with a withdrawal of morphine" in a case where there was "already a complicated hysteria present" (Breuer and Freud, 1893–1895, p. 249). And these references prompt us to wonder why the two authors failed to clarify matters further—when referring to the "artificial means," Freud could as easily have stated "an injection of morphine"; and, in referring to an acute hysteria accompanying a morphine withdrawal, Breuer identified the patient involved as merely "another case" (Breuer and Freud, 1893–1895, p. 249), when in all probability it was "Frau Cäcilie M . . ." to whom he was referring.

There are a number of possible reasons for such a hiatus—during the years 1885–1887, Freud's scientific credibility had suffered damage following his incautious advocacy of cocaine as a means of curing morphine addiction (cf. Jones, 1953, p. 94); there are also certain indications that Breuer may have been somewhat hasty in dispensing morphine to his patients,[53] on which basis he might well have incurred criticisms from certain of his colleagues. It is conceivable, then, that drugs represented for the two authors a somewhat sensitive issue—but the hiatus could as well have had tendentious motives, besides. Possibly the authors were concerned that critics might question whether it was not in fact the central effects of the morphine, rather than the cathartic treatment per se, which had been responsible for restoring the patient's clarity of mind and emotional stability. And possibly the authors were concerned to preclude another objection—namely, and here to state the matter rhetorically: Was it not hazardous to generalize with respect to the psychological mechanism of hysteria on the basis of a woman addicted to morphine and therefore especially liable to alternating states of intense nervous excitation and sopor?

This last question can also now be posed in a more general way: viz., was it not hazardous to universalize with respect to the psychological mechanism of hysteria on the basis of a woman who, given her aristocratic station and so much else about her, was not only a highly atypical member of the human species but also so actively given to fantasy as her poetry shows her to have been—a propensity to fantasizing that may have been yet further stimulated by the influence of Morpheus, God of Dreams? Is Anna's penchant for turning pains into images and images into pains not to be directly related to her poetic bent and the flights of fantasy that these involved? Note how her hallucinatory conversion of the "counterparts" Breuer and Freud into two men hanging on a tree, by means of the pun contained in the French word *pendant* (Breuer and Freud, 1893–1895, p. 181), is, besides being very "poetic," a symbolization produced contemporarily with the actual treatment— inviting the question, then, as to whether similar interpretations, involving mimetic relationships between symptoms and ideas that were supposedly forged on the occasion of events long forgotten, were not in fact *current* flights of mutual fantasy between patient and doctor in the manner of a *folie à deux*.

But even if all this were so, would it necessarily detract in any way from the authenticity and the universality of the phenomenon of "symbolic conversion" in hysteria? Earlier it was noted how "the mere contact with sickness or with misery" tended to produce both "psychological and physical pain" (Ewart, 1907, p. 78) in the case of so many of the women members of Anna's family circle. And now, taking such a fact into account, and proceeding to turn the whole argument on end: In the very phenomenon of unrestrained fantasy, as perhaps exemplified by Anna von Lieben, have we perhaps an explanation for hysteria of the classical form so prevalent among unfulfilled women during that period? In other words, was hysteria in truth an illness of fantasy and a fantasy of an illness? And here I might point out that what is also absent from the fragments of case history in the *Studies on Hysteria* is any reference, or even so much as an allusion, to what I characterized earlier as the "pathogenic milieu *par excellence*" of which Anna was a product—a truly fantastical milieu almost geared to begetting the syndrome of incontinent fantasy; a milieu where, indeed, art and neurosis tended to fuse into one.

One might say that—being a child of his time and having, through Breuer, a close association with Vienna's *haute bourgeoisie;* and being, moreover, reliant upon the latter for his own financial welfare—Freud would have lacked, understandably enough, the social and historical perspective that would be prerequisite to any impugnment of that milieu. We should recall, though, that, in 1886, Theodor Gomperz had himself ascribed the illnesses of the women in his family circle to "the inheritance of a very old civilized race and of the urban life"—an atavistic cum environmental explanation, albeit perhaps a somewhat unsophisticated one. But, at any rate, it is certainly of note that, while ostensibly wedded to Charcot's principle of environmental trauma in the genesis of hysteria, the whole thrust of Freud's concern, even at this early stage of his thinking, was nevertheless with the intrapsychic processes of the "unconscious" whose existence he was postulating rather than with any objective features of the supposed traumas, per se.[54]

It is to be supposed that Freud's commitment to treating Anna von Lieben twice a day for some three years would have entailed some restrictions on his own life and movements—but the treatment must have been a very lucrative one for him to undertake. And indeed, it can be said with certainty that Frau Anna was the "most important patient [*Hauptklientin*]" referred to by Freud in writing to his friend Wilhelm Fliess on August 1, 1890, partly on whose account he felt unable to visit his friend in Berlin because just then—as was so often the case—she was undergoing "a kind of nervous crisis . . ." (Freud to Fliess, 1 August 1890, in Bonaparte, A. Freud, and Kris, 1954, pp. 59–60). The ellipsis, as found in the published version of the letter, replaces the remark "and perhaps in my absence [she] might get well" (see note 4)—betraying, of course, the fact that Freud had a powerful vested interest in continuing her treatment. In that same letter, ironically enough, Freud mentioned to Fliess that he was especially sorry about not being able to see him "because for years now I have been without a teacher [*Lehrmeister*]" (Freud to Fliess, 1 August 1890, in Bonaparte, A. Freud, and Kris, 1954, p. 60) —ironical, because this was precisely the role that in subsequent years he would attribute to his *Hauptklientin* of that time.

Freud's letter to Fliess was sent from Reichenau, a fashionable resort in the Semmering district some 50 miles southwest of Vienna which he and his family then used to patronize each summer.[55] As we would presume on the basis of his continuing daily treatment of Anna and his letter to Fliess of July 12, 1892 in which he mentions to his friend that his "prima donna has just moved into the Brühl," it was Freud's custom during these summers—that is to say, during the years 1890 through 1892, also possibly during the summers of 1889 and 1893—to visit her regularly at the Villa Todesco in Hinterbrühl. The Brühl was connected with the town of Mödling by an electric railway—in fact the first one in Europe, opened in 1883. And Mödling, just to the south of Vienna, stands on the main railway line linking the city with the Semmering. Thus, Freud could manage regular visits to the Villa Todesco, whether travelling from Vienna or from Reichenau.[56]

Now these were the years when, as Freud would later recall, he found it "highly flattering to enjoy the reputation of being a miracle worker"—a reputation then bestowed upon him if not in virtue of any "huge, enormous halo" then at least his role as a professional hypnotist (Freud, 1925, p. 17; cf. Freud to M. Bernays, 20 June 1885, in E. Freud and L. Freud, 1968, p. 158). And, whether or not the suggested miracles were actually forthcoming, there can be no mistake about it—these were the days when he was popularly conceived of in Vienna not as a regular physician but as a *magnétiseur*. A glimpse of just such a Freud we get from the biography of the legendary violinist Fritz Kreisler, born in 1875, who is quoted as reminiscing:

> Freud made a deep impression on me, even though [being so young] I was unable to grasp fully what he was discussing with my father [Dr. Samuel Kreisler, physician to Freud's parents and a friend of Freud]. . . . He was then by no means the famous man he later came to be, but a practicing *magnétiseur*. He tried, in fact, to help my

ailing mother [Anna Kreisler, born Reches] by suggesting [to her] that she really wasn't crippled at all but would be able to move about after hypnotic treatments. I never saw her walk, however! [in Lochner, 1950, p. 13; cf. Freud to Martha Bernays, 26 November 1885, in E. Freud and L. Freud, 1968, pp. 190–191].

And it is in this somewhat Mesmeresque context—that of Freud as *magnétiseur* making use of the "mystical" medium hypnosis (Freud, 1910, p. 22)—that we must understand the young Lieben children's reaction upon seeing him constantly arriving at their home, or visiting the nursery to talk with Meja, twice a day for some years. They feared and detested him—for them he was *"der Zauberer,"* the "magician," come to put their mother into a trance yet again and to accompany her through her fits of ravings, screamings, and long declamatory speeches.

And indeed, the atmosphere in Anna's sickroom must have had something of the séance, something of the black magic, about it, not to mention the decadent—what with the injections of morphine, the cocaine?,[57] the caviar and the champagne, and the opulence of the setting; also the passionate and—as we shall learn shortly—perhaps on occasion somewhat lurid content of Anna's reminiscences as she lay there abreacting them on a *chaise longue;* also certain physical aspects of the treatment. Possibly from time to time, if Anna was suffering particular kinds of pains, Freud would have proceeded to massage her (cf. Breuer and Freud, 1893–1895, pp. 51–56); and it is probable that, in endeavoring to retrieve many of her memories, he used the so-called "pressure technique," which involved taking his patient's head in his hands or laying his hand on his patient's forehead, à la Bernheim—a technique plainly related to the messianic or magical traditions. Moreover, an entry from many years later in the diary of Sandor Ferenczi would indicate that Freud must have described to his pupil how, during his early years in practice, he had even lain on the floor, sometimes for hours at a time, accompanying a patient through hysterical crises—most surely a reference to his treatment of Anna von Lieben before any other of his patients.[58]

Now it remains to be said that, according to descendants of the family, there existed some extraordinary kind of rapport—some extraordinary intensity of mutual "infatuation"—between Anna von Lieben and Freud. And, after all, who would really doubt as much when, half a century later, Freud would remember this woman out of *all* his many hundreds of patients as having been nothing less than his "teacher"—his *Lehrmeisterin?* Now one might reasonably wonder how Leopold von Lieben felt about his wife's infatuation with her young doctor; and it should come as no surprise that, having had to put up with a hysterically ill wife for so many years, he sought his female company elsewhere. Around the time of Freud's arrival on the scene, he took up with a certain Frl. Molly Filtsch—an intimate of Anna's father and mother but someone intensely disliked by most of the family.[59] How Anna felt about her husband's infidelity, assuming she got to learn about it, we do not know. But over the course of time the liaison became respectable and most of the members of the family circle eventually came to tolerate the woman.

But it has yet to be said in respect of Anna von Lieben and Freud that her side of their rapport—her side of the mutual "trans-ference"—was entirely conditional upon his willingness to dispense her morphine, meaning to say that, if he refused her the drug, then he jeopardized or forfeited the rapport. It was surely on this ac-count, then, that, at some point during the treatment, Freud took a step which probably cost him the good will of Meja Ruprecht. A French-speaking German governess, Frl. Lina Baumann, had been appointed to supervise the education of the children, and soon she set about gaining influence over the mother. A severe and unsym-pathetic woman, for a time she vied with Meja over who should dispense morphine to Frau Anna—as whoever had this job auto-matically won great power in the household. As a result, Meja was gradually displaced and Anna demanded that the keys to the drug cabinet should be handed over to the governess. And, although Meja was surely very hurt, Freud agreed to this in the hope he would thereby placate his patient.

Of special interest is that Freud reportedly made Anna keep a diary of her analysis. However—and now comes a sad story—a son-in-law is said to have destroyed it some years later on the grounds that it was full of private and indecent things, even perhaps outright obscenities. Nevertheless, from the published fragments of case his-tory it is clear that, in treating "Frau Cäcilie M . . .," Freud gained many of his earliest insights not only into the essential process of "abreaction" but also—particularly, no doubt, through their inno-vation of the "free association" method, although its use in her case is not explicitly stated—into so many of those mechanisms of mind postulated by him as being manifestations of the "unconscious." From the *Studies on Hysteria* it is evident that the phenomena of conversion and symbolization, counter-will, conflict and defense, even perhaps wit and superstition—all of these are to be found occurring in the treatment of this one patient, all of them presented themselves daily before Freud's eyes and ears. Indeed, without fear of exaggeration one might say that Anna von Lieben presented the "unconscious" to Freud on a silver platter.

But to all of these mentioned things we can now also add the rapport—in other words, the phenomenon of "transference." Also, no doubt—seeing as it is clear enough from her poetry that Anna's own understanding of her illness was that it was largely consequent upon earlier disturbances of passion (Lieben, 1901, pp. 19, 25, 29, 34–35, 56, 115, 155–156)—Freud was brought into direct confrontation with the realm of sexuality, blatant rather than latent.[60] We may also venture to suppose that Anna, a woman hitherto concerned with dreams and their interpretation, would surely have been among those who encouraged Freud in his recognition of their significance.[61] And allowing that, as a hypnotist, Freud's formal technique was to have his subject *sit* directly in front of him,[62] we might again go so far as to suppose that his introduction of the analytic couch may have owed a very great deal to his treatment of this patient—a woman who spent much of her life, and probably all of her treatment, reclining on a *chaise longue*.

Thanks to the existence of a letter, since published, which Breuer sent to Auguste Forel on 21 November 1907, we know that, during the course of the treatment, in the process of retrieving and abreacting those memories supposedly responsible for her illness, under Freud's guidance Anna plunged further and further back, right to her childhood. As Breuer recalled for the benefit of Forel: "We were skeptical and astonished"—and he went on to explain that, while "these were only Freud's findings," they were nevertheless "constantly discussed" at the time between the two of them (Breuer to Forel, 21 November 1907, in Ackerknecht, 1957, p. 170). So in every respect, then, in discussing Freud and his "teacher," there can be no question but that we are talking about the very *birth* of psychoanalysis; and it is indeed an extraordinary reflection on Freud scholarship that nothing has been known until now about a woman who, in truth, was instrumental to its very conception.[63]

On June 28, 1892, Freud wrote to Fliess announcing that Breuer had agreed to full publication of their investigations into hysteria—as he would remark a little facetiously in another letter, "it has cost enough in battles with Mr. Collaborator" (Freud to Fliess, 28 June 1892, 18 December 1892, in Bonaparte, A. Freud, and Kris, 1954, pp. 62, 64). For some years past, unable to properly present the fruits of his own investigations unless permitted to take the case history of Bertha Pappenheim as his point of departure, Freud had been attempting to seduce Breuer into publication (cf. Freud, 1925, p. 21; Jones, 1953, p. 250)—in 1888 he had even sought to force his mentor's hand by announcing Breuer's novel therapeutic method in a published essay on hysteria (Freud, 1888a, p. 56). More than that, though, Freud had reason to desire a joint publication with Breuer in virtue of the latter's scientific reputation and prestige (cf. 1925, pp. 19, 26). Despite attempts at 'psychophantasizing' him, howev-er—as with his 1886 inscription to "the secret master of hysteria," and the formal dedication of his 1891 book *On Aphasia* to his respected friend[64]—Breuer had steadfastly resisted Freud's persua-sion (cf. Freud to Minna Bernays, 13 July 1891 in E. Freud and L. Freud, 1968, pp. 238–239; Jones, 1953, p. 213). And there were probably a number of reasons for his recalcitrance.

Contrary to the two authors' subsequent representations (Breuer and Freud, 1893–1895, pp. 40–41, 47; Freud, 1916–1917, pp. 274, 279; 1923, p. 235; 1924, p. 193), Breuer had by no means succeeded in finally curing Bertha Pappenheim (Freud to Zweig, 2 June 1932, in E. Freud and L. Freud, 1968, p. 428; Bjerre, 1916, p. 67; Jones, 1953, p. 225; Ellenberger, 1972, pp. 270, 277–279; Hirschmüller, 1978, pp. 152–157, 362–381). Given her family's prominence in the local Jewish community, moreover, publication of her case history would have appeared difficult without compromising her identity; and Breuer had reason not to want to stir up the past in that his own conduct at the time had fallen short of being exemplary (Freud, 1925, p. 26; Jones, 1953, p. 224; Hirschmüller, 1978, p. 366). Also to be reckoned, in my opinion, is the hostility of Theodor Meynert—not only in respect of hypnosis[65] and, on that account, towards Freud in particular; but also, as Breuer could anticipate, in respect of a psychological as opposed to an organic theory of hys-teria. Meynert was a figure of great power and influence in the Viennese medical establishment; and it is perhaps very significant that, under pressure from Freud, Breuer finally "gave way" and agreed to a joint publication (Freud, 1925, p. 21) only a matter of weeks following Meynert's sudden death on May 3, 1892 at the age of 58. That July, incidentally, as he informed Fliess, Freud had "a rare human delight" in being able to choose for himself whatever books he liked from his former teacher's library—"a little like when a savage drinks mead out of the skull of the enemy."[66]

But, in his later autobiographical sketch, Freud would indicate that an important factor in his finally being able to persuade Breuer to agree to a publication was the fact that, in the meantime, in published works, Pierre Janet had anticipated several of Breuer's findings (Freud, 1925, p. 21; cf. McGuire and Burnham, 1983, p. 254); while, in the *Studies on Hysteria,* Freud states that it was the study of the "remarkable case" of "Frau Cäcilie M . . .," jointly with Breuer, which led directly to the publication in a Viennese medical journal in January 1893 of their "Preliminary Communica' tion"—the paper that had heralded the *Studies* (Breuer and Freud, 1893–1895, p. 178). One is tempted to assume, then, that Freud must have succeeded in convincing Breuer that the "first case" of Bertha Pappenheim had not been in any way atypical; and that the cathartic method, used with or without hypnosis, was indeed effec' tive in treating hysteria. It is of note, though, that the members of Anna von Lieben's family circle shared neither the enthusiasm of Freud nor the confidence of Breuer. Indeed, convinced of Anna's physician's impotence, they would have preferred to have no more of it and see him thrown to the dogs.

According to descendants, the members of the family became ever more skeptical and had no confidence at all in what Freud was doing. In fact, they quite detested the man and kept on asking each other why he seemed powerless to really help her—to effect some permanent improvement in her condition—rather than going on month after month with all this "talking," which seemed to be leading nowhere at all. And, in this general connection, some con' temporary statements of Anna's uncle, Theodor Gomperz, are awfully significant. Towards the end of 1892, Gomperz's wife Elise, then 44 years old, sought relief from Freud of her neuralgic pains; and reportedly Freud promised her a cure through hypnotic sug' gestion (Kann, 1974, p. 234). This was not to be so easily accom' plished, however, and Theodor Gomperz felt deeply ambivalent— at one time optimistic, another time pessimistic—as to whether anything permanent could be accomplished through such treatment (Kann, 1974, pp. 234–236).

On November 13, 1892, in writing to his son Heinrich, Gomperz remarked:

> Mama seems through hypnosis to be really on the way to a cure. Would only that the means of healing was not so uncanny [*unheimlich*] and so little experimented with. . . [in Kann, 1974, p. 234].

Then, two months later, on January 8, 1893, he wrote to his wife Elise, then staying at a spa near Vienna:

> I am very pleased to learn that . . . you are starting to feel better, and regret only that you also consult Freud from a distance [i.e., presumably by letter]. . . . Only and always only ear-confession and hypnosis—from that we have seen no wonders; I could only ever see increasing deterioration. All reasonable people—Breuer and Freud here excepted—warn incessantly about the continuation of these until now more than fruitless experiments. . . . Hypnosis appears to me to be like a newly invented medicine which no one understands yet how to dose and which, like other (and particularly the effective) healing medicines, has an effect of poison when not properly measured. . . [in Kann, 1974, p. 235].[67]

In another letter to his wife, dated April 7, 1893, Gomperz accuses Freud's hypnotic treatment of actually being responsible for engendering his wife's hypernervosity—in other words, then, of being the very illness of which the treatment purported to be a cure. Elise was automatically transforming each idea that entered her head into a pain, usually of a physical kind (Kann, 1974, p. 236). And still in early 1894 she was turning to Freud for hypnotic relief of her neuralgia (Kann, 1974, p. 251).[68]

Now why, when, and how did Freud discontinue his treatment of Anna von Lieben? We know from the "prima donna" remark that Freud was anticipating continuation of his treatment in the Brühl during the summer of 1892. And a reference to the Brühl in a letter to Fliess dated July 24, 1893 (see note 4) could, although cryptic, be construed to imply that Freud still at that time considered Anna his patient. But, at some point before autumn 1893, the treatment ceased; in a letter to Fliess of November 27, 1893 (see note 4), Freud mentions having "lost" Frau von Lieben, and he says his head has since been missing the "usual overwork." The family's descendants are inclined to suppose Freud was bound to end his treatment as otherwise the woman would have devoured him— reportedly she talked so much that he instructed her to write every-thing down, but eventually even that got out of hand. Whether there is truth in that version of the finale, it is difficult to say. But I am myself inclined to the view that, having seen the treatment was bringing no permanent improvement, the family intervened and, probably with Breuer's agreement, brought it to a halt.

And here it is perhaps not inappropriate to reflect for a moment on Gomperz's comparison between hypnotic suggestion—if not ac-tually catharsis, per se—and those effective "healing medicines" that have "an effect of poison when not properly measured." In late 1896, Breuer wrote Gomperz a letter in which he discussed the concept of catharsis in some detail and, in that general connection, elaborated on the fact that "the same agents used in small measure have a stimulating and pleasure-inducing effect while, used heavily, they have a destructive and death-causing effect" (in Hirschmüller, 1978, p. 210). Nearly 20 years later, in writing to one of his friends and patients, Breuer would make a similar observation in noting how alkaloids such as caffeine and cocaine can be used both as "poisons and useful medicine; like the proverb, what is useful is harmful and what is harmful can be useful" (Breuer to Ebner-Es-chenbach, 7 July 1914, in Kann, 1969, p. 151).

Now whether or not it was so that the family of Anna von Lieben intervened to bring the treatment to a halt having realized it was doing no more for her than an addictive drug, and whether or not Breuer approved of the treatment being terminated, this brings us to a fact which I consider very important and that, given the significance of the case of "Frau Cäcilie M . . ." in the development of Freud's thinking, and given also the need for the readers of the *Studies on Hysteria* to be able to obtain some realistic assessment of the relative efficacy or inefficacy of the therapeutic method, I feel should have been explicitly stated in the book—namely the fact that there was no final cure of the hysteria of Anna von Lieben, only at most the temporary alleviation of her symptoms, a matter possibly related to the issue which I raised earlier in respect of the "pathogenic milieu" of which she was a product to the extent that one might be inclined to ascribe etiological significance to the latter.

In the summer of 1894—probably a year or so, then, following the termination of Freud's treatment—the well-known Viennese poet Ferdinand von Saar visited Anna at the Villa Todesco in the Brühl and, in two letters, reported back to her cousin, Franzi von Wertheimstein. On August 25, 1894, he noted:

> During daytime Anna remains out of sight, though she is a little better now. Last night she even made the effort to go out for a drive. The evenings and part of the night she spends on one of the two terraces where, wrapped in three coats, I chat with her. She speaks with more difficulty than before and tires easily; the effect of all the poisons which she takes is devastating. But her characteristic spirit, free and humorous, has remained faithful to her. At particularly good moments her old face even reappears—only the eyes have become smaller and duller. On the whole, a depressing picture, and I am gripped with a deep melancholy when I see her like that, lying before me covered with plaids [tartan blankets] on the chaise longue. By the way, as Dr. Karplus has told me, and as I do sincerely believe, she can be brought up to a certain status quo ante—although a healing [i.e., a complete recovery] is out of the question.[69]

Elsewhere it is stated that, despite her obesity, Anna retained something truly girl-like in her being—an aura of purity or, as it is said, "virginity" (Winter, 1927, p. 42). Ten days later, on September 4, 1894, von Saar wrote again to Franzi—herself nearly as much an invalid as Anna (cf. Holzer, 1960; H. Gomperz, manuscript, pp. 57, 1586):

> From all at the Brühl I have to send warmest greetings with the agreeable news that Anna has recovered remarkably of late. Now she has not merely moments but even hours and half-days [presumably of lucidity and composure]. Of course, that doesn't amount to very much. But one thing is certain: what would be good for her is the company of a person congenial to her. For that reason, my departure from here will be somewhat regretted. But . . . I absolutely cannot stay any longer; I have already given the utmost.[70]

The physician referred to in the first letter is 27-year-old Paul Karplus—a former tutor of Anna's son Robert and, from 1894, an assistant to Richard von Krafft-Ebing at the local psychiatric clinic. In 1897 he would marry Anna's daughter Valerie—it was he who is said to have destroyed Anna's diary of her analysis. Presumably he had taken over Anna's treatment by arrangement with Breuer—

certainly Karplus was acquainted with Breuer around this time (Breuer and Freud, 1893–1895, p. 213n).

But, within a year or two, Anna's treatment fell into the hands of a certain Josef Winter, a Viennese physician born in 1857 who would marry into the Auspitz family. A published poet, he is said to have been a gifted but melancholy individual. For a time, though, he succeeded in winning Anna's confidence, took over control of her drug use, and exerted a favorable influence on her (cf. Winter, 1927, p. 82). This would not prove to be of any real duration; and, over the course of the next few years, Anna was cared for much of the time by a faithful old friend, Julie Schlesinger.[71] It does seem, however, that—excepting the oldest child Ilse who, late in 1895, married a Dutch baron—the children did get to see rather more of their mother during these years than had hitherto been the case, and were thereby able to come to love her a little more. The summers of 1896 and 1897 Anna spent with her family at Aussee in the Alps— coincidentally, the same resort where Freud and his family stayed those two summers.[72] And on December 3, 1896 she and her husband had their silver wedding anniversary, an occasion celebrated by the whole family (Winter, 1927, p. 82).

On October 31, 1900, at the age of 53, Anna von Lieben died suddenly in the arms of the faithful housekeeper, Meja Ruprecht, at the Oppolzergasse apartment. The cause of death was stated to be "myocardial degeneration" and she was buried two days later in the family's vault. The following year, her family published the selection of her poems; and, of course, a copy of that book would reach the hands of Sigmund Freud. But, as I mentioned early on, there is a *second* book in Freud's library bearing the name Anna Lieben— those two words handwritten inside it. Maybe Freud borrowed the book and forgot to return it; maybe Anna actually gave it to him; possibly after her death he chose it *in memoriam* from her collection of books as he had done in the case of Meynert. At any rate, whatever the circumstances, the book in question was Francis Bacon's *Novum Organum*, the founding work of modern scientific philosophy.[73] Published in 1620, this is Bacon's treatise on his new inductive method of interpreting nature and organizing knowledge, commencing with the injunction *dissecare naturam*—dissect Nature!— the basic principle of scientific analysis. How apt that of all the books once belonging to Anna von Lieben—Freud's "prima donna"; his avowed "teacher"; the first person ever to undergo a psychoanalysis; indeed, a woman instrumental to its very conception and birth—how appropriate, then, that, of all her books, Freud should have inherited this one. Now there is surely some poetry in that.

Notes ————————————————————————————

1. In a lecture on hysteria presented on January 11, 1893, however, Freud stated of this patient that she had been "overcome with fear that she might not 'find herself on a right footing,' " resulting in "violent pains in her right heel," at a time "when she made her first appearance in society" (1893c, p. 34).

2. The letter is one of five letters of Freud to Fliess which, together with three other letters of Freud addressed to herself, Fliess's wife Ida retained when, in 1936, her son Conrad sold the bulk of Freud's letters to his father for the purpose of securing their preservation. In 1977 they were donated to the Jewish National and University Library in Jerusalem by Fliess's daughter Pauline (cf. Swales, in preparation).

3. Prof. Gerhard Fichtner of Tübingen, a spectator during the early stages of this project, is responsible for having alerted me to the cited article of Lingens (August 27, 1981). One would generally translate the word *Lehrmeister* as "master" (correlative with "apprentice"). However, the female form *Lehrmeisterin* does not lend itself to equivalent translation in that to do so would incur an unwanted connotation. So let us then settle for "teacher."

4. In the present paper I cite information contained in unpublished portions of three letters of Freud to Fliess other than those preserved in Jerusalem and there accessible for scholarly inspection. So here it behooves me to note that, on August 25, 1983, Mr. Mark Paterson, Director of Sigmund Freud Copyrights Ltd., provided me with a transcript of what purports to be the complete letters of Freud to Fliess towards assisting me in the completion of a comprehensive biography of Fliess (Swales, in preparation). An expression of my great gratitude is therefore due to this gentleman—also to Freud's grandchildren, Prof. Sophie Loewenstein and Mr. Clement Freud M.P., and Fliess's daughter Mrs. Pauline Jacobsohn, for their moral support in the face of a complete lack of cooperation from the Sigmund Freud Archives.

5. A comprehensive account of all the various vicissitudes involved in the project must await the completion and publication of a forthcoming autobiography. But here it is necessary that I give at least an outline of all the circumstances leading up to publication of this paper. Having in August 1979 made the connection between Freud's "Frau Cäcilie M . . ." and the poetess Anna von Lieben, it was in January 1980 that I met in London with one of her granddaughters—and she was ecstatic to receive me. A decade or so earlier, in her presence, Dr. Kurt R. Eissler, Secretary of the Sigmund Freud Archives in New York, had tape-recorded an interview with her mother Henriette, and they had begged to be told whether

Freud had ever published Anna Lieben's case history. He told them nothing, however (cf. his interview no. 74-910B, restricted in the Library of Congress till the year 2000)—in fact, he failed to even supply them with a transcript of the interview—and Henriette died in 1978, denied any vindication of her *idée fixe, viz.*, that her mother must have been the most important of all Freud's early patients. Concerned for the truth finally to be told, Henriette's daughter now proceeded to communicate to me various facts and material and promised me copies of two journals of Anna Lieben in her possession. By mutual understanding, then, I under-took to invest considerable time, effort, and money into extensive research on Anna Lieben—(in that connection, incidentally, I owe thanks to Prof. Hanns Jäger-Sunstenau, Direktor of the Heraldisch-Genealogische Gesellschaft "Adler" in Vienna, who provided me with basic genealogical data on the von Lieben, von Todesco, Gomperz, Auspitz, and von Wertheimstein families which I was later able to elaborate through research of my own, mainly in the israelitische Kultusge-meinde in Vienna; however, my biggest debt of gratitude is to my dear wife, but for whose linguistic capabilities so much of the documental material on which large portions of this reconstruction depend would have been inaccessible to me)—and after some months I fulfilled a promise to supply the granddaughter with a detailed reconstruction of the first 30 years of her grandmother's life. But by then having fallen under the malevolent influence of a befriended hack who simply detested the very nature of my work—and in spite of the attempts of a befriended lawyer, enthusiastic about the project, to quell her *folie du doute*—she withheld any fur-ther cooperation and failed to honor her promise to supply me with copies of the two journals, now claiming that she was beholden to honor her ancestors' wish for privacy. Thus, in autumn 1980, I reluctantly put the whole project on ice. In 1982, though, I was approached by a Dutch woman who sought my professional as-sistance in connection with a study she was undertaking on Freud and Theodor Gomperz—it was her firm conviction that "Frau Cäcilie M . . ." was in fact Gomperz's wife Elise. I advised her in reply that the patient in question was, in truth, a *niece* of Gomperz—but soon I regretted disclosing as much, on learning that the woman was a truly wild and reckless thinker, having published the non-sensical thesis that "Frau Cäcilie M . . ." and the widowed "Irma" of Freud's famous dream were actually, both of them, Elise Gomperz. Needless to say, now knowing where to look, soon enough the woman was bound to ascertain and to concede the truth of what I had advised her; with which, motivated by an ill-considered generosity, I sought to help her straighten out her work on the Gom-perzes and Freud by granting her access to considerable unpublished material obtained through my research—including, that is, all my documentation on Anna Lieben, the niece of Gomperz. But then in 1984 I found mysterious the fact that, without clarifying the basis for her interest, the woman addressed to me certain queries specifically in respect of Freud's treatment of Anna von Lieben; whereupon I chanced to learn that, having gone behind my back, she had recently interviewed Henriette's daughter—who was now intending to give her copies of the two journals in order that the woman could expand her project to include Anna von Lieben. This I learned from a befriended independent historian—himself a respon-sible and outstandingly competent researcher—who also saw fit to advise me that, a year or two before, the granddaughter had permitted *him* to make copies of the two journals. Of course, all this made nonsense of the earlier claim that a wish for privacy had to be honored—as, indeed, did the simple fact that, in 1901, the von Lieben family had printed the volume of poems which, like the 1927 book of their relative Josefine Winter, documents many facts about Anna Lieben's illness. Furthermore, the large part of all that I had been able to learn from the granddaughter during several meetings in January 1980 was subsequently communicated to me by another grandchild and by a granddaughter of one of Anna Lieben's sisters—the first of whom voiced no objection to the truth being told; and the second of whom felt strongly that it ought to be. In January 1984, in presenting a lecture on Anna von Lieben at the Payne Whitney Clinic in New York, I proceeded to take upon myself the same responsibility earlier assumed by persons such as Ernest Jones in undertaking to reveal the true identity of one of Freud's early patients—except that, in my case, the fact that Anna von Lieben had been Freud's "patient" and "teacher" had already been published in 1981 in an essay in the *Sigmund Freud House Bulletin* (Lingens, 1981); while the fact that Anna von Lieben had suffered chronic mental illness had been revealed in print in 1901 and 1927 (Lieben, 1901; Winter, 1927). Thus, I had merely to identify Freud's early patient, Anna Lieben, as being one and the same woman as "Frau Cäcilie M . . ." in the *Studies on Hysteria*. In the knowledge that the daughter of Henriette has cooperated with two other investigators, one of whom has acted in bad faith towards me, I now proceed, then, with publication—and I offer my paper in the spirit of a "preliminary communication." Here I present what is essentially a skeletal reconstruction of the life, illness, and treatment of Anna von Lieben and her role in the origins of psychoanalysis—considerable research work, to be informed in part by important historical material presently restricted of access, remains still to be undertaken. Towards accounting for my sources and assisting serious scholars, then, I am depositing two copies of my text, both of them comprehensively annotated in respect of the precise sources of all information herein that is not explicitly attributed, in the Unrestricted Section of the Sigmund Freud Archives in the Library of Congress, Washington, D.C., and at the Institut für Geschichte der Medizin in Tübingen, West Germany (—*in memoriam*, as it were).

6. Winter (1927, p. 42) simply states that Anna began to display "severe psychic symptoms." That she must have exhibited psychic symptoms of a hysterical nature even at the age of 15 is inferred from remarks in the *Studies on Hysteria* (Breuer and Freud, 1893–1895, pp. 69–70, 180), also from a statement found in Freud's later dream-book (1900, p. 522).

7. *Vide*: H. Gomperz (manuscript); J. Gomperz (1903); T. Gomperz (1905); Ewart (1907); Winter (1927); Stockert-Meynert (1930); T. Gomperz (1936); Grunwald (1936, pp. 338–341); Holzer (1960); Hennings (1963); Barea (1966, pp. 293–311); Spiel (1967); Kann (1974); Schwarz (1979); Holzapfel-Gomperz (1980); Schorske (1980); see also: letter of Theodor Gomperz, 11 September 1907 (Handschriftensammlung, H.I.N. 25415, Vienna Stadtbibliothek).

8. In Egham, during the mid-19th century, a Dr. John James Furnivall operated a mental institution in a 16th-century manor, "Great Fosters," built on the site of a former home of Anne Boleyn. In light of this fact and certain other material, it seemed to me *prima facie* probable that during her illness Anna von Todesco was

confined to bed in this establishment, rather than at the home of her sister. I am therefore very much indebted to my fellow independent Freud researcher, Mr. Anthony Stadlen of London, for sparing me such a misconception. He has managed to ascertain that, at the time of Anna's arrival in Egham, the institution in question had recently ceased to operate—also that it had functioned more as an asylum for incorrigible lunatics than as a sanatorium.

9. These few details—like most of the chronology with respect to Anna's travels between 1868 and 1871—derive from a brief inspection of her two surviving journals (January 15, 1980).

10. Leopold von Lieben to Moritz Hartmann (Handschriftensammlung, I.N. 45034, Vienna Stadtbibliothek)—cf. poem of Anna von Todesco written shortly before her marriage, also addressed to Hartmann (Handschriftensammlung, I.N. 43807, Vienna Stadtbibliothek).

11. I have reason to wonder whether this testimony is accurate—it is something told me by the granddaughter of Anna von Lieben who is in possession of the two mentioned journals. Nevertheless, the statement is certainly in accord with the fact, as documented in the *Studies on Hysteria,* that for some time Anna experienced "great mental irritability towards her husband" (Breuer and Freud, 1893–1895, p. 178). It is said of Leopold von Lieben, incidentally, that he was "abrupt and not very approachable" in his manner (letter of his sister, Ida Brentano, to Heinrich Glücksmann, 15 June 1889—Handschriftensammlung, österreichische Nationalbibliothek, Vienna).

12. Concern existed that the children, too, would one day fall victim to "this dangerous madness" (Ida Brentano to Heinrich Glücksmann, 3 September 1889—Handschriftensammlung, österreichische Nationalbibliothek, Vienna)—part of the reason, perhaps, why the children were kept away from their mother.

13. Apropos this statement, there need be no fear of any exaggeration. In 1895 in the *Studies on Hysteria,* Freud would state that the "hysteria" of "Frau Cäcilie M . . ." was of the "severest type" and characterize the woman as his "most severe case" (Breuer and Freud, 1893–1895, pp. 103, 176). Writing in 1907, Breuer would refer generally to cases of "severe hysteria (especially 'Cäcilie M.' in the book)" whose treatment by Freud he had personally witnessed (in Ackerknecht, 1957, p. 170). In note 54 below, I address the issue of whether Anna von Lieben's condition was less of a hysteria and more of a psychosis. For the moment, though, it is to be noted that, while in the interests of providing an adequate depiction of the woman's condition I have resorted to certain psychiatric terminology of modern coinage and currency (in which connection, incidentally, I have benefited from discussions with John Kerr, Dr. Larry Friedman, and the late Dr. Ed Hornick), I do not thereby mean to insinuate any nosological partisanship. After all, I am no psychiatrist, nor even a psychoanalyst. I am simply my own person.

14. Any readers disposed to find objectionable such a cynical interpretation are respectfully asked to suspend all judgment until, at a later point in this essay, they have had an opportunity to take into account an important statement of Freud in respect of his treatment of this woman (see p. 48–49).

15. *Nauheimer Kurliste*, 29 May 1880 (No. 5) through 21 August 1880 (Nr. 17). Here to be assumed is that Anna von Lieben departed from the spa around the time when her name ceased to appear in the weekly cure lists—viz., 28 August 1880 (Nr. 18). I owe thanks to Frau Molitor of the Nauheimer Kurverwaltung for making the cure lists available for inspection (August 6, 1980). Cure lists survive from the year 1877 and all those up to 1887 were inspected excepting those from the year 1883 which are missing. A possibility does exist, then, that Anna von Lieben visited the spa during 1883 and that, at the time, Breuer had only recently been appointed her physician—but probability would speak against that being the case. However, through his own research work, Mr. Anthony Stadlen is privy to important unpublished information on Anna von Lieben; and he has been good enough to inform me that, in point of fact, the woman also visited Bad Nauheim as early as 1876. It is therefore possible that the poem dates, in fact, from that year; and that Breuer was therefore already, by the year 1876, her physician.

16. Like Anna's uncle, Max Ritter von Gomperz, Franz Brentano was a great chess player; like Anna, he could play more than one game at a time (Winter, 1927, pp. 19–20).

17. Ida Brentano to Frl. Sophie Lotheissen, circa 1887–1891 (Handschriften-sammlung, I. 135.390, Vienna Stadtbibliothek).

18. It is generally supposed that Freud first became acquainted with Breuer during the late 1870s while pursuing studies in Ernst von Brücke's Institute of Physiology (Jones, 1953, p. 223). In his book on Breuer, Hirschmüller dates their first meeting in 1877 at the latest (1978, p. 179). By autumn 1874, however, Freud had become quite closely befriended with his fellow student, Josef Paneth, 17 years old, who was in close contact with Breuer. The son of a wealthy clothes merchant, Paneth was orphaned in 1872 following an accident near Berchtesgaden when, surely in a carriage, he and his parents plunged into an abyss (data from the Sterberegister, israelitische Kultusgemeinde, Vienna—13 and 19 September 1872). On that occasion, the poet and physician Ludwig August Frankl—a prominent figure in the Jewish community in Vienna (cf. Stockert-Meynert, 1930, pp. 157–159)—happened to be nearby, did what he could for the parents, and took care of the injured boy (Paneth to Frankl, 5 January 1873—Handschriftensammlung, I.N. 103453, Vienna Stadtbibliothek). It would appear that Frankl was one of those well-meaning persons who must then have played some role in looking after the boy's interests and future (Paneth to Frankl, 27 August 1873)—another one of whom was probably Josef Breuer. For, on or about July 28, 1874, Breuer and Paneth together checked into the Gasthof Sonne in the Alpine resort of Aussee (*Ausseer Cur- und Fremdenliste*, 1874, Nr. 15, # 686–687). Thus it may well have been the case that it was through Paneth that Freud first became acquainted with Breuer, as early as 1874; and that Breuer may therefore have fulfilled his role as mentor and benefactor of Freud rather longer than has been supposed.

19. One of Bernfeld's files, preserved in the Library of Congress, contains a sheet of paper which states simply: "Lieben, Anna von/Ref. by Chrobak—/Information/Hartman [sic]/March 1950." Hartmann's wife Dora was a niece of Dr. Paul Karplus, who married one of Anna von Lieben's daughters (see p. 57).

20. Because Freud's association with Chrobak is obscure, and because the gynecologist's name appears in Freud's works in only one connection, I append the following information towards indicating the extent of their association during Freud's earliest years in medical practice. In May 1886 Freud consulted Chrobak about the wife of an American physician—Freud was treating both husband and wife at the time (Freud to Martha Bernays, 13 May 1886, in E. Freud and L. Freud, 1968, p. 224). In August 1886 Theodor Gomperz proposed that his wife Elise should seek treatment from Freud "under Chrobak's supervision"—she was a patient of both Breuer and Chrobak (Kann, 1974, pp. 60, 170). In October 1887, Freud was asked to consult with Chrobak over "Frau L."—whoever she may have been (Freud to Emmeline and Minna Bernays, 24 October 1887, in E. Freud and L. Freud, 1968, p. 233). In 1888, Freud was treating a certain "Frau B . . ." in collaboration with Chrobak (Freud to Fliess, 4 February 1888, in Bonaparte, A. Freud, and Kris, 1954, p. 54). Circa 1889 (cf. Lesky, 1976, p. 429), Chrobak asked Freud to take over the treatment of a married woman whose illness, reputedly, Chrobak attributed to her being a virgin in virtue of her husband's impotence (Freud, 1914, pp. 14–15; 1925, p. 24; Nunberg and Federn, 1962, p. 360). And in 1895 Freud treated another young woman who had remained a virgin for some time following her marriage—"which Professor Chrobak confirmed to her" (Draft J, in Bonaparte, A. Freud, and Kris, 1954, p. 139). Chrobak, born in 1843 and not a Jew, died on October 1, 1910—he was therefore the "university teacher whom I greatly admired" whose recent death Freud mentions in the third edition of *The Interpretation of Dreams* (1900, p. 168; cf. 1914, p. 13).

21. This letter, like the vast majority of Freud's surviving letters, is of course unavailable in the original for scholarly inspection. It is not clear, therefore, whether Freud used the initial in his original, or whether that is actually a subterfuge of his editors.

22. I have no knowledge, unfortunately, of how Brentano felt about the treatment. Freud had first had personal contact with Brentano when, between 1874 and 1876, shortly following the philosopher's arrival in Vienna, he attended his seminars at the university (Bernfeld, 1951, pp. 204, 216). In 1875, he and Josef Paneth visited Brentano at his home and received advice from him on their future studies and careers (Stanescu, 1971, p. 200). Many years later Freud would state that it was on the recommendation of Brentano that Theodor Gomperz had commissioned him in 1879 to translate a volume of the works of John Stuart Mill (Jones, 1953, pp. 55–56). Around that time, incidentally, Freud received two stipendia from a certain Freiherr von Eckeles, paid to him through a brother of Gomperz living in Brünn (note of Siegfried Bernfeld based on research by Prof. Viktor Kraft, 13 May 1950, in the Siegfried Bernfeld Collection, Library of Congress; cf. Freud to Knöpfmacher, 6 August 1878, in E. Freud and L. Freud, 1968, p. 14); and it was during the same period that Freud heard Gomperz speak of the role played by dreams in the mental life of so-called "primitive man" (Freud to E. Gomperz, 12 November 1913, in E. Freud and L. Freud, 1968, p. 316). In 1866 Gomperz had published an essay on dream interpretation, magical thinking, and superstition in which he contended that traditional dream interpretation was based on the mere thought associations of the interpreter (Gomperz, 1866; cf. Freud, 1900, p. 98n).

Gomperz was very closely befriended, by the way, with Freud's teacher and later friend, Ernst Fleischl von Marxow (cf. H. Gomperz, manuscript, pp. 853–860, 901–924, 949, 1044, 1120, 1498; Kann, 1974, pp. 75–79, 84–90).

23. Mrs. Hortense Becker, daughter of Carl Koller, kindly provided me with a copy of the original letter (January 4, 1979). It is written on the stationery of Koller & Hoppen, Teplitz, and is apparently dated 24 March 1887—however, the dating is problematic. Prof. Josef Sajner (January 22, 1980) was kind enough to obtain details for me from the Jewish cemetery in Teplitz on Gabriel Koller, who died of a brain seizure aged 62 on March 22, 1887—that is, two days before the date on the letter. From the letter's content, however, it is clear that Koller's uncle, a victim of progressive paralysis, was still living, though expected to die in about two weeks' time. Possibly, then, Freud's date reads not 24 März but 2er März—that is, 2nd March, 1887.

24. Betty Paoli to Hermine Villinger (Badische Landesbibliothek, Karlsruhe, K. 1847). Cf. letter of Betty Paoli to Ida von Fleischl, 16 July 1891 (Handschriften-sammlung, 48489, Vienna Stadtbibliothek).

25. Mathilde Schleicher inscribed the book: "To the excellent Dr. Freud/in affectionate memory./As a token of the greatest gratitude and respect/Mathilde Schleicher/June [1]889"—thanks are overdue to Ms. Anna Freud for allowing me to inspect this and other books in her father's library (October 4, 1979). It was from Prof. Gerhard Fichtner and Dr. Albrecht Hirschmüller that I first received particulars about Mathilde Schleicher's father and age (May 3, 1979)—facts which I then reencountered in summer 1980 while undertaking research in the israelitische Kultusgemeinde, Vienna (Sterberegister, 24 September 1890).

26. Elise Gomperz attributed her nervous suffering and neuralgic pains to the severe anxieties and excitement which she had experienced during 1876 in connec-tion with a major family upset (H. Gomperz, manuscript, p. 924; Kann, 1974, p. 85). It was expected for some time that Ernst Fleischl von Marxow would propose marriage to Franzi von Wertheimstein—instead, though, he suddenly announced his plans to marry Elise's younger sister, Sophie von Sichrovsky. The von Wertheimsteins perceived this as a terrible insult and were convinced that Elise and Theodor Gomperz had engineered things in favor of her sister—the final outcome of the whole miserable episode was that Fleischl remained a bachelor (H. Gomperz, manuscript, pp. 900–924; Kann, 1974, pp. 84–90). However, in point of fact, Elise Gomperz had displayed nervous symptoms during the years before 1876. Already in 1870 she was suffering from nerves, headaches, and pains in her feet (H. Gomperz, manuscript, pp. 772–773).

27. Meynert regarded Freud's espousal of hypnosis as a betrayal of his strictly physicalistic scientific training (cf. Freud, 1889, p. 95). As a student, Freud had attended Meynert's lectures in clinical psychiatry during the winter semester of 1878–1879 (Bernfeld, 1951, pp. 205, 216); and it was Meynert who, in autumn 1882, recommended Freud to Hermann Nothnagel for a position in the latter's department in the General Hospital (Jones, 1953, p. 63). For five months beginning May 1883, Freud worked under Meynert in his psychiatric clinic and, at the same time, received permission to undertake histological research in his laboratory

(Bernfeld, 1951, pp. 210–211)—permission which held good until 1886 (Jones, 1953, pp. 142, 144). Meynert was among those who, in 1885, approved Freud's application for an appointment as *Privatdozent* (Bernfeld, 1951, p. 215); but it was Meynert who, at a meeting of the Society of Physicians in Vienna on October 15, 1886, some months following Freud's return from Paris, was sufficiently skeptical of his claims as to challenge him to produce before the society a male patient display-ing somatic symptoms of the kind understood by Charcot to be characteristic of male hysteria (cf. Lebzeltern, 1973).

28. The letters in question were recently subjected to a "discovery"—they had been lying all these years in Freud's house in London so that locating them involved a feat of "research" (cf. Malcolm, 1984, p. 147). The cited assertion is made by Jeffrey Moussaieff Masson on page one of his unpublished 1981 lecture "The Seduction Hypothesis in the Light of New Documents" (cf. Malcolm, 1984, p. 130) and lacks corroboration as such. A reading of all the letters might not warrant such a conclusion—however, Masson's claim is compatible with what is inferred in the present paper to the extent that at least two such visits to Paris are here postulated (see below). In a letter to Anna Freud, dated October 11, 1981, I formally re-quested copies of the letters in question in the interests of rendering this historical reconstruction as comprehensive as possible. She declined to oblige me, however (cf. Malcolm, 1984, p. 131), and in her letter of response, dated November 20, 1981, sought to assure me there was no mention of any patients in the letters in question.

29. There is a strong possibility that, already by 1886, Elise Gomperz had received treatment from Charcot (cf. Kann, 1974, p. 170). In the Sigmund Freud Archives in the Library of Congress is Charcot's side of a correspondence with Theodor Gomperz—sealed, however, till the year 2009 (Restricted Series, Catalog Entry No. 1069).

30. Note in the Siegfried Bernfeld Collection, Library of Congress. Mr. Mark Micale of Yale University has been good enough to provide me with a copy of the title page of Freud's *Zur Auffassung der Aphasien* ([July] 1891) inscribed to: "J M Charcot/hommage de son ancien élève, Dr. Freud."

31. While revising my manuscript for publication, I have received a copy of the new edition of what purports to be the complete letters of Freud to Wihelm Fliess (Masson, 1985). The passage from Charcot's letter is to be found quoted in an editor's footnote—Masson dates the letter "October (?) 26, 1888" (p. 20). Possibly the reason for Masson's query is that during the last century it was common practice to abbreviate October as "8bre." Masson does not quote the French original so, in taking the liberty of rendering the published English less clumsy, I have been unable to compare it with the original text. I have confined myself to changes, then, only where the meaning can be in no doubt. Masson quotes Charcot as having written "Mrs. X."—presumably, then, "Mme. X." But in 1980 I in-formed him of the true identity of "Frau Cäcilie M . . ." (letter of April 17, 1980) and also made him aware that she was also treated by Charcot (meeting on May 11, 1980). So it is to be supposed that she must be the woman referred to in Charcot's letter, as Masson understands to be so.

32. Calling card of Charcot preserved in the Unrestricted Section of the Sigmund Freud Archives, Library of Congress. Charcot's undated inscription reads: "All my congratulations, may he be welcome, may the evangelist and the generous centurion be propitious for him; may their names which are his bring him happiness! Present my respectful compliments to Mme. Freud and believe me always/your devoted/Charcot." Charcot must have been referring to Jean Martin Freud, born on December 7, 1889.

33. It is clear from the poem written in Paris in 1889 (Lieben, 1901, pp. 151–152) that Anna von Lieben was undergoing a profound mental crisis at the time in the belief that, having been too trustworthy, she had been wickedly deceived. It is altogether unclear what the circumstances were—her reaction could have been a response to certain news from home. Given, however, that the purpose of her visit to Paris was presumably to consult Charcot, then one wonders if this poem does not perhaps record the fate of his treatment. A faint possibility does exist, though, that Anna's visit to Paris in 1889 was for the purpose of consulting the eye specialist Richard Liebreich—he had treated her mother who was then responsible for referring Theodor Gomperz and his son Heinrich to him in August 1889 (H. Gomperz, manuscript, p. 1506; cf. Kann, 1974, p. 211). Between June and September 1889, Heinrich Glücksmann, 25 years old, was a guest at the Villa Todesco in the Brühl. Anna von Lieben found him to be stimulating company—however, Glücksmann betrayed too clearly his interest in her two teenage daughters, Ilse and Valerie, causing her husband to disapprove of him (Ida Brentano to Glücksmann, 15 June 1889 and 3 September 1889—Handschriftensammlung, österreichische Nationalbibliothek, Vienna).

34. Normally, wanting to get to Nancy from Vienna, one would have travelled on the Orient Express via Munich and Stuttgart—a trip via Zürich taking substantially longer. For this information I am very grateful to Dr. Shettek of the österreichische Bundesbahnen Bibliothek in Vienna (February 25, 1980). Andersson (1965, p. 11) and Ellenberger (1977, p. 530) state that Forel was befriended with Fanny Moser. Forel's signature is to be found in her guest book (see note 35) dated June 19, 1897, and in 1893 he referred her to the Stockholm hypnotherapist Otto Wetterstrand (Andersson, 1965, pp. 9, 11; cf. Walser, 1968, pp. 299, 330–331). Almost certainly, then, Forel was the "prominent physician" from the neighborhood of Zürich who, "a few years later at a Scientific Congress," gave Freud some follow-up information on the patient (Breuer and Freud, 1893–1895, p. 105); for it would appear that, in late September 1894, Forel attended the Congress of German Natural Scientists and Physicians in Vienna (Walser, 1968, p. 299), a meeting in which Freud actively participated (Freud to Fliess, 7 February 1894, in Bonaparte, A. Freud, and Kris, 1954, p. 81).

35. I am grateful to Herr Hans Lieb of the Staatsarchiv Schaffhausen for enabling me to inspect the guest book (July 5, 1979), the existence of which was first reported by Ellenberger (1977, p. 526). Otto Wetterstrand signed her book, incidentally, on September 26, 1893, then again in August 1896. In a letter preserved with the guest book dated September 2, 1896, the psychiatrist Eugen Bleuler mentions having met Wetterstrand, among other important people, during a recent

visit to Fanny Moser's home. One wonders whether, when reviewing the *Studies on Hysteria* that same year (Bleuler, 1896), he was doing so with knowledge of the actual identity of "Frau Emmy von N . . ."—also, in that case, whether she was herself aware of her published case history. For yet another very positive review of the *Studies on Hysteria,* see Moebius (1895) who, like Bleuler, considered Breuer and Freud to have accomplished "an advancement and a deepening of medical psychology in general."

36. I owe thanks to Dr. Leon Chertok of Paris and Prof. D. Barrucand of Nancy for having sought in vain to oblige me in this respect back in 1979–1980.

37. 21 May 1894—after his wife Martha, his *"nächste Vertraute."*

38. Also to be taken into account is that Minna was reputedly the only person, other than Fliess, sympathetic to discussing Freud's ideas with him during the late 1890s and the early years of the new century (Jones, 1955, pp. 6, 387; cf. recollections of Ernst Waldinger dated October 25, 1951, in the Siegfried Bernfeld Collection, Library of Congress; Dr. Frank Hartman of New York informs me that Freud ascribed just such a role to Minna in conversation with Marie Bonaparte, as attested by the latter's unpublished journal of her own analysis). Cf. Swales (1982a).

39. Freud is also said to have been reading Liébeault's 1889 book *Le Sommeil Provoqué et les États analogues* at the time of writing his letter (cf. Lewis and Landis, 1957, p. 352, # 734). I am in receipt of letters from Mr. Clement Freud M.P. (June 14, 1983) and Prof. Sophie Loewenstein (June 16, 1983) which make it perfectly clear how strongly they disapprove of the state of affairs presently obtaining with respect to the restriction imposed by the Sigmund Freud Archives—and enforced by the Library of Congress—on the bulk of documents, etc., that comprise their grandfather's literary estate. Both express the view that all of the material should be made immediately available for public scrutiny (—although both are heirs to Freud's copyrights, they themselves have no right of access to his estate). Myself, I consider all such historical data on Freud to constitute part of the public domain. And because, furthermore, I consider that the mentioned letters of Freud's grandchildren provide me with the express moral warrant for doing so, here I have no hesitation in citing the information from Freud's letter to his sister-in-law—information learned about adventitiously thanks to the indiscretion of one granted privileged access to the letter in question; a letter that is, after all, absolutely indispensable to this *bona fide* project of historical reconstruction.

40. Of course, repression had yet to be invented.

41. So surely rather cheaper than a standard psychoanalysis.

42. There is, however, an amazing catch to the story—one of very special interest to students of Freud. To reveal it, though, would be to spoil completely any future reader's enjoyment of the novel. So I refrain from doing so.

43. Of note in this general respect is that the name Heidenhoff seems to have been conjured by Bellamy out of two German words—*Heiden* meaning "heathen"; and *-hoff,* probably suggesting *Hoffnung,* meaning "hope." Thus—as the actual content of the novel affirms—there is the suggestion that the doctor's therapy is fundamentally anti-Christian in nature (cf. Swales, 1982b; Swales, 1983a, pp. 14–

15n, 61–62). Prof. Eric Carlson and Mr. John Kerr have raised the question of whether Bellamy may not have conceived the name Heidenhoff after learning of Rudolf Heidenhain's experimentation with hypnosis (see p. 39). Heidenhain's work on the subject was published at some point in 1880, the same year as Bellamy's book. But I suppose it is possible that word of his investigations in Breslau reached Bellamy early on; and that, indeed, his name might well have been Bellamy's source of inspiration.

44. In a footnote to his edition of what purports to be the complete letters of Freud to Fliess, Masson (1985) cites a letter to Minna Bernays dated July 28, 1889 in which Freud states that the thought of his having to stay in Nancy till the following Saturday makes him feel sick (pp. 17–18n). Because July 28, 1889 fell on a Sunday, this information would strongly support the chain of inference that culminates in the above sentence. However, the letter constitutes yet another document unavailable for scholarly inspection—so its content can be cited only with caution.

45. That Freud made Delboeuf's personal acquaintance while visiting Paris in August 1889 (if not already during 1885–1886) is a conclusion which, in 1979, I communicated to Prof. Malcolm Macmillan of Monash University, Australia. In a letter of reply dated May 30, 1980, he states that, in his view, this is indeed very plausible—he notes the apparent absence in Delboeuf's works of the remark attributed to him by Freud in the *Studies on Hysteria*, viz., that if as Bernheim asserts suggestion is everything, then "there is no such thing as hypnotism" (Breuer and Freud, 1893–1895, p. 101). Delboeuf's remark, then, may have been communicated orally.

46. Born in Odense, Denmark, in 1833, Hansen gave public demonstrations in Vienna during January and February 1880 which provoked considerable controversy among members of the medical community (cf. miscellaneous material in the Siegfried Bernfeld Collection, Library of Congress; Hirschmüller, 1978, pp. 127, 130). In an unpublished postcard to Eduard Silberstein dated February 3, 1880 and written in English, Freud declines to attend a demonstration by Hansen and expresses the hope that his friend will remain very skeptical when doing so (cf. Malcolm, 1984, pp. 96–97). However, in his 1925 autobiographical sketch, Freud would recall how, when a student, he had attended a demonstration by Hansen that convinced him of the reality of the phenomenon of hypnosis; and of how scientific support for the authenticity of the phenomenon was soon afterwards forthcoming in the work of Rudolf Heidenhain (Freud, 1925, p. 16). Here to be mentioned, incidentally, is the fact that, shortly following his visit to Breslau in 1880, Brentano recommended that Heidenhain's unmarried sister Marie, 40 years old, should come to Vienna and take over management of the Auspitz household— Rudolf Auspitz's wife Helene having recently been confined to a sanatorium. In July 1881 she joined the family for that purpose, also to supervise the education of all the Auspitz and von Lieben children (Winter, 1927, pp. 13–16).

47. So here I am opposing the view of Macmillan (1979, p. 307), who considers it highly improbable that Freud, Delboeuf, and Janet could have simultaneously evolved a strikingly similar method while proceeding altogether independently of one another. In my understanding, they—also Bourru and Burot, Benedikt, and

very possibly others—were all simply responding to, yet at the same time were actively constituting, the post-Hansen-Charcot-Bernheim Zeitgeist. Cf. Ralph Waldo Emerson: "In history an idea always overhangs like a moon and rules the tide which rises simultaneously in all the souls of a generation."

48. Calling card of Theodor Gomperz addressed to Wilhelm Jerusalem and dated 20 April 1892 (Edmond Jerusalem Archive, Ms. Var. 445/11, Department of Manuscripts and Archives, Jewish National and University Library, Jerusalem). Münsterberg, yet to emigrate to America, was working at the time in Freiberg im Breisgau, where Heinrich Gomperz then visited him in June 1892 (H. Gomperz, manuscript, pp. 1661–1663). No reference is to be found to Münsterberg in any of Freud's published letters or works, though he did have a few of his early works in his library (Lewis and Landis, 1957, p. 347, # 542–545). In an 1887 letter to his wife, incidentally, Gomperz mentions how, at the spa of Vöslau, he had recently been speaking about Jacob (and Michael) Bernays with Gustav Freitag (Kann, 1974, p. 189). So it is virtually inconceivable that, at some point or other, Bernays would not have come up in conversation between Gomperz and Freud. Frequently Freud used to visit Gomperz's home for the purpose of treating his wife Elise (Kann, 1974, p. 106, cf. pp. 301, 319). On February 2, 1896, the literature historian and director of Vienna's Burgtheater Alfred Freiherr von Berger, a close friend of Gomperz (cf. Winter, 1927; Kann, 1974), published a glowing review of the Studies on Hysteria in the Morgenpresse under the title "Surgery of the Soul." Quite possibly, through Gomperz and perhaps also Breuer, Berger had long been aware of the novel mode of "cathartic" therapy being developed by Freud under Breuer's auspices—on February 24, 1890 he had presented a lecture to the Philosophical Society in Vienna entitled "On the Dramatic Expression of Psychical Phenomena," and on March 2, 1896 he lectured again on "The Aristotelian Theory of Catharsis in the Light of Modern Neuroscience" (Berichte der Philosophischer Gesellschaft, 3er Bericht, p. 2; 9er Bericht, p. 3). Berger believed that Jacob Bernays had succeeded beyond doubt in showing that, in truth, Aristotle's "catharsis" entailed a specifically medical purgation (Kann, 1974, p. 266). During 1895 or 1896, the library of the Philosophical Society acquired a copy of the Studies on Hysteria (9er Bericht, p. 6). The society had been formed in 1888 with Brentano, Gomperz, Meynert, and Exner among its founding members (1er Bericht, p. 5). Breuer enrolled as a member in 1897–1898 (11ter Bericht, p. 10)—already on February 26 and March 5, 1894, though, he had presented a two-part lecture to the society on "The Sense of Stasis" (7er Bericht, p. 2) which Gomperz characterized as "equally wonderful in subject and treatment" (Gomperz to Wilhelm Jerusalem, 26 February 1894—Edmond Jerusalem Archive, Ms. Var. 455, Department of Manuscripts and Archives, Jewish National and University Library, Jerusalem).

49. That Gomperz would have readily discussed intellectual matters with suitably receptive women members of his family is indicated by the fact that, in July 1869, he notified his fiancée Elise—then visiting Franzensbad, apparently in the company of her future niece Anna—that soon he intended mailing her a copy of his 1866 essay on dream interpretation (H. Gomperz, manuscript, p. 759). That Anna had a powerful intellectual curiosity is strongly suggested by the book inscribed with her name to be found in Freud's library (see p. 58). Also cf. Kann (1974, p. 76).

50. Here one feels bound to draw special attention to the coincidence that Bertha Pappenheim and Anna von Lieben should have both displayed for a time a hysterical aphasia (Hirschmüller, 1978, p. 369; cf. Freud, 1893a, p. 164).

51. Here we have a more or less literal translation of the poem and not all of its metaphors and allusions are necessarily clear. Whether the three asterisks were inserted by the poetess, or whether they represent lines or verses deleted by her subsequent editor(s), I am not in a position to be able to say.

52. Interesting is how, in later years, Bernheim would assert that "modern psychotherapy, emancipated from hypnotism, is the creation of the Nancy school" (Bernheim to Ludwig Darmstaedter, 1 August 1910—Sammlung Darmstaedter, 3 1 1884 [2], Handschriftensammlung, Staatsbibliothek Preussischer Kulturbesitz, West Berlin). Cf. Ellenberger (1970, pp. 804–805).

53. In mid-June 1882, in a letter to Robert Binswanger in connection with Bertha Pappenheim, Breuer acknowledges that "a considerable measure of guilt apparently lies on my head" in virtue of his patient's dependence on morphine and chloral hydrate (in Hirschmüller, 1978, p. 366). Breuer was physician to Ernst Fleischl von Marxow who, at least by 1883, had become addicted to morphine in attempting to overcome pains associated with a severe neurological affliction (Jones, 1953, p. 90). In May 1894, Fliess's sister-in-law Melanie Bondy, whose family physician was Breuer, was administered morphine merely on account of her severe dysmenorrhea (Swales, in preparation). Early in 1907, Breuer spread "a veil of shut-off consciousness" over Franzi von Wertheimstein following her lapse into a mental illness that must have precipitated her death shortly thereafter (Holzer, 1960, p. 139). In 1905–1906 Breuer sought with morphine to spare Rudolf Auspitz all pain during his terminal illness—though Auspitz feared he would thereby develop a habit. A medical colleague questioned the wisdom of administering the drug, saying, "Then the patient is lost"—to which Breuer replied: "No, but rather, when the patient is lost, then I give morphine" (Winter, 1927, pp. 96–97). As should go without saying, two physicians might have quite different ideas about when exactly a patient is to be given up for "lost."

54. That the five featured patients in the *Studies on Hysteria* were not hysterics but actually schizophrenics is a view first advanced by Goshen (1952), then partially disputed by Reichard (1956) who concedes this to have been so only in the cases of "Anna O . . ." and "Frau Emmy von N . . . ." In reference to the case history of "Anna O . . .," Macalpine and Hunter (1956, pp. 138–142) and Bram (1965) argue likewise that Bertha Pappenheim was in the throes of a psychosis; Karpe (1961) affirms that she was suffering "from severe hysteria, bordering on a psychotic state, which some psychiatrists would label schizophrenia" (p. 23); while Hurst (1982) and Thornton (1983, pp. 130–147) suppose her to have been suffering from one or more diseases organic in nature—possibly even tuberculous meningitis. By contrast, Ellenberger (1972, p. 279), Hollender (1980), Pappenheim (1980b, 1981), and Wykert (1980) incline to the view, more or less explicit, that her condition was contingent upon a variety of psychosocial and interpersonal factors such as would support, at most, the continuing utility of hysteria as a diagnostic label. As for the case history of "Frau Emmy von N . . .," Pappenheim (1980a), Hurst (1983), and Thornton (1983, pp. 202–206) contend that, far from

being a hysteric, Fanny Moser was a victim of Gilles de la Tourette's disease; De Boor and Moersch (1980), however, suppose that she was indeed a case of hysteria. Reichard (1956) contends that hysteria remains a tenable diagnosis in the cases of "Miss Lucy R.," "Frl. Elisabeth von R . . .," and "Katharina . . ."; however, Hurst (1983) considers all three of these women to have been suffering, in truth, from a variety of organic conditions. As I can assert on the basis of a historical investigation of Freud's case history involving an extensive reconstruction of her life and circumstances (Swales, 1985), it is altogether untenable to suppose that "Katharina . . ." was liable to anything much more than a temporary emotional crisis attended by certain somatic symptoms of a plausibly hysterical kind. As for "Frau Cäcilie M . . .," on the other hand, seen from a modern viewpoint she would hardly qualify for a diagnosis of hysteria despite the fact of her somatizations being virtually paradigmatic in that respect. A possibility does exist, then, that, following publication of this paper, this patient too will be subjected to revisionist diagnostic interpretations—and these could prove interesting enough. However, to be remembered is that hysteria as a concept has shifted significantly since the fin-de-siècle period (cf. Hirschmüller, 1978, p. 178)—indeed, in virtue of the disappearance of hysteria of the classical kind prevalent during the 19th century, and in virtue of the increased atomization of psychopathological symptomatology, the very concept of hysteria has by now become minimized virtually to the point of meaninglessness. It would not necessarily follow, then, that Freud and Breuer were under a serious diagnostic misapprehension in characterizing "Frau Cäcilie M . . ." as a case of severe hysteria.

55. It was while staying at Reichenau in August 1893, and probably within days of Charcot's death on August 16, that Freud encountered the girl "Katharina . . .," whose case history he would then present in the *Studies on Hysteria*. This summer resort, and Freud's personal association with it, are comprehensively discussed in Swales (1985).

56. It is to be supposed that, when visiting both Oppolzergasse 6 and the Villa Todesco, Freud would surely from time to time have come into contact with other members of the family circle—including Franz and Ida Brentano and Marie Heidenhain. Born into a family of doctors, Marie Heidenhain is said to have been able to get along with physicians only if they would acknowledge what she supposed to be her own superior authority in all matters of medicine (Winter, 1927, p. 13). Circa 1889, Rudolf Auspitz announced his intention of divorcing his wife Helene, who by then had been in permanent confinement for the best part of a decade, and marrying Marie Heidenhain. This was strongly opposed by almost all of his family circle—even to the point where in March 1890, the time of the divorce, Brentano broke off all relations with him. Significantly, though, in the conviction that his sister would never recover, Leopold von Lieben was the one person who supported his brother-in-law in his course of action (Winter, 1927, pp. 45–46).

57. Several of Freud's letters to Fliess attest to the fact that, between the years 1893 and 1896, he often resorted to personal use of cocaine for the treatment of nasal conditions—but such nasal application of the drug would certainly have produced central and psychoactive effects (Prof. Robert Byck, personal communica-

tion, April 29, 1980). It is therefore quite possible that, during the years 1887 through 1892, Freud continued to employ cocaine as he had done formerly for the purpose of abolishing his migraines and depressions and artificially boosting his self-confidence (cf. Jones, 1953, pp. 84–85; Freud to Martha Bernays, 17 May 1885, 18 January 1886, 20 January 1886, 2 February 1886, in E. Freud and L. Freud, 1968, pp. 149, 199, 201–202, 207–209). During his first decade in medical practice, Freud frequently had cause to administer various drugs to his patients (cf. Swales, 1983b, p. 12n). Whether he ever used them to facilitate the induction of hypnosis is not known—but this represents a distinct possibility. In 1891, Schrenck-Notzing reported on how the administration of narcotics is sometimes necessary for the purpose of diminishing resistance to hypnosis (1895, pp. 10, 209). And, writing circa 1914, the Russian journalist P. D. Ouspensky noted: ". . . although the use of narcotics in hypnosis has been very little studied, and description of their use is hard to find even in special literature on the subject . . . narcotics are used far more often than is thought, and for two purposes: first the weakening of the resistance to hypnotic action, and second for the strengthening of the capacity to hypnotise. . . . Almost all professional hypnotists use morphia or cocaine in order to be able to hypnotise. Different narcotics are used also for the person hypnotised . . ." (Ouspensky, 1971, p. 266). The further possibility exists, then, that drugs such as cocaine and morphine played a decisive role in the very inception of Freud's "free association" method and its employment with patients other than Anna von Lieben (cf. Scheidt, 1973, p. 425; 1983, pp. 60–62; Swales, 1983a, p. 12n)—in 1886, Freud had resorted to "a little cocaine, to untie my tongue"; and the drug had had the effect of inducing him to make "silly confessions" about his own person (Freud to Martha Bernays, 18 January 1886, 2 February 1886, in E. Freud and L. Freud, 1968, pp. 199, 209). Of note is that Schott (manuscript) directly equates the "hypnoid state" obtaining during the practice of "free association" with the euphoria induced by cocaine; for a corollary, see Swales (1983b, pp. 19n, 20n).

58. Masson, in possession of material restricted by the Sigmund Freud Archives, quotes this entry dated 1 May 1932 from an unpublished diary of Ferenczi (Masson, 1984, p. 186; cf. p. 224, note 2).

59. Molly Filtsch was reportedly born circa 1850, so she was not very much younger than Anna. In a letter to a friend dated 13 October 1893, the poet Hugo von Hofmannsthal, then 19 years old, stated of her: "I really dislike Frl. Filtsch, but she is really intelligent and sees many things with remarkable clarity, doesn't she?" (to Fürstin Elsa Bruckmann, transcript, Handschriftensammlung, Bayerische Staatsbibliothek, Munich). By this time, Hofmannsthal had become very friendly with Josephine von Wertheimstein and Sophie von Todesco, who worshipped his poetic gifts. The youth had cause to visit the Brühl from time to time and it is said that Anna von Lieben was also befriended with him. One wonders whether, when consulting the *Studies on Hysteria* in researching his play *Elektra* (Ellenberger, 1970, p. 773), Hofmannsthal saw through the pseudonym "Frau Cäcilie M . . . ." Certainly Anna von Lieben would have better fulfilled Hofmannsthal's desire to depict his heroine as a hysterical fury than any other of the women featured in the book.

60. In their joint introduction to the *Studies on Hysteria,* dated April 1895, Breuer and Freud state that, in the book, they have been unable to present adequate evidence "in favour of our view that sexuality seems to play a principal part in the pathogenesis of hysteria as a source of psychical traumas and as a motive for 'defence'—that is, for repressing ideas from consciousness" because it would be "a grave breach of confidence to publish material of this kind, with the risk of the patients being recognized and their acquaintances becoming informed of facts which were confided only to their physician" (Breuer and Freud, 1893–1895, p. xxix). During the few years previous to 1895, active collaboration between Breuer and Freud had been gradually dwindling. Yet in 1907 Breuer would assert that he had been able "in company with Freud . . . to witness the encroachment of sexuality" during the treatment of cases of hysteria (in Ackerknecht, 1957, p. 170)— strongly indicating, then, that this must have happened during the early 1890s, if not already during the late 1880s. The great probability, then, is that Freud had encountered sexuality in analyzing his "teacher"—a possibility even exists that she may have been the acquiescent patient who, once upon a time, on waking up from her hypnosis, "threw her arms" around her physician's neck, much to his consternation (Freud, 1916–1917, p. 450; 1925, p. 27; cf. pp. 17–18). In a striking anticipation of Freudian-style logic, incidentally, Anna supposes in one of her poems that frequently women smoke cigarettes because, in truth, they yearn to be kissed (Lieben, 1901, p. 90). Whether she herself smoked, I cannot say. But her sister Fanny—following her divorce from Henry de Worms, and reputedly a very "liberated" woman—certainly did so.

61. But Freud had himself long had a superstitious preoccupation with his own dream life (Jones, 1953, pp. 351–352) and had been actively concerned with dream theory since at least as early as 1886—which is when he obtained a book by W. Robert on dreams as a vital function that he would later cite prominently in *The Interpretation of Dreams* (Trosman and Simmons, 1973, p. 659, # 115; cf. Freud, 1900, pp. 17–18, 79–81, 163, 164n, 177–178, 189, 579, 591). In the latter work, Freud would also devote substantial discussion to a book on sleep and dreams by Josef Delboeuf, published in Paris in 1885 (Freud, 1900, pp. 11–12, 20–21, 51, 52n, 58, 60, 105, 179n, 184n)—quite possibly Freud had acquired this work in 1889, if not already in 1885–1886. At any rate, his statement in 1914 that his interest in dreams and their interpretation was a spontaneous byproduct of his adoption of the "free association" technique, and that he knew of no "outside influence" which "drew" his "interest" to them or "inspired" him with any "expectations" in regard to them (1914, p. 19), was plainly disingenuous, to say the least.

62. In his autobiographical sketch of 1925, Freud would imply that he had had all his early hypnotic subjects "lie on a sofa" (p. 28). But his two formal discussions of the hypnotic technique, dating from 1890 and 1891, indicate that, in point of fact, he had had his subjects "sit down" in a "comfortable chair" while he would then "sit down opposite" so as to permit the employment of ocular fixation or related techniques of inducing hypnosis (Freud, 1890, p. 294; 1891b, p. 108; Strachey, 1966a, pp. 63–64; 1974, p. 428). Beginning May 1889, Freud seems to have induced hypnosis in the case of "Frau Emmy von N . . ." while she reclined "on a sofa"—however, she was in a nursing home at the time and was spending

much of her time in bed (Breuer and Freud, 1893–1895, pp. 48, 50–51). In mid-1890, Freud hypnotized a patient so that she was soon "lying back"—however, the woman was confined to bed following the birth of a child (1892–1893, p. 119). But by late 1892, by then in the process of abandoning hypnosis, it was customary for Freud to have at least some of his patients "lie down"—see the cases of "Miss Lucy R." and "Frl. Elisabeth von R . . ." in the *Studies on Hysteria* (Breuer and Freud, 1893–1895, pp. 113, 139). It seems likely that Freud's treatment of the latter took place in her own home (de Swaan, 1977, p. 386; cf. Breuer and Freud, 1893–1895, p. 155). But probably it was during the years 1891–1892 that Freud first began to employ his neurologist's couch as an integral element in his psychotherapeutic technique—which is to say, some three or four years after he had begun the treatment of Anna von Lieben. No doubt the introduction of the "free association" method, superseding catharsis, was directly related to this innovation—the induction of hypnosis via ocular fixation not being required with the new method. And possibly this innovation had something to do, in turn, with Freud's move from a smaller apartment to Berggasse 19 in September 1891.

63. In his *The Assault on Truth: Freud's Suppression of the Seduction Theory* (1984), Masson seeks to portray Emma Eckstein as Freud's first and most important analytic patient (cf. pp. 57, 245). Freud himself identifies "Frl. Elisabeth von R . . ." as the subject of his "first full-length analysis of an hysteria" (Breuer and Freud, 1893–1895, p. 139). While both of these women played important enough roles in the origins of psychoanalysis (cf. Swales, 1982c, pp. 8–15; 1983a, pp. 38–40; 1983c, p. 4), neither stands comparison with Anna von Lieben, his "prima donna" and "teacher."

64. Freud's dedication reads: "Dedicated to Dr. Josef Breuer in friendship and respect" (Freud, 1891, p. v). In a footnote in *On Aphasia*, Freud states that "the stimulus to this study came, in fact, from the papers published by Exner jointly with my late friend Josef Paneth . . ." (1891a, p. 66n). Afflicted with tuberculosis, Paneth had died on January 4, 1890 during a severe influenza epidemic; and it is revealing that, while closely befriended with his widow Sophie (cf. Breuer and Freud, 1893–1895, pp. 162–164; Freud, 1900, pp. 110–111, 117; Freud to Fliess, 7 November 1899, in Masson, 1985, pp. 383–384n), Freud did not see fit to dedicate the book to his memory. Nor, for that matter, did he dedicate this, his first real book, to his devoted wife—as Fliess would later do with one of his works (1924, p. v). Jones states that, in dedicating the book to Breuer, Freud was not merely expressing "gratitude" to the man but "hoped thereby to win Breuer into a better humour" (1953, p. 213).

65. Meynert's contempt for hypnosis is nicely reflected in a letter of his dated 18 April 1891, apparently addressed to Prof. Ludwig Darmstaedter (Sammlung Darmstaedter, 3 1 [2] 1880, Handschriftensammlung, Staatsbibliothek Preussischer Kulturbesitz, West Berlin). While affirming his esteem for certain advocates of hypnosis such as Krafft-Ebing and Forel, he nevertheless considers them gullible and points out that Helmholtz and du Bois-Reymond, two men whose opinions certainly do not count for little, number among those who, like himself, consider hypnotism to be essentially a fraud.

66. Freud to Fliess, 12 July 1892, preserved in Jerusalem.

67. All of the ellipses in this passage appear in the published version of the letter; I have been unable to locate the original.

68. It is implied in a statement of Heinrich Gomperz, though, that Freud did eventually succeed through hypnosis in curing his mother of her pains (H. Gomperz, manuscript, p. 1464).

69. Handschriftensammlung, 122.204, Vienna Stadtbibliothek.

70. Handschriftensammlung, 122.203, Vienna Stadtbibliothek.

71. See the poem of Anna Lieben dedicated to Julie Schlesinger and dated 24 March 1898 (Handschriftensammlung, I.N. 123.787, Vienna Stadtbibliothek). Cf. Winter (1927, pp. 73–74).

72. Aussee comprises three distinct resorts, Altaussee, Bad Aussee, and Grundlsee, all of them adjacent—while between Altaussee and Bad Aussee is situated the district of Obertressen where, accompanied by two servants, the Freud family stayed during the summers of 1896–1898 in the farmhouse of Ferdinand and Maria Mauskoth (*Ausseer Cur- und Fremden-liste,* 6 June 1896, # 217; 25 May 1897, # 54; 24 May 1898, # 15). Around July 16, 1896, Anna von Lieben arrived in Grundlsee accompanied by her family, servants, housekeeper, and the children's governess—a total of 17 people—and set up home for the summer in the Villa Jurie (*Ausseer Cur- und Fremden-liste,* 1896, # 2204). The following year, accompanied by her family and servants, she arrived at the resort around July 17, 1897—her party consisted of 13 persons—and moved into Bräuhof 15 (*Ausseer Cur- und Fremden-liste,* 1897, # 2313). Around the same time, Dr. Josef Winter arrived and took up residence in the nearby Gasthof Schraml (# 2302), where he was joined just a few days later by Dr. Paul Karplus (# 2781) who was by then courting Valerie von Lieben. Many years later, Anna's youngest daughter Henriette would recall that the family stayed in Grundlsee at the villa of Count Meran—presumably a recollection of the year 1897 because the von Meran family had stayed at Bräuhof 15 the previous year (*Ausseer Cur- und Fremden-liste,* 1896, # 1101). According to Henriette, Josef Winter did not see eye to eye with Frl. Lina Baumann—with the result that she was shortly dismissed from her position as governess. To be noted is that the Auspitz family owned a villa in Fischerndorf just to the north of Altaussee; while Jella Oppenheimer, Anna's younger sister, owned a villa, Das Ramgut, in Obertressen, where Anna is said to have sometimes stayed and which was also frequented by Hofmannsthal. During the years 1896–1898, as the cure lists attest, an average of some 8500 people patronized this Alpine resort each summer. During the 1896 season, its visitors included, besides Sigmund Freud and his former patient Anna von Lieben, Emma Eckstein's widowed mother Amalie accompanied by two of her daughters, Freud's current patient Emma surely being one of them (# 2260); Hugo von Hofmannsthal (# 4387); Theodor Herzl (# 1056—cf. Stewart, 1974, p. 253); Carl Lueger (# 989); Karl Kautsky (# 289); and a certain Dr. Karl Krauss (# 2306)—possibly a misspelling of Kraus. I am greatly indebted to Herr Alois Mayrhuber, Aussee's local historian and law enforcement officer, for having kindly arranged for me to inspect all the surviving cure lists (August 5–7, 1980); also for arranging for me to interview Frau Maria

Baschlberger, a daughter of Mirzl Kals, born Mauskoth, a redhead born in 1881 (cf. M. Freud, 1957, p. 54).

73. The book is listed as No. 250 in the catalogue of Freud's London library published in 1973 by Trosman and Simmons—their entry reads: "Bacon, Francis, Viscount St. Albans. Neues Organ der Wissenschaft. 1830. Few markings. 'Anna Lieben,' not in Freud's writing" (p. 665). However, when inspecting all the books in Freud's library on October 4, 1979, I was unable, despite a considerable expenditure of effort on the part of the librarian Ms. Gertrud Dann and myself, to find the book in question.

References

Ackerknecht, E. H. (1957), Josef Breuer über seinen Anteil an der Psychoanalyse. *Gesnerus,* 14:169–171.

Andersson, O. (1965), A supplement to Freud's case history of "Frau Emmy von N." in *Studies on Hysteria,* 1895. Paper read at the International Psychoanalytic Congress, Amsterdam.

Bakan, D. (1975), The authenticity of the Freud Memorial Collection. *J. Hist. Behav. Sci.,* 11:365–367.

Barea, I. (1966), *Vienna: Legend and Reality.* London: Secker & Warburg.

Bellamy, E. (1880), *Dr. Heidenhoff's Process.* New York: D. Appleton & Co.

Bernfeld, S. (1951), Sigmund Freud, M.D., 1882–1885. *Internat. J. Psycho-anal.,* 32:204–217.

Bjerre, P. (1916), *The History and Practice of Psychanalysis.* Boston: Gorham Press.

Bleuler, E. (1896), Review of *Studien über Hysterie,* by J. Breuer & S. Freud. *Münchener medizinische Wochenschrift,* Jg. XLIII, pp. 524–525.

Blumenthal, R. (1984), Freud: Documents reveal years of strife as analysis evolved. *New York Times,* January 24.

Bourru, H., & Burot, P. (1888), *Les Variations de la Personnalité.* Paris: Baillière.

———&——— (1889), Un Cas de neurasthénie hystérique avec double personnalité. In: *First International Congress of Experimental and Therapeutic Hypnotism.* Paris: Dorn, pp. 228–240.

Bram, F. M. (1965), The gift of Anna O. *Brit. J. Med. Psychol.,* 38:53–58.

Brentano, F. (1874), *Psychology from an Empirical Standpoint.* London: Routledge & Kegan Paul, 1973.

Breuer, J., & Freud, S. (1893–1895), *Studies on Hysteria. Standard Edition,* 2. London: Hogarth Press, 1955.

Brill, A. A. (1921), *Fundamental Conceptions of Psychoanalysis.* New York: Harcourt, Brace.

Charcot, J.-M. (1889), *Clinical Lectures on Diseases of the Nervous System,* Vol. 1. London: The New Sydenham Society.

Chertok, L. (1961), On the discovery of the cathartic method. *Internat. J. Psycho-Anal.,* 42:284–287.

Dalma, J. (1963), La catarsis en Aristoteles, Bernays y Freud. *Revista de Psiquitria y Psicologia Medical,* 6:253–269.

De Boor, C. & Moersch, E. (1980), Emmy von N.—eine Hysterie? *Psyche,* 34:265–279.

de Swaan, A. (1977), On the sociogenesis of the psychoanalytic setting. In: *Human Figurations: Essays for Norbert Elias,* ed. P. R. Gleichmann, J. Goudsblom, & H. Korte. Amsterdam: Amsterdams Sociologisch Tijdschrift, pp. 381–413.

Delboeuf, J. (1889), *Le Magnétisme Animal: A Propos d'une Visite à L'école de Nancy.* Paris: Alcan. (Published under the same title in 1888–1889 in *Revue de Belgique,* 50:241–260, 387–408; 51:5–33, 286–324.)

Eissler, K. R. (1979), Bericht über die sich in den Vereinigten Staaten befindenen Bücher aus S. Freuds Bibliothek. *Jahrbuch der Psychoanalyse,* 11:10–50.

Ellenberger, H. F. (1970), *The Discovery of the Unconscious: The History and Evolution of Dynamic Psychiatry.* New York: Basic Books.

———— (1972), The story of "Anna O": A critical review with new data. *J. Hist. Behav. Sci.,* 8:267–279.

———— (1977), L'histoire d' 'Emmy von N.' *L'Evolution Psychiatrique,* 42:519–540.

Ewart, F. [= Exner, Emilie] (1907), *Zwei Frauen-Bildnisse zur Erinnerung.* Privately printed, Vienna.

Fliess, W. (1924), *Vom Leben und vom Tod: Biologische Vorträge.* Jena: Eugen Diederichs.

Forel, A. (1937), *Out of My Life and Work.* New York: W. W. Norton.

Freud, E., & Freud L., Eds. *Sigmund Freud: Briefe 1873–1939.* Frankfurt: S. Fischer.

Freud, M. (1957), *Glory Reflected: Sigmund Freud—Man and Father.* London: Angus & Robertson.

Freud S. (1886), Report on my studies in Paris and Berlin. *Standard Edition,* 1:1–15. London: Hogarth Press, 1966.

———— (1888a), Hysteria. *Standard Edition,* 1:37–59. London: Hogarth Press, 1966.

———— (1888b), Preface to the translation of Bernheim's *Suggestion. Standard Edition,* 1:71–85. London: Hogarth Press, 1966.

———— (1889), Review of August Forel's *Hypnotism. Standard Edition,* 1:89–102. London: Hogarth Press, 1966.

———— (1890), Psychical (or mental) treatment. *Standard Edition,* 7:281–302. London: Hogarth Press, 1953.

———— (1891a), *On Aphasia: A Critical Study,* trans. E. Stengel. New York: International Universities Press, 1953.

———— (1891b), Hypnosis. *Standard Edition,* 1:103–114. London: Hogarth Press, 1966.

———— (1892–1893), A case of successful treatment by hypnotism. *Standard Edition,* 1:115–128. London: Hogarth Press, 1966.

———— (1893a), Some points for a comparative study of organic and hysterical motor paralyses. *Standard Edition,* 1:160–172. London: Hogarth Press, 1966.

———— (1893b), Charcot. *Standard Edition,* 3:7–23. London: Hogarth Press, 1962.

_____ (1893c), On the psychical mechanism of hysterical phenomena: A lecture. *Standard Edition*, 3:25–39. London: Hogarth Press, 1962.

_____ (1900), *The Interpretation of Dreams. Standard Edition*, 4 & 5. London: Hogarth Press, 1953.

_____ (1905), On psychotherapy. *Standard Edition*, 7:255–268. London: Hogarth Press, 1953.

_____ (1910), Five lectures on psycho-analysis. *Standard Edition*, 11:7–56. London: Hogarth Press, 1957.

_____ (1914), On the history of the psycho-analytic movement. *Standard Edition*, 14:7–66. London: Hogarth Press, 1957.

_____ (1916–1917), *Introductory Lectures on Psycho-Analysis (Part III). Standard Edition*, 16. London: Hogarth Press, 1963.

_____ (1923), Two encyclopaedia articles. *Standard Edition*, 18:233–259. London: Hogarth Press, 1955.

_____ (1924), A short account of psycho-analysis. *Standard Edition*, 19:189–209. London: Hogarth Press, 1959.

_____ (1925), An autobiographical study. *Standard Edition*, 20:7–74. London: Hogarth Press, 1959.

_____ (1927), Postscript to "The question of lay analysis." *Standard Edition*, 20:251–258. London: Hogarth Press, 1959.

Gomperz, H. (manuscript), Theodor Gomperz. Bibliothek der österreichischen Akademie der Wissenschaften, Vienna (published in part by Kann, 1974).

Gomperz, J. von (1903), *Jugend-Erinnerungen*. Privately printed.

Gomperz, T. (1866), Traumdeutung und Zauberei: Ein Blick auf das Wesen des Aberglaubens. In: *Essays und Erinnerungen*. Stuttgart: Deutsche Verlagsanstalt, 1905, pp. 72–86.

_____ (1905), *Essays und Erinnerungen*. Stuttgart: Deutsche Verlagsanstalt.

_____ (1936), *Briefe und Aufzeichnungen*, Vol. 1 (1832–1868), ed. H. Gomperz. Vienna: Gerold.

Goshen, C. E. (1952), The original case material of psychoanalysis. *Amer. J. Psychiat.*, 108:829–834.

Grunwald, M. (1936), *Vienna*. Philadelphia: Jewish Publication Society of America.

Hartman, F. R. (1983), A reappraisal of the Emma episode and the specimen dream. *J. Amer. Psychoanal. Assn.*, 31:555–585.

Heidenhain, R. (1880), *Der sogenannte thierische Magnetismus: Physiologische Beobachtungen*. Leipzig: Breitkopf & Härtel.

Hennings, F. (1963), *Ringstrassen Symphonie*. Vienna & Munich: Herold.

Hirschmüller, A. (1978), *Physiologie und Psychoanalyse in Leben und Werk Josef Breuers*. [*Jahrbuch der Psychoanalyse*, Suppl. 4.] Bern: Hans Huber.

_____ (1979), Eine bisher unbekannte Krankengeschichte Sigmund Freuds und Josef Breuers aus der Entstehungszeit der 'Studien über Hysterie.' *Jahrbuch der Psychoanalyse*, 10:136–168.

Hollender, M. H. (1980), The case of Anna O.: A reformulation. *Amer. J. Psychiat.*, 137:797–800.

Holzapfel-Gomperz, B. (1980), *Reisnerstrasse 13: Meine Jugend im Wien der Jahr-*

hundertwende. Vienna & Munich: Österreichische Verlagsanstalt & A. Schroll-Verlag.

Holzer, R. (1960), *Villa Wertheimstein: Haus der Genien und Dämonen*. Vienna: Bergland.

Hurst, L. C. (1982), What was wrong with Anna O? *J. Royal Soc. Med.*, 75:129–131.

—— (1983), Freud and the great neurosis: Discussion paper. *J. Royal Soc. Med.*, 76:57–61.

Janet, P. (1889), *L'Automatisme Psychologique*. Paris: Alcan.

Jensen, E. M. (1984), *Streifzüge durch das Leben von Anna O./Bertha Pappenheim: Ein Fall für die Psychiatrie—Ein Leben für die Philanthropie*. Frankfurt am Main:ZTV.

Jones, E. (1953), *The Life and Work of Sigmund Freud*, Vol. 1. New York: Basic Books.

—— (1955), *The Life and Work of Sigmund Freud*, Vol. 2. New York: Basic Books.

—— (1957), *The Life and Work of Sigmund Freud*, Vol. 3. New York: Basic Books.

Kann, R. A., Ed. (1969), *Marie von Ebner-Eschenbach—Dr. Joseph Breuer: Ein Briefwechsel, 1889–1916*. Vienna: Bergland.

—— (1974), *Theodor Gomperz: Ein Gelehrtenleben im Bürgertum der Franz-Josefs-Zeit*. Vienna: Österreichischen Akademie der Wissenschaften.

Karpe, R. (1961), The rescue complex in Anna O's final identity. *Psychoanal. Quart.*, 30:1–27.

Lebzeltern, G. (1973), Sigmund Freud und Theodor Meynert. *Wiener klinische Wochenschrift*, Jg. 85, Heft 23, 8 June 1973, pp. 417–422.

Lesky, E. (1976), *The Vienna Medical School of the 19th Century*. Baltimore: Johns Hopkins University Press.

Lewis, N. D. C., & Landis, C. (1957), Freud's library. *Psychoanal. Rev.*, 44:327–354.

Lieben, A. von (1901), *Gedichte: Ihren Freunden zur Erinnerung*. Privately printed [K. u. k. Hofbuchdruckerei Carl Fromme, Vienna].

Lingens, E. (1981), Sigmund Freud und die Deutsche Akademie im Exil. *Sigmund Freud House Bull.*, 5:25–35.

Lobner, H. (1975), Some additional remarks on Freud's library. *Sigmund Freud House Bull.*, 1:18–29.

Lochner, L. P. (1950), *Fritz Kreisler*. New York: Macmillan.

Macalpine, I., & Hunter, R. A. (1956), *Schizophrenia 1677: A Psychiatric Study of an Illustrated Autobiographical Record of Demoniacal Possession*. London: William Dawson, 1956.

Macmillan, M. B. (1979), Delboeuf and Janet as influences in Freud's treatment of Emmy von N. *J. Hist. Behav. Sci.*, 15:299–309.

Malcolm, J. (1984), *In the Freud Archives*. New York: Knopf.

Masson, J. M. (1984), *The Assault on Truth: Freud's Suppression of the Seduction Theory*. New York: Farrar, Straus & Giroux.

——, Ed. & Trans. (1985), *The Complete Letters of Sigmund Freud to Wilhelm Fliess: 1887–1904*. Cambridge: Belknap Press/Harvard University Press.

McGuire, W., & Burnham, J. C. (1983), *Jelliffe: American Psychoanalyst and Physician: & His Correspondence with Sigmund Freud and C. G. Jung*. Chicago: University of Chicago Press.

Moebius, P. J. (1895), Review of *Studien über Hysterie*, by J. Breuer & S. Freud. *Schmidt's Jahrbücher der Gesammten Medicin*, Jg. 248, S. 96.

Moll, A. (1890), *Hypnotism*. London: Contemporary Science Series, Walter Scott.

Nunberg, H. & Federn, E., Eds. (1962), *Minutes of the Vienna Psycho-Analytic Society, Volume 1: 1906–1908*, trans. H. Nunberg, E. Federn, & M. Nunberg. New York: International Universities Press.

Ouspensky, P. D. (1971), *A New Model of the Universe*. New York: Vintage.

Owen, A. R. G. (1971), *Hysteria, Hypnosis and Healing: The Work of J.-M. Charcot*. New York: Garrett Publications.

Pappenheim, E. (1980a), Freud and Gilles de la Tourette: Diagnostic speculations on 'Frau Emmy von N.' *Internat. Rev. Psycho-Anal.*, 7:265–277.

——— (1980b), Letter to the editor. *Amer. J. Psychiat.*, 137:1625–1626.

——— (1981), A postscript to the case of Anna O. *Bull. Psychoanal. Assn. N. Y.*, 18:8, 15.

Reichard, S. (1956), A re-examination of "Studies in [sic] Hysteria." *Psychoanal. Quart.*, 25:155–177.

Roback, A. A. (1957), *Freudiana*. Cambridge, Mass: Sci-Art Publishers.

Scheidt, J. vom (1973), Sigmund Freud und das Kokain. *Psyche*, 27:385–430.

——— (1983), Von der Droge zum Traum. *Freiburger Universitätsblätter*, 82:49–64.

Schorske, C. E. (1980), *Fin-de-Siècle Vienna: Politics and Culture*. New York: Knopf.

Schott, H. (manuscript), Freuds Selbstversuche mit Kokain als Moment Seiner Selbstanalyse, 1982. (Publication pending.)

Schrenck-Notzing, A. von (1895), *The Use of Hypnosis in Psychopathia Sexualis*. New York: Julian Press, 1956.

Schwarz, G. (1979), *Villa Wertheimstein: Geschichte eines Döblinger Hauses*. Vienna: Jugend & Volk.

Sextus, C. (1893), *Hypnotism: Its Facts, Theories and Related Phenomena, with Explanatory Anecdotes, Descriptions and Reminiscences*. Privately printed, Chicago.

Simitis, I. G.- (1978), *Sigmund Freud: His Life in Pretty Pictures and Words*. New York: Harcourt Brace Jovanovich.

Spiel H. (1967), Jewish women in Austrian culture. In: *The Jews of Austria: Essays on Their Life, History and Destruction*. London: Vallentine, Mitchell, pp. 97–110.

Stanescu, H. (1971), Young Freud's letters to his Rumanian friend, Silberstein. *Israel Ann. Psychiat. & Rel. Disc.*, 9:195–207.

Stewart, D. (1974), *Theodor Herzl*. New York: Doubleday.

Stockert-Meynert, D. (1930), *Theodor Meynert und seine Zeit: Zur Geistesgeschichte Österreichs in der zweiten Hälfte des 19. Jahrhunderts*. Vienna: Österreichischer Bundesverlag.

Strachey, J. (1955), Editor's Introduction to *Studies on Hysteria. Standard Edition*, 2: ix–xxviii, London: Hogarth Press.

Strachey, J. (1966a), Editor's introduction to "Papers on hypnotism and suggestion." *Standard Edition*, 1:63–69. London: Hogarth Press.

———— (1966b), Editor's note to "Preface to the translation of Bernheim's *De La Suggestion*." *Standard Edition*, 1:73–74. London: Hogarth Press.

———— (1974), Addenda and Corrigenda [to the *Standard Edition*]. *Standard Edition*, 24:405–468. London: Hogarth Press.

Swales, P. J. (1982a), Freud, Minna Bernays, and the conquest of Rome: New light on the origins of psychoanalysis. *New American Review*, 1:1–23.

———— (1982b), Freud, Minna Bernays, and the Imitation of Christ. Presented at the New School for Social Research, New York, May 20. (Publication pending.)

———— (1982c), Freud, Johann Weier, and the status of seduction: The role of the witch in the conception of fantasy. Privately printed, New York. (Condensed as: "A Fascination with Witches," *The Sciences*, 22:21–25.)

———— (1982d), Freud, Fliess, and fratricide: The role of Fliess in Freud's conception of paranoia. Privately printed, New York.

———— (1983a), Freud, Martha Bernays, and the language of flowers: Masturbation, cocaine, and the inflation of fantasy. Privately printed, New York.

———— (1983b), Freud, cocaine, and sexual chemistry: The role of cocaine in Freud's conception of the libido. Privately printed, New York.

———— (1983c), Freud, Krafft-Ebing, and the witches: The role of Krafft-Ebing in Freud's flight into fantasy. Privately printed, New York.

———— (1985), Freud, Katharina, and the first "wild analysis." Presented at the History of Psychiatry Section, Payne Whitney Clinic, New York, January 9. (Publication pending.)

———— (in preparation), *Wilhelm Fliess: Freud's OTHER—A Biography*. New York: Random House.

Thornton, E. M. (1983), *Freud and Cocaine: The Freudian Fallacy*. London: Blond & Briggs.

Trosman, H. & Simmons, R. D. (1973), The Freud library. *J. Amer. Psychoanal. Assn*. 21:646–687.

Wagner-Jauregg, J. (1950), *Lebenserinnerungen*. Vienna: Springer.

Walser, H. H., Ed. (1968), *Auguste Forel: Briefe/Correspondance*. Bern: Hans Huber.

Winter, J. (1927), *Fünfzig Jahre eines Wiener Hauses*. Vienna & Leipzig: In Kommission bei Wilhelm Braumüller, Universitäts-Verlagsbuchhandlung.

Wykert, J. (1980), Anna O.—a re-evaluation. *Psychiatric News*, May 2, pp. 4–5, 22.

Edwin R. Wallace, IV ⸻⸻⸻⸻⸻⸻

Freud as Ethicist

Among the many intersections of psychoanalysis with other realms, that of psychoanalysis with ethics is perhaps the most problematic, seminal, and interesting. Since virtually all the issues pertaining to this connection were elaborated or adumbrated by Freud himself, a thorough consideration of his position is prerequisite to any evaluation of the relationship between psychoanalysis and ethics.

The approach of this essay is thematic rather than historical. Although I shall touch on aspects of the chronological development of Freud's ethical thinking, and although I shall address at times the work of Freud's commentators and critics (especially Hartmann [1960] and Rieff [1959, 1966], by whom I have been much influenced), I am concerned neither to write a prehistory or history of Freud's ethical thought nor to provide a historical survey of the numerous commentaries on his relationship to ethics.

Since there are as many definitions of "ethics" or "morality" as there are ethicists and moralists, I should indicate that I shall be using the term "ethics" in a very broad way indeed, to embrace the domains of both theoretical and applied ethics, as well as what is popularly considered "morality." In so doing I cannot help but encroach upon what many consider the domain of social theory or social philosophy (issues previously treated in Wallace, 1977, 1983).

The definition of "ethics" by Abelson and Nielsen in their excellent history of the subject (1967) approximates as closely as any to what I mean by the term: "(1) a general pattern or 'way of life,' (2) a set of rules of conduct or 'moral code,' and (3) inquiry about ways of life and rules of conduct" (p. 81). In the first sense, one might speak of Buddhist or Christian ethics, in the second of professional, public, or private ethics and of moral or immoral behavior, and in the third of that branch of philosophy—metaethics—that systematically and analytically studies the premises, rules, and procedures of ethical reasoning. In his writing, clinical work, and private life Freud was directly or indirectly concerned with all three of these areas, although primarily with the second.

Freud's relationship to ethics is subject to at least two profound ironies. First, although he wrote chiefly as a scientist and physician and rarely treated ethical issues explicitly, he was, as he himself occasionally acknowledged, continually dealing with what was traditionally considered the domain of ethics, pure and applied (whether secular or religious). Second, even though he did not consider himself a moralist or philosophical ethicist, he has had more impact on ethics and public and private morality than perhaps any individual since Christ or Paul, and certainly more than such self-consciously ethical theorists as Hobbes, Hume, Kant, Bentham, and Mill. Freud himself, despite his disavowals of the moralist's role, was hardly unaware of the ethical implications of his psychological thought or of his lifelong fascination with the "origins of religion and morality" (1935, p. 72).

In this essay I shall consider those aspects of Freud's thought that address ethical or moral concerns directly and those that, although not couched as ethical propositions, nevertheless have powerful implications for the moral domain. One's perception of Freud as ethicist very much depends on one's perspective; there are numerous, and in some respects contradictory, sides to his ethical thinking and professional and private morality. There is no better proof of this than that some, such as D. H. Lawrence, Norman O. Brown, and Wilhelm Reich, have seen Freud as antinomian and "remissive" (to use Rieff's term), others, such as Rieff and Hartmann, as favoring a balance between remissions and interdicts, and still others, such as Küng (1979), as bolstering traditional, largely Judeo-Christian interdicts and imperatives.

The overarching theme of Freud's relationship to ethics, and the source of its creative tension, was his attempt to apply a dispassionate scientific mode of investigation to matters that had hitherto been evaluated in moral terms and considered to be within the exclusive purview of philosophers and clerics. This, I shall argue, constituted his greatest contribution to theoretical and practical ethics at the same time that it posed the greatest threat to traditional ethical formulations. In short, in this essay, as in most other treatments of the matter, one cannot escape questioning the degree to which Freud was supportive of or antithetical to traditional Western moral values (imperatives and interdicts, and the system of rewards, punishments, and valuations that supports them; by "traditional" I mean Judeo-Christian with some Greco-Roman elements).

Embedded within this central theme are a number of subsidiary ones, many of which overlap, but each of which I shall treat separately, insofar as possible. The essay is divided into five sections. The first, and longest, is a miscellany of the following themes: the role of what Freud termed "ethical motives" in the instigation of repression, and the importance of the conflict between morality and impulse in pathogenesis; Freud's ambivalence about the use of traditional moralistic terminology in reference to psychopathology; his equation of immorality with childishness, and his insistence on the universality of sexual trends that traditional morality had generally treated harshly; his psychological theory of moral development; sexist trends in his pronouncements about feminine morality; his phylogenetic–Lamarckian theory of moral development, with reference to his ambiguity on the relative influence of social and biological factors in that development; his emphasis on the narcissistic and egoistic aspects of one's moral demand system and the impact of the pleasure principle on moral behavior; his consideration of the pathological vicissitudes of "conscience"; his elucidation of the unconscious aspects of morality, with particular regard to his increasing emphasis on the role of the unconscious sense of guilt in promoting and maintaining psychopathological (and even criminal) behavior and in impeding the recovery process; and his stance on the relationship between ethics and religion. I shall also consider a certain "levelling," almost Nietzschean tone toward certain aspects of traditional Western morality in his treatment of these issues.

The second section is concerned with Freud's considerations of the impact of remissions and interdicts (especially in regard to sexuality and aggression) on the maintenance of civilization and on the mental health of the individual, including his sophisticated "costs/benefits analysis" of culture's imperatives. The third section attempts more clearly to define Freud's own moral values and eth-

ical desiderata, as explicit and implicit in his writing and his personal and professional life. The fourth section examines Freud's stance
on determinism and its implications for ethics, and the fifth draws
on the preceding four in an assessment of Freud's impact on ethics
and public and private morality.

MISCELLANY: SOME THEMES IN FREUD'S
RELATIONSHIP TO ETHICS

For a man who wrote, "I do not break my head very much about
good and evil" (Freud to Pfister, 9 October 1918 in Meng and E.
Freud, 1963, p. 61), "What is moral is always self-evident" (Freud
to Putnam, 8 July 1915 in Hale, 1971, pp. 189–190), and "Why I—
as well as my six children—are compelled to be thoroughly decent
human beings is quite incomprehensible to me" (Freud to Putnam, 8
July 1915, in Hale, 1971, p. 190), Freud was in fact preeminently
concerned with ethical–moral issues from the outset of his career to
its culmination in *Moses and Monotheism.*

As early as 1896 Freud deemed "shame and morality" the "repressing forces" (1892–1899, p. 221). That view is reiterated in
numerous places, including the Clark University lectures (1909c),
wherein "ethical and aesthetic standards" (p. 24) are said to initiate
repression, and in the essay on Popper-Lynkeus (1923a), in which
the motives for dream censorship are declared to be "ethical and
aesthetic" (p. 262). As late as 1933 "repression" is characterized as
the "work of the superego [the structural equivalent of "shame and
morality"] . . . carried out either by itself or by the ego in obedience
to its orders" (p. 69). Hence, the pathogenic conflict in neurosis is
that between "firmly-rooted complexes of moral ideas in which one
has been brought up and the recollection of actions or merely
thoughts of one's own which are irreconcilable with them; when, in
other words, one feels the pangs of conscious . . . [mostly over]
ideas and processes connected with sexual life" (Breuer and Freud,
1893–1895, p. 210), such as, Freud adds, adolescent masturbation
or fantasies of adultery.

As I suggested earlier, one of Freud's primary aims was to apply
dispassionate scientific and clinical analytic methods and terminology to what had hitherto been viewed in moral terms. *Three
Essays on the Theory of Sexuality* (1905a) is characterized by its
aseptic treatment of such "moral" issues as infantile sexuality, sexu-

al fantasies, and perversions and inversion. Freud puts the word "ethical" in quotation marks in his published lecture to B'nai B'rith, and throughout his writing often uses quotation marks around the words "good," "bad," and "evil" when they refer to certain human impulses—sexual, egoistic, aggressive, and so forth. Indeed, at times (as we shall see in *Jokes,* "'Civilized' Sexual Morality," and elsewhere) Freud could be acerbically critical of traditional morality, especially where it dealt with sexual matters.

Nevertheless, he consistently used—and without quotation marks—the adjectives "moral" and "immoral" to refer to the repressing and the repressed mental forces respectively. For instance, the popular tendency to excuse parapraxes is considered a "compliant tolerance of the immoral," the "immoral" meaning, in this case, the "egoistic, jealous, and hostile feelings and impulses" (1901, p. 276). This practice is evident in his very earliest writings (1895, pp. 210, 245; 1900, p. 72; 1901, p. 276) right on through the Rat Man case (1909b), in which Freud refers to the "contrast between [the patient's] moral self and [his] evil one—the moral self [being] the conscious, the evil self the unconscious" (p. 276). In "A Short Account of Psycho-Analysis" (1923b) he declares the "impulses . . . subjected to repression [to be] those of selfishness and cruelty, which can be summed up in general as evil, but above all sexual wishful impulses, often of the crudest and most forbidden kind" (p. 197). And in "The Ego and the Id" (1923c) he is concerned to rebut, calling it "unjust," the reproach that psychoanalysis has ignored the "higher, moral, supra-personal side of human nature" (p. 35), adding that, with the doctrine of the superego, psychoanalysis affirms that "the normal man is not only far more immoral than he believes but also far more moral than he knows" (p. 52). Wortis (1954, p. 147) recalls the moralistic tinge in Freud's comments about Ellis's and Hirschfeld's perversion and inversion, and indeed about homosexuality in general. In his private life, as we shall see in the third section, Freud could be quite moralistic—in the traditional way and about the traditional matters: sexuality, egoism, fidelity and trustworthiness, aggression, and so forth. (May not his characterization of the symptom as a "compromise" carry a subtle moralistic connotation?)

Despite Freud's persistent (although at times ironic) use of traditional moral terminology and in spite of a certain puritanism in his private life, his large intent was to rescue psychopathology, fantasy life, dreams, and major areas of sexual behavior from the moral judgments that had generally surrounded them. He wished to conquer much of this territory for science and medicine and to enhance medical and public tolerance for the psychopathological and sexually deviant, to extend the "compliant tolerance of the immoral" from parapraxes to other spheres of human life.

That intent is illustrated nowhere more clearly than in his equation of immorality with childishness, his hypothesis of the universality of the bisexual disposition, and his assertion that we all pass through perverse modes of sexual pleasure in childhood (which remain latent, ready to resurrect themselves, in many of us).

> The character of even a good child is not what we should wish to find it in an adult. Children are completely egoistic; they feel their needs intensely and strive ruthlessly to satisfy them—especially as against the rivals, other children, and first and foremost as against their brothers and sisters. But we do not on that account call a child 'bad'; we call him naughty; he is no more answerable for his evil deeds in our judgment than in the eyes of the law. And it is right that this should be so; for we may expect that, before the end of the period which we count as childhood, altruistic impulses and morality will awaken in the little egoist. . . . If this morality fails to develop, we like to talk of 'degeneracy,' though what in fact faces us is an inhibition in development [1900, p. 250].

Freud (1905a) refers to the "aptitude for [perversions] innately present in [children's] disposition." In children there is little resistance to seduction, "since the mental dams against sexual excesses—shame, disgust, and morality—have either not yet been constructed at all or are only in the course of construction. . . . In this respect children behave in the same kind of way as an average uncultivated woman in whom the same polymorphously perverse disposition persists. . ." (p. 191).

Years later, in "An Autobiographical Study" (1925a), Freud makes it quite plain that when he referred to children as "polymorphously perverse" he was simply using language then current and that no moral judgment was implied: "psycho-analysis has no concern whatever with such judgments of value" (p. 38). Assertions such as "this disposition to perversions of every kind is a general fundamental human characteristic" (1905a, p. 191), and there is "some trace of homosexual object-choice in everyone" (1925a, p. 38) tend to remove such dispositions from the moral domain, and have the ultimate effect—as I believe Freud intended them to have—of increasing medical and public tolerance for them. (Recall, moreover, Freud's comforting and nonjudgmental letter of 9 April 1935 [in Jones, 1957, pp. 195–196] to the mother of a homosexual.) Freud is aware of what he is undercutting: The "authoritative prohibition by society" is perhaps "chief" among the factors, apart from the innate attraction for the opposite sex, that diminish the incidence of homosexuality (1905a, p. 229). There is also perhaps a subtle antinomian irony implicit in Freud's (1905a) reference to the neurotic (the very caricature of what society deemed "a refined organization . . . [with] great moral purity" [Breuer and Freud, 1893–1895, p. 245]) as suffering from the "negative" of the perversions, in the sense that the latter had traditionally been subject to the severest moral judgments.

If Freud equated much of what had traditionally passed for immorality with childishness, he also put forward a systematic theory of the childhood origins of morality. As early as 1895 he considers the initial helplessness of human beings as the primal source of all moral motives (p. 318). In view of the infant's total dependence on the good will of its parent, loss of the latter's love and nurturance constitutes the infant's greatest danger: "If he loses the love of another person upon whom he is dependent, he also ceases to be protected from a variety of dangers. Above all, he is exposed to the danger that this stronger person will show his superiority in the form of punishment. At the beginning, therefore, what is bad is whatever causes one to be threatened by loss of love" (1930, p. 124). With regard to the oral instinct, Freud (1925b) proposes another ontogenetic prototype for the moral sense of "good" and "bad" : " 'I should like to eat this" or " 'I should like to spit it out' " (p. 237). A good deal of what is considered "character," in both the popular moral and the technical psychoanalytic senses, is posited to arise from sublimation of, and reaction formation to, perverse instinctual impulses of the preoedipal phase (1905a, p. 178). In "Character and Anal Erotism" (1908a) "morality" is defined as a species of reaction formation, as are shame and disgust (p. 171).

But although the beginnings of the moral sense could be located in the oral and anal periods (with regard to the latter, the "sphincter morality" associated with toilet training), its development was determined by the events of the oedipal stage. Freud's theory of superego formation—through the child's repression of his incestuous and parenticidal fantasies and his identification (primarily) with the parent of the same sex—is too well known to require recapitulation here. The concept of the superego completed the structural vision of the moral system toward which Freud's thinking had been moving for years. I shall limit myself to three, somewhat paradoxical, points:

(1) Insofar as the parent determines the character of the child's superego it is through the child's identification with the parent's superego, rather than with the parent himself : "Whatever under-standing [the parents'] ego may have come to with the superego, they are severe and exacting in educating children. They have for-gotten the difficulties of their own childhood and they are glad to be able now to identify themselves fully with their own parents, who in the past laid such severe restrictions upon them" (1933, p. 67).

(2) The more powerful the sexual and aggressive impulses of the child, the stricter his superego: "The more powerful the Oedipus complex was and the more rapidly it succumbed to repres-sion . . . the stricter will be the domination of the superego over the ego later on—in the form of a conscious or perhaps of an uncon-scious sense of guilt" (1923c, pp. 34–35). Morality (or at least its unconscious aspects as organized in the ego ideal–superego) is thus subject to the paradox that, as the "heir of the Oedipus complex," it is "also the expression of the most powerful impulses and most important libidinal vicissitudes of the id. . . . What has belonged to the lowest part of the mental life of each of us is changed, through the formation of the ideal, into what is highest in the human mind by our scale of value" (p. 36). "Kant's 'Categorical Imperative,'" Freud (1924) triumphantly asserts, "is thus the direct heir of the Oedipus complex" (p. 167).

(3)The degree of harshness of the superego is determined, in large measure, by the intensity of the child's parenticidal impulses, and not by the parent's aggressiveness. In *Civilization and Its Discon-tents* (1930) Freud emphasizes that the aggressiveness of the super-ego is mainly determined by the child's introjection of hostility hitherto projected onto the same-sexed parent. The child's superego then trains on his ego the hostility that he would like to level at the parent.

That the second and third points, when coupled with the concept of reaction formation, can be used cynically—to conceptualize the ostensibly most saintly as actually the most sinful—is all too appar-

ent. As early as 1900 Freud was using psychogenetics as an instrument to demolish man's moral pretensions: "[The Oedipus story]
compel[s] us to recognize our own inner minds, in which the same
impulses, though suppressed, are still to be found. . . . [Oedipus
Rex] strikes as a warning at ourselves and our pride, at us who since
our childhood have grown so wise and mighty in our own eyes" (p.
263). Recall such comments as "Each of these excessively virtuous
individuals [obsessionals] passed through an evil period in his infancy—a phase of perversion which was the forerunner and precondi-
tion of the later period of excessive morality" (1913, pp. 160–161);
"[the] pre-existence of strong 'bad' impulses in infancy is often the
actual condition for an unmistakable inclination towards 'good' in
the adult. . . . Most of our sentimentalists, friends of humanity, and
protectors of animals have been evolved from little sadists and animal tormentors" (1915, p. 282); in a letter to Putnam, Freud writes:
"You are suffering from a too early and too strongly repressed sadism expressed in over-goodness and self-torture" (5 October 1911,
in Hale, 1971, p. 130); of his lack of enthusiasm for the "doctor
game" and for "any craving in my early childhood to help suffering
humanity" he quips, "My innate sadistic disposition was not a very
strong one, so that I had no need to develop this one of its derivates"
(1927a, p. 253); Dostoevsky is termed a "sadist"—"that is to say
the mildest, kindliest, most helpful person possible" (1928, p. 179).

In fine, although Freud repeatedly protested (1923d, p. 252;
1925c, p. 218) that by deriving the "higher," "moral" capacities
from infantile factors and "animal instinctual" tendencies he implied nothing demeaning or debunking, he was nevertheless capable
of adopting a sardonic, levelling, almost Nietzschean tone. Such a
tone, coupled with psychogenetic reductionism, could well lead
one, as Rieff (1959) suggests, to understand both "a Saint Augustine and a de Sade . . . as fixated on the fantasies formed during
childhood. . ." (p. 166). Moreover, Freud's position overlooks the
alternative possibility—that the little sadist might grow up to be a
big one, rather than a humanitarian and animal lover. Might not the
psychogenetic instrument, in the hands of those less humane and
more reductionistic than Freud, serve to provide a sinister and
cynical rationalization for what former ages have viewed as moral
laxity?

The sexist bias in Freud's theory of the psychogenesis of feminine
morality is by now well known. In brief, Freud (1925d) argues that

the girl, already feeling castrated, lacks the motive, fear of castration, that leads the boy to renounce his oedipal strivings and form
the core identification of the superego. The putative moral deficien-
cies of women resulting from their infantile sense of castration are
said to include: "Their super-ego is never so inexorable, so impersonal, so independent of its emotional origins as we require it to be
in men . . . they show less sense of justice . . . are less ready to
submit to the great exigencies of life . . . are more often influenced
in their judgments by feelings of affection or hostility" (Freud,
1925d, pp. 257–258). Furthermore, "women [are] weaker in their
social interests . . . and have less capacity for sublimating their instincts than men" (Freud, 1933, p. 134). We shall re-encounter such
psychoanalytic name-calling, or pseudomoralizing, in Freud's work
on religion.

Alongside Freud's psychosocial theory of the origin and development of conscience ran a phylogenetic–Lamarckian one. As early as
1897 Freud (1892–1899, pp. 269–270) suggested that man's adoption of an upright carriage and the consequently diminished role of
the olfactory sense led formerly pleasurable smells to become re-
pulsive: "To put it crudely, the current memory stinks just as an
actual object may stink; and just as we turn away our sense organ
(the head and nose) in disgust, so do the preconscious and our
conscious apprehension turn away from the memory. This is *repression*" (p. 232). Such ideas are reiterated in *Civilization and Its
Discontents*.

Freud's phylogenetic–Lamarckian theory of the origins of man's
sense of guilt, religion, and social interdicts (taboos) in the primal
parricide is, as Rieff and others have pointed out, a sort of secu-
larized version of original sin. The primal parricide thesis forms the
nucleus for all Freud's subsequent biogenetic theories of morality
(see Wallace, 1983).

I have already referred to the tension in Freud's theoretical work
with regard to the relative influences of phylogenetic and social
determinants of the individual's moral sense. For example, in *Three
Essays on the Theory of Sexuality* (1905a) Freud characterizes the
incest taboo as "essentially a cultural demand made by society" (p.
225), and yet, in a footnote added to the same page in 1915, opines
that this interdict, "like other moral taboos, has no doubt already
established itself by organic inheritance." In another 1915 footnote

to *Three Essays* Freud reasserts that the "forces which act like dams upon sexual development—disgust, shame, and morality—must also be regarded as historical precipitates of the external inhibitions to which the sexual instinct has been subjected during the psychogenesis of the human race." Even while "upbringing and external influences" are accorded a role in determining when those forces arise, there is still a tendency to emphasize the phylogenetic and Lamarckian—with regard to the inhibitions of the latency period, for example, which are said to be "organically determined and fixed by heredity," with the role of "education" limited to "following the lines which have already been laid down organically and to impressing them more clearly and deeply" (pp. 177–178). Such ideas, including the parricide hypothesis, are reissued in *Moses and Monotheism* (1939), wherein a phylogenetic–Lamarckian basis is claimed for the ethics and religion of the Jewish people. The notion that the "ethical motives" for repression have a hereditary–constitutional component quite as much as the drives they oppose suggests once again that the "higher" capacities of man are not so high after all. I shall return to these matters in my discussion of Freud's attitudes toward religion.

Let us turn now to a different aspect of Freud's theorizing about the nature and development of the moral system—the role of the pleasure principle and narcissism in conscience formation. On the question of whether moral behavior is ultimately egoistic, Freud followed in the footsteps of Hobbes (1651) and Locke (1690), who emphasized "self-preservation" and the drive to achieve "satisfaction" and avoid "uneasiness," respectively, as the mainsprings of all behaviors. Man's egoism was harnessed, thought these philosophers, by the rational recognition that some form of social contract made life longer and less "brutish" and "nasty" than the *Homo homini lupus* state of nature.

Freud conceptualized all human behaviors—with the possible exceptions of certain aspects of the fate and transference neuroses, post-traumatic dreams, and repetitive children's play—as motivated by the pleasure principle, in accordance with which the organism seeks to reduce the intrapsychic tension of unfulfilled striving or conflict to a minimum. The reality principle is but its adaptive modification, the goal remaining reduction in psychic tension, albeit through means that involve a postponement of gratification or perhaps even a temporary heightening of unpleasure. The inhibitions, sublimations, and reaction formations that constitute the unconscious basis of morality and character are all motivated by the unpleasure (signal anxiety) associated with the ontogenetic danger situations, the most advanced of which is superego condemnation.[1]

From "On Narcissism" through "Mourning and Melancholia" to "Group Psychology and the Analysis of the Ego" Freud focuses on the narcissistic aspects of moral development. "Repression," he asserts (1914), "proceeds from the self-respect of the ego. . . ." The "ideal ego"—or "ego ideal," as he would generally come to call it— "becomes the target of the self love which was enjoyed in childhood by the actual ego. The subject's narcissism makes it appearance displaced on to this new ideal ego which, like the infantile ego, finds itself possessed of every perfection that is of value. . ." (p. 94). "Conscience" is defined as that agency which sees to it that "narcissistic satisfaction from the ego ideal is insured and which, with this end in view, constantly watches the actual ego and measures it by that ideal" (p. 95). In "Group Psychology" (1921a), which offers a much more differentiated concept of the ego ideal, Freud reiterates the narcissistic aspect of its origin and functioning.

Freud's subsumption of moral behavior under the pleasure principle (or its modification in the reality principle), along with his emphasis on the narcissistic aspects of conscience formation, could serve further to rationalize cynicism toward morality in general. If all behavior, that of Mother Teresa no less than that of Charles Manson, is motivated by the desire to diminish the tension associated with unfulfilled strivings (including moral demands) and intrapsychic conflict, if the saint is indulging his narcissism as much as the sinner, then what makes moral behavior intrinsically different from or better than, immoral behavior? I doubt that Freud would countenance the drawing of such antinomian conclusions from his ideas, but the implications are there nevertheless and it would be easy for those not familiar with the depth, complexity, and ambiguity of Freud's corpus to use them to bolster a remissive or morally nihilistic philosophy.

Hartmann (1960) offers a much-needed corrective to Freud's thinking on the role of the pleasure principle in moral behavior, one that softens the antinomian edge just addressed. The problem, as Hartmann sees it, is Freud's failure to appreciate the "different pleasure conditions" obtaining in the mental systems id, ego, and superego. "The three types of gratification are, descriptively, of a very different kind," a datum that Hartmann feels is an obstacle to any purely "hedonistic" theory of morality :

> It would seem promising to attempt . . . a qualitative differentiation of pleasure experiences. . . . It appears that the three types of satisfac-tion (and this is true of different elements comprised in these types) cannot completely be substituted for one another. Instinctual grati-fication can often take the place of the other two types of gratifica-tion—of ego gratification and of moral or aesthetic gratification—although not fully nor under all conditions. Moral satisfaction, on the other hand, can replace even less completely, in most people, the gratification of instinctual demands [pp. 36–37].

Hartmann states that the "widespread expectation that a maximal consideration of self-interest would provide solutions most satisfac-tory from all the points of view . . . is not borne out by psycho-analytic experience and is unlikely to prove true" (p.33).

One of Freud's most seminal contributions to ethics came in his study of the pathological vicissitudes of morality. "Mourning and Melancholia" (1917) is an exquisite analysis of the diseased con-science : "The patient represents his ego to us as worthless, incapa-ble of any achievement and morally despicable; he reproaches him-self, vilifies himself, and expects to be cast out and punished"; his self-reproaches are out of all proportion to any realistic justification for them (p. 246). The pathological mechanism is understood to be the patient's identification with a lost or disappointing formerly loved object. Toward the portion of the patient's ego altered by identification with the object, his conscience levels reproaches that would actually apply to the lost, ambivalently cathected object. The centrality of this dynamic to melancholia is reiterated in several works (1926, p. 223; 1933, pp. 60–61).

In the same general regard Freud examines the role of the uncon-scious sense of guilt in psychopathology. In 1897, in attempting to understand Hamlet's difficulty avenging his father, he broaches the idea for the first time (1892–1899, pp. 265–266). In 1907 he speaks of the unconscious sense of guilt as motivating the obsessional's rituals. In 1916 he considers two pathological character types deter-mined by the unconscious sense of guilt: "those wrecked by suc-cess" (p. 318) and the "criminal from a sense of guilt" (p. 332). In the latter, the sense of guilt attaching to an unconscious *fantasy* leads the individual to commit a criminal *deed* in reality, for which he can then receive the punishment he unconsciously seeks. Freud (1924) presses that irony home in his dissection of the pathological, apparently hypermoral superego that leads to a "sin in order to repent" morality(p.169).

As the years went by Freud accorded an increasingly prominent role to the unconscious sense of guilt in neurotogenesis (see, for example, 1923c, pp. 26–27). It came to be denominated "perhaps the most powerful bastion in the subject's (usually composite) gain from illness—in the sum of forces which struggle against his recovery and refuse to surrender his state of illness" (1924, p. 166; see also 1930, p. 139; 1937; 1940, pp. 179–180). Indeed, in *Civilization and Its Discontents* (1930) the unconscious sense of guilt is considered "the most important problem in the development of civilization" (p. 134). Freud's experience with the pathological vicissitudes of morality ultimately generates his sardonic response to Kant's encomium of the categorical imperative—that it ranked with the starry heavens as a magnificent specimen of divine handiwork: "As regards conscience God has done an uneven and careless piece of work" (1933, p. 61).

Freud's focus on the unconscious sense of guilt and its role in pathogenesis has led some to accuse him of undermining the concept of "existential," "ontic," or "real" guilt. Foremost among these are the Christian psychologist O. H. Mowrer (1950) and the Jewish philosopher Martin Buber (1965). The former conceptualizes the neurotic as a "bona fide sinner," whose distress "comes not from acts which the individual would commit but dares not, but from acts which he has committed but wishes he had not" (p. 537). Although he acknowledges the importance of Freud's concept of "neurotic guilt," Buber reminds us that there is also such a thing as real, or what he calls "existential," guilt. By undertaking to "relativize guilt feeling genetically"—that is, to explain it by reference to human ontogenesis—Freud was denying the existential character of guilt, according to Buber. The risk is that the patient will become diverted, albeit to his great relief, from his "authentic guilt" to an "unambiguous neurotic one that . . . allows itself to be discovered in the microcosmos of his dreams or in the stream of his free associations" (pp. 124–128). Likewise, Tillich (1952) insists that neurotic anxiety must be differentiated from that related to man's existential guilt.[2]

Although there is some substance to such criticisms, it must be remembered that Freud was writing out of his experience with those who were victimized by their own pathological moral systems—by what Catholics would call "overscrupulousness." Their sense of guilt was associated with *fantasies*, not *deeds*, and largely *unconscious* fantasies at that.[3]

For Freud, it was *action* and not fantasy that was moral or immoral. In speaking of neurotics he states : "We find no deeds, but only impulses and emotions, set upon evil ends but held back from their achievement. What lie behind the sense of guilt of neurotics are always psychical realities and never actual ones" (1913, p. 159). Of course this carries with it, as Buber suggests, the danger of ignoring that there may be "real" sources of guilt (i.e., actual deeds) as well. In *Civilization and Its Discontents* (1930) Freud differentiates "remorse" for an act committed from a "sense of guilt" for one unconsciously contemplated (p. 131). Similarly, in "Psycho-Analysis and the Establishment of the Facts in Legal Proceedings" (1906) he takes pains to distinguish the conscious from the unconscious secret, which seems akin to the differentiation of a real and conscious source of guilt from a fantasied and unconscious one:

> In the neurotic the secret is hidden from his own consciousness; in the criminal it is hidden only from you [the jurist]. In the former, there is a genuine ignorance, though not an ignorance in every sense, while in the latter there is nothing but a pretense of ignorance. Connected with this is another difference, which is in practice of importance. In psycho-analysis the patient assists with his conscious efforts to combat his resistance, because he expects to gain something from the investigation, namely, his recovery. The criminal, on the other hand, does not work with you; if he did, he would be working against his whole ego [pp. 111–112].

He then warns the jurist that he may be "led astray" by a neurotic who, although innocent, reacts as if he were guilty "because a lurking sense of guilt that already persists in him seizes upon the accusation made in the public instance" (p. 113).

When Freud turns to the relationship between religion and ethics we encounter him at his least objective and most ambivalent. I have previously examined (1984) Freud's complex, in part psychodynamically determined, stance toward religion and the uneven quality of his work on the subject.

In a remarkable passage of 1897 Freud adumbrates what was to be the central thesis of *Totem and Taboo* 16 years later, one to which he would adhere all his life—*that morality and religion arise together:* "'Holiness' is something based on the fact that human beings, for the benefit of the larger community, have sacrificed a portion of their sexual liberty and their liberty to indulge in perversions. The horror of incest (something impious). . ." (1892–1899, p. 257). In *Totem and Taboo* Freud (1913a) would give this unity of religion and morality a cultural-historical and biogenetic basis: The rites (totem meal) and taboos (against incest) were motivated by the sons' remorse over patricide and the necessity to prevent fratricidal strife; these rituals and interdicts were then said to be determined by phylogenetic–Lamarckian transmission of the ambivalence and remorse vis-à-vis the primal father.

This unity of origin of religion and ethics is reiterated in *Moses and Monotheism* (1939), which underscores the importance of the social contract and instinctual renunciation to the formation and preservation of civilization: "The last form of a social organization came about with a *renunciation of instinct,* a recognition of mutual *obligations,* the introduction of definite *institutions,* pronounced inviolable (holy)—that is to say, the beginnings of morality and justice" (p. 82).

Freud (1927b, p. 37) had high praise for certain aspects of religion—the historical role it played in enforcing the imperatives and interdicts that are necessary to community life and the Christian ethos of *caritas,* which he compared to his own concept of Eros (1921a, p. 91). He even offered that the Christian emphasis on spiritual or affectionate love was a necessary counterbalance to what he viewed as the too purely sensual love of antiquity (1912, pp. 180, 187). Freud (1939) conceded that many of the Judeo-Christian injunctions were "justified rationally by the necessity for delimiting the rights of society as against the individual, the rights of the individual as against society, and those of individuals as against one another" (p. 122).

Nevertheless, Freud (1927b) charged religion with careless handiwork in its promulgation of morality and its promotion of moral behavior:

> It is doubtful whether men were in general happier at a time when religion held unrestricted sway; *more moral they certainly were*

not. . . . One sinned, and then one made a sacrifice or did penance and then one was free to sin once more. . . . In every age immorality has found no less support in religion than morality has [pp. 37–38; my italics].

Recall Freud's (1907a) earlier thesis that religious rituals were group compromise formations, invariably (and, Freud thought, increasingly directly) expressing bits and pieces of the impulses they were designed to ward off: "How commonly all the acts which religion forbids—the instincts it has suppressed—are committed precisely in the name of, and ostensibly for the sake of, religion" (p. 125). In fact, Freud charged, "complete backslidings into sin are more common among pious people than among neurotics" (p. 126).

Although Freud viewed certain of the ethics promoted by religion as justified by their survival value for humankind, he wanted them supported on the grounds of adaptation and rationality rather than belief in God. He favored (perhaps influenced by Bayle and a host of other Enlightenment thinkers) an "independent ethic"— that is to say, a moral system founded on principles other than belief in God or reward or retribution in an afterlife:

So long as [the masses] do not discover that people no longer believe in God, all is well. But they will discover it, infallibly, even if this piece of writing of mine is not published. . . . If the sole reason why you must not kill your neighbor is because God has forbidden it and will severely punish you for it in this or the next life—then, when you learn that there is no God and that you need not fear his punishment, you will certainly kill your neighbour without hesitation, and you can only be prevented from doing so by mundane force [1927b, p. 39].

Freud's solution: "Leave God out altogether and admit the purely human origin of all the regulations and precepts of civilization . . . [then] people could understand that they are made, not so much to rule them as, on the contrary, to serve their interests; and they would adopt a more friendly attitude to them, and instead of aiming at their abolition, would only aim at their improvement" (p. 41).

If Freud found little in favor of basing ethics on religious tenets, he was positively acerbic toward the "golden rule." Positing that the commandment was formulated out of awareness of the necessity to "set limits to man's aggressive instincts and to hold the manifestations of them in check with psychical reaction formations" (1930, p. 112), he nevertheless held that the injunction was not only psychologically unworkable and maladaptive for the individual, but that it cheapened the love for family and friends, being "an injustice to them if I put a stranger on a par with them" (pp. 109–110). "Indeed, if this grandiose commandment had run 'Love thy neighbour as thy neighbour loves thee,' I should not take exception to it" (p. 110).

In Freud's approach to religion we find something else that, with his pronouncements on feminine morality and character, is peculiar to his ethical thinking in these areas—the use of psychoanalytic and psychodiagnostic terms and concepts in a moralizing manner. Religion is compared to paranoia (1901, pp. 258–259; 1913, p. 92) and to the childhood neurosis through which all must pass (1927b). The religious question, regarding the "meaning and value of life," is declared pathological: "By asking this question one is merely admitting to a store of unsatisfied libido to which something else must have happened, a kind of fermentation leading to sadness and depression" (Freud to Bonaparte, 13 August 1937, in E. Freud, 1960, p. 436). Other characterizations of religion as a "neurotic relic" (1927b, p. 44), a "mass delusion" (1930, p. 81), and "blissful hallucinatory confusion" (1927b, p. 43) support Ackerknecht's (1943, p. 57) charge that Freud is making "hidden moral judgments."

THE REMISSIONS VERSUS THE INTERDICTS

Rieff (1966) conceptualizes culture—correctly, in my opinion—as "a system of moralizing demands, including remissions that ease the pressure of communal purposes" (p. 15). By this way of thinking a society or age can be characterized by its particular patterning and balancing of remissions and interdicts.

Freud was vitally concerned, both as a clinician and a psychological and social theorist, with the relationship between these remissions and interdicts. The works considered in this section of my essay constitute the most forceful and unblinking "cost/benefits analysis" of civilization ever undertaken. To capture the subtlety, ambiguity, and many facets of Freud's analysis—and his pronounced ambivalence on the matter—it would be necessary to render verbatim whole passages from *Jokes*, " 'Civilized' Sexual Morality," and virtually the entire text of *Civilization and Its Discontents*. Indeed, I beg the reader's indulgence for engaging in a substantial amount of direct quotation and paraphrasing of Freud, but I believe that is necessary in order to convey the tortuous complexity and ambiguity of his thinking and attitudes. This section bears more intimately than any of the others on the assessment of Freud's impact on contemporary ethics that is offered in the final section of the essay.

In this part I proceed chronologically because it is important to appreciate the evolution of—and vacillation in—Freud's thinking over time. In large measure, as the reader will see, he never resolved his mind on these matters—but it is precisely his ambiguity, realism, and lack of closure that is his greatest contribution to our comprehension of these issues. The first half of the section deals largely with Freud's costs/benefits analysis in relation to sexuality, and the second portion primarily with that in regard to aggression.

From the outset of his work as a psychoanalyst Freud was aware that he was dealing with the pathogenic effects of culturally induced repressions (Breuer and Freud, 1895, pp. 245–246). He was thrust out of the comfortable sphere of the purely medical into the problematic spheres of social and ethical theory. Due largely, one might suppose, to his experience with the neurotogenic effects of repression, Freud's writing assumed a strongly antinomian and remissive tone by 1905, in *Jokes and Their Relation to the Unconscious*.

Speaking of jokes that were intended to express in disguised fashion the general human desire, given the uncertainty of tomorrow, to throw off moral interdicts and indulge the pleasures of the day, Freud (1905b) urges us to acknowledge that there have been times when we have admitted the "rightness of this philosophy of life [*carpe diem*]" and "reproached moral doctrine with only understanding how to demand without offering any compensation" (p. 109):

> What these jokes whisper may be said aloud: That the *wishes and desires* of men have a right to makes themselves acceptable alongside of *exacting and ruthless morality*. And in our days it has been said in forceful and stirring sentences that this morality is only a selfish regulation laid down by the few who are rich and powerful and who can satisfy their wishes at any time without any postponement. So long as the art of healing has not gone further in making our life safe

and so long as social arrangements do no more to make it more enjoyable, so long will it be impossible to stifle the voice within us that rebels against the demands of morality. *Every honest man will end by making this admission, at least to himself* [p. 110; my italics].

Among those witticisms that assail the institutions inhibiting our pleasure Freud gives a prominent place to jokes of marital infidelity: "One does not venture to declare aloud and openly that marriage is not an arrangement calculated to satisfy a man's sexuality, unless one is driven to do so perhaps by the love of truth and the eagerness for reform of a Christian von Ehrenfels [whose advocacy of the abolition of monogamy and the nuclear family we shall return to shortly]" (pp. 110–111).

Even here, however, alongside these remissive and antinomian sentiments, Freud acknowledges the indispensability of instinctual renunciation, sublimation, and identification to culture:

> One must bind one's own life to that of others so closely and be able to identify oneself with others so intimately that the brevity of one's own life can be overcome; and one must not fulfill the demands of one's own needs illegitimately, but must leave them unfulfilled, because only the continuance of so many unfulfilled demands can develop the power to change the order of society [pp. 110–111].

And in the same year in which he expresses the antinomian opinions of *Jokes,* he writes in *Three Essays on the Theory of Sexuality* (1905a) of the "inverse relation holding between civilization and the free development of sexuality" (p. 242), and deems the sexual repression of the latency period necessary for the "aptitude of men for developing a higher civilization" (p. 234).

Nevertheless, Freud's fierce realism, precursive of that of *Civilization and Its Discontents,* requires him to state that "not every personal need can be postponed in this way and transferred to other people, and *there is no general and final solution of the conflict*" (1905b, p. 111; my italics). For example, the very latency period that Freud declares necessary for the development of civilization is also responsible for man's "tendency to neurosis" (1905a, p. 234).

" 'Civilized' Sexual Morality and Modern Nervousness" (1908b), the next great entry in Freud's accounting of culture, displays him at his most antinomian, although even here, as we shall see, he never completely abandons his recognition of the indispensability of cultural interdicts. And the remissive Freud of " 'Civilized' Sexual

Morality," while considerably more optimistic than the dour analyst of *Civilization and Its Discontents,* never approaches the utopian libertinism of a Wilhelm Reich, D. H. Lawrence, or Norman O. Brown. Freud was no believer in the possiblity of an Islamic heaven on earth.

Freud's essay takes off from Ehrenfels's argument that our repressive sexual morality (one aspect of which Ehrenfels considered to be monogamy and the nuclear family) impairs the vitality of the race and works against natural selection. To these criticisms, Freud adds his own: the etiological role of sexual repression in neurosis (p. 185).

He writes a brief for the many "perverts" and "inverts" constitutionally incapable of cleaving to the "civilized" morality that permits only maritally sanctioned heterosexual genital intercourse (p. 189). He deems it an "injustice" to demand genital sexuality of those "constitutionally inclined in other directions" (p. 192). (Recall the sardonic implications of referring to the neuroses as the "negative" of the perversions.) He speaks of the many who fall ill precisely because they attempt to be too "noble-minded": "They would have been more healthy if it could have been possible for them to be less good" (p. 191). In this regard, he contrasts the "healthy" but "immoral" men in many families with their "high-minded" but "neurotic" women (p. 192). He mocks the hypocrisy of civilization's unacknowledged double standard (for males and females) of sexual morality.

Not only does Freud deem society unwise and unjust for attempting to inhibit all forms of sexual activity outside of marital genital intercourse, he believes that its heavy-handed repression of premarital sexual activity ill prepares men and women for marital sex; it produces "impotent men," "frigid women," "well behaved weaklings," and a general prohibition of thought and curiosity that extends to intellectual areas.

Freud goes on to attack "civilized" sexual morality on its own terms as well, not merely as unjust and hypocritical: It leads to masturbation, which "teaches people to achieve important aims without taking trouble and by easy paths instead of through an energetic assertion of force"; it promotes "ethically objectionable" forms of intercourse that "degrade the relationship of love between two human beings from a serious matter to a convenient game, attended by no risk and no spiritual participation"; it contributes to

an increased incidence of homosexuality. Finally, its aim of promoting civilization backfires, both by producing large numbers of people
who are antipathetic to civilization and by engendering neuroses
that sap psychic energy that might otherwise be expressed in useful
cultural pursuits (pp. 199–201).

Certainly when one juxtaposes these contentions ("We may well
raise the question whether our 'civilized' sexual morality is worth
the sacrifices which it imposes upon us. . . ." [p. 204]) with those of
Jokes, one winds up with a fairly remissive prescription for sexual
ethics, exemplified in Freud's (1908b) frank opinion that "marital
unfaithfulness" would be the cure for neurotic illness in many (p.
195).

One must remember, however, the ambience in which Freud
wrote. Although the prudery of the Victorians has been much exag-
gerated and although sexual interdicts were already beginning to
give way when Freud began work in fin-de-siècle Vienna, there
were many more restrictions on the sexual life, even between law-
fully married men and women, than in our day. Furthermore, one
wonders to what extent—given Freud's well-known comments
about the quiescence of his sexual life in early middle age and the
claims and speculations about his relationship with Minna Bernays—he was writing out of his personal experience. He may well
have numbered himself among the victims of "civilized" sexual
morality, whether or not he ever took the infidelity cure. One can
read the Freud of 1905 and 1908 as arguing, not for the abolition of
all restraint in sexual matters, but for a more equitable balance
between remissions and interdicts. Even in " 'Civilized' Sexual Morality" he was not unaware of the necessity for the latter: "Generally speaking, our civilization is built up on the suppression of instincts" (p. 186). In a meeting of the Vienna Psycho-Analytic
Society in December, 1908, at which Ehrenfels himself was present,
Freud opposed Ehrenfels's advocacy of the abolition of the monog-
amic family—on the grounds that "family life is the basis for the
striving for propagation!" (in Nunberg and Federn, 1962–1975, p.
100)! As a medical man Freud was aware of the pathogenic role of
sexual repression; as a man of high culture he was aware of the
necessity for some degree of sexual inhibition and sublimation for
the maintenance of civilization; out of the tension between the two
grew his social and ethical thought.

On the issue of balance, moreover, one must recall that Freud (1912, pp. 180–187) considered sensuality divorced from affection, as Rieff (1959, p. 163) reminds us, a "degrading" state of affairs. I do not believe that Freud would have endorsed the current ethic of promiscuity that many have mistakenly inferred as his mandate. The indiscriminate acting out of the conscious derivatives of unconscious incestuous fantasies, as well as the aggressive aspect of much of the "love 'em and leave 'em" ethos, probably causes quite as much pain, in its own way, as did the cultural repressions of Freud's day. Freud was concerned to heal the split between sensuality and affection (or "aim-inhibited libido," if one prefers); in his day that meant easing repressions and pleading the case for sensuality.[4]

In the Clark lectures (1909c), Freud's next treatment of the subject, he is much less antinomian than in " 'Civilized' Sexual Morality" the year before (perhaps because he is addressing an American audience?). We find him explcitly concerned to counter the charge that by enhancing the patient's awareness of repressed sexual impulses the doctor is "overwhelming his higher ethical trends and . . . robbing him of his cultural acquisitions" (p. 52). Freud's rebuttal:

> The patient's personality may be convinced that it has been wrong in rejecting the pathogenic wish and may be led into accepting it wholly or in part; or the wish itself may be directed to a higher and consequently unobjectionable aim (this is what we call its 'sublimation'); or the rejection of the wish may be recognized as a justifiable one, but the automatic and therefore inefficient mechanism of repression may be replaced by a condemning judgement with the help of the highest human mental functions—*conscious control of the wish is attained* [p. 28; my italics].

> [When unconscious the wish is far stronger and is] independent of any contrary tendencies, whereas a conscious one is inhibited by whatever else is conscious and opposed to it. Thus the work of psycho-analysis puts itself at the orders of precisely the highest and most valuable cultural trends, as a better substitute for the unsuccessful repression. . . . The most frequent outcome is that while the work is actually going on, these wishes are destroyed by the rational mental activity of the better impulses that are opposed to them. *Repression* is replaced by a *condemning judgement* carried out along the best lines [p. 53].

In the Little Hans case and in a meeting of the Vienna Psycho-
Analytic Society, both in the same year as the Clark lectures, Freud
expresses similar sentiments:

> Analysis replaces the process of repression, which is an automatic
> and excessive one, by a temperate and purposeful control on the part
> of the highest agencies of the mind. In a word, analysis replaces
> repression by condemnation [1909a, p. 145].

> We liberate sexuality through our treatment, but not in order that
> man may from now on be dominated by sexuality but in order to
> make a suppression possible—a rejection of the instincts under the
> guidance of a higher agency [in Nunberg and Federn, 1962–1975,
> p.89].

All the same, and this illustrates Freud's balance, he warns his
Clark University audience that, in the interests of hygiene and
culture, "we ought not to exalt ourselves so high as to completely
neglect what was originally animal in our nature. . . . just as we do
not count on our machines converting more than a certain fraction
of the heat consumed into useful mechanical work, we ought not to
seek to alienate the whole amount of the energy of the sexual instinct from its proper ends" (p. 54).

This suggestion was hammered home by the parable of the "horse
of Schilda," the concluding note of the five lectures, which is paradigmatic of Freud's Aristotelian, Stoic–Epicurean, and Enlightenment ethic of reason and balance. According to this parable, the
horse of Schilda was so widely renowned for his strength and capacity for work that from far and wide people came to the village to
admire him. Still, the good people of Schilda, being a thrifty sort,
were disturbed by the enormous quantity of oats the horse consumed. Determined to break him of his expensive habit, they re-
duced his feedings bit by bit and day by day. Finally he was weaned
to one stalk a day, and thence to nothing! When, soon afterward,
"the spiteful animal was found dead . . . the citizens of Schilda
could not make out what it had died of. We should be inclined to
think that the horse was starved and that no work at all could be
expected of an animal without a certain modicum of oats" (pp. 54–
55).

In the *Introductory Lectures on Psycho-Analysis* (1915–
1917)Freud returns to this theme, with an even more remissive
twist. While he wishes to disabuse his audience of any misconcep-

tion that psychoanalysis gives the patient a "direct injunction" to disregard the "ethical restrictions demanded by society" and to "live a full life sexually," he asserts that the reasons for this reticence are purely pragmatic: Since the conflict between the "sexual" and "ascetic" currents is unconscious, it could not be solved simply by the analyst's lending support to one side or the other. Moreover, "anyone on whom the doctor could have so much influence would have found the same way out without the doctor" (pp. 432–433). Let no one mistake him of refraining from such influence on traditional moral grounds:

> . . . you must not conclude from my eagerness in defending myself against the charge that neurotics are encouraged in analytic treatment to live a full life—you must not conclude from this that we influence them in favour of conventional virtue. That is at least as far from being the case. It is true that we are not reformers but merely observers; nevertheless, we cannot help observing with a critical eye. . . . We can present society with a blunt calculation that what is described as its morality calls for a bigger sacrifice than it is worth and that its proceedings are not based on honesty and do not display wisdom. We do not keep such criticisms from our patients' ears, we accustom them to giving unprejudiced consideration to sexual matters no less than to any others; and if, having grown independent after the completion of their treatment, they decide on their own judgement in favour of some midway position between living a full life and absolute asceticism, we feel our conscience clear whatever their choice [p. 434].

In "Two Encyclopedia Articles" (1923d), written five years later, Freud gives vent to his more conservative side, averring that psychoanalysis aims, not to give "free rein to sexuality," but to enable the neurotic to "obtain a mastery" over it and to set him "free from the chains of his sexuality" (p. 252).

Yet two years later, while reasserting that "psycho-analysis has never said a word in favour of unfettering instincts that would injure our community" (1925c, p. 219), Freud repeats the admonitions of 1916. Society errs in setting up "a high ideal of morality—*morality being restriction of the instincts*—and insist[ing] that all its members shall fulfill that ideal without troubling itself with the possibility that obedience may bear heavily on the individual" (p. 219; my italics). This, coupled with the inadequacy and inequity of society's compensation to its members for this renunciation, leads him to accuse it of *"cultural hypocrisy"* (p. 219). Freud prescribes a "reduction in the strictness with which instincts are repressed and . . . correspondingly more play . . . given to truthfulness." Once more, however, this is liberty, not license: "Certain in-stinctual impulses with whose suppression society has gone too far should be permitted a far greater amount of satisfaction; in the case of certain others the inefficient method of suppressing them by means of repression should be replaced by a better and securer procedure" (p. 220).

In 1927 Freud again admonishes society, although this time with the more revolutionary tone of his earlier (1905b, 1908b) writings. He indicts it for excessive interdiction, not merely of sexuality, but of a broader class of strivings as well—aggressive, egoistic, and so forth. After making the customary obeisance to the necessity of instinctual renunciation to civilization and bemoaning the fact that "most people" have not internalized the external coercions (in the form of the superego), he criticizes culture for basing the satisfaction of one portion of its participants on the suppression of another : "In such conditions an internalization of the cultural prohibitions is not to be expected. . . . *a civilization which leaves so large a number of its participants unsatisfied and drives them into revolt neither has nor deserves the prospect of a lasting existence*" (1927b, pp. 11–12; my italics).[5]

Still, Freud was never so naively utopian as to suppose that man's innate strivings, unfettered, would lead society and the individual to unimagined heights of perfection: "Every civilization must be built up on coercion and renunciation of instinct. . . . It is only through the influence of individuals who can set an example and whom masses recognize as their leaders that they can be induced to perform the work and undergo the renunciation on which the exis-tence of civilization depends" (pp. 7–8).

From this brief survey of Freud's costs/benefits analysis of sexual interdicts we can see that it is difficult to characterize his thinking succinctly. There is a degree of waffling throughout. At times it appears that his ideas and opinions vacillate from year to year; indeed, he was capable of making highly remissive and highly inter-dictory statements literally back to back. I suspect that part of this ambivalence was determined, not merely by Freud's awareness of the cultural and psychological complexity of the problem, but by his own unresolved oedipal and sexual issues. In his personal sexual life, insofar as we can judge from his letters [(e.g., 1892–1899, p. 267)] and comments to friends, and from observations of him by others (Jones, 1955, p. 5; Hartmann, 1960, p. 98), and with the exception of a possible liaison with his sister-in-law, he was fairly puritanical (see also Roazen, 1975).

On balance, it is probably correct to say that the earlier Freud was more remissive with regard to sexuality than the later. The strident and revolutionary tone of *Jokes* and "'Civilized' Sexual Morality" grows softer. In "Analysis Terminable and Interminable" (1937), for example, Freud conceptualizes the means and ends of analysis as "eliminating the influence of an increase in instinct . . . increasing the power of resistance of the inhibitions . . . cur[ing] neuroses by ensuring control over instinct" (pp. 228–229). In Freud's last work but one, we witness Freud's identification with, and adulation of, a great interdictory hero—Moses. One might wonder how much this subtle shift back toward the interdicts was a function of changing times—society's increasing remissiveness on matters sexual and, as we shall see momentarily, aggressive and egoistic. What was true of society's attitudes on such matters in 1905 and 1908 did not hold in the 1920s and certainly not in the final decade of Freud's career.

And we must reckon of course with the development of Freud's clinical and metapsychological theorizing over the years. Although the simplistic "strangulated affect–catharsis" theory of pathology and therapy was discarded well before 1900, its vestiges remained until 1926, when Freud formulated his structural theory of anxiety. Shifting the etiological emphasis from dammed up libido to the ego's interpretive and defensive activities would seem to carry with it a corresponding de-emphasis on the socially and individually therapeutic potency of sheer instinctual discharge. The structural theory itself reflects, as Freud himself pointed out, an increasing acknowledgment (in the form of the ego, ego ideal, and superego) of what has been traditionally considered the "moral" side of life.

Furthermore, Freud's work on social cohesion (see Wallace, 1977) emphasizes the necessity for self-restraint, sublimation, reaction formation, and particularly the enhancement of mutual identifications and aim-inhibited libidinal ties: "Those sexual instincts which are inhibited in their aims have a great functional advantage. . . . Since they are not capable of really complete satisfaction, they are especially adapted to create permanent ties" (1921a, p. 139); "[civilization must set limits to sensual love in order to summon up] aim inhibited libido on the largest scale so as to strengthen the communal bond by relations of friendship" (1930, pp. 108–109). Freud also emphasizes the divisiveness that sexual license would engender. This idea, as we have seen, appeared as early as 1897 and was reiterated strongly in *Totem and Taboo* and *Civilization and Its Discontents*; in the latter work Freud (1930) asserts that restrictions on sensual libido contribute, indirectly, to culture's efforts to inhibit aggression, since sexuality has a propensity to become the "source of the strongest dislike and the most violent hostility among men who in other respects are on an equal footing" (p. 114). The necessity "to set limits to man's aggressive instincts . . . [with] psychical reaction formations" (p. 112) is explicitly declared one of the *raisons d'etre* for a certain degree of sexual inhibition.

In the *New Introductory Lectures on Psycho-Analysis* (1933) Freud assumes the Stoic, Enlightenment, and prudential stance that is perhaps most characteristic of his thought and attitudes on the matter as a whole: "The ego develops from perceiving the instincts to controlling them; *but this last is only achieved by the [psychical] representative of the instinct being allotted its proper place in a considerable assemblage, by its being taken up into a coherent context*" (p. 76; my italics). The passions are not to be denied wholesale, but rather governed by reason and indulged or restrained with an eye to adaptation and to the impact of that choice on the health and well-being of self and others. For Freud, as for Socrates and Aristotle, *balance* was the central metaphor.[6]

Freud's accounting of the credits and debits of culture takes a turn in *Civilization and Its Discontents,* where he is more concerned with the interdictive–remissive balance in relation to aggression than to sexuality. The themes of *Civilization and Its Discontents* are adumbrated in "The Ego and the Id" and "The Economic Problem of Masochism." In the former work (1923c) Freud considers a dilemma inherent in morality (quite apart from his treatment of the pathological vicissitudes of conscience). He suggests that "the more a man checks his aggressiveness toward the exterior the more severe—that is aggressive—he becomes in his ego ideal—the more intense . . . his ideal's inclincation to aggressiveness against his ego" (p. 54). This is complicated further by his thesis that identification with the parent (which forms the nucleus of the ego ideal–superego) leads to an "instinctual defusion" whereby "the erotic component no longer has the power to bind the whole of the destructiveness that was contained with it." This destructiveness is released "in the form of an inclination to aggression and destruc-tion." It becomes "the source of the harshness and cruelty exhibited by the ideal—its dictatorial 'Thou shalt'" (pp. 54–55). The dilem-ma is reiterated in 1924: The "suppression of an instinct can—frequently or quite generally—result in a sense of guilt" (p. 167); "a person's conscience becomes more severe and sensitive the more he refrains from aggression against others" (p. 170).

In *Civilization and Its Discontents* (1930) the dilemma reap-pears in this form: "Civilization is built up upon a renunciation of instinct" at the same time that this "non-satisfaction" causes the "hostility with which all civilizations have to struggle" and the "serious disorders" with which the physician contends (p. 97). Freud approaches, unblinkingly, man's central "struggle": "finding an expedient accommodation—one that is, that will bring hap-piness—between this claim of the individual and the cultural claims of the group" (p. 96).

As in *Jokes*, "'Civilized' Sexual Morality," and "The Future of an Illusion," Freud indicts civilization for its insufficient compensa-tion of most persons for the renunciations it demands and for doing no more to ease their suffering. "But"—and this possibility few social theorists have had the courage to face for long—"*perhaps we may also familiarize ourselves with the idea that there are difficulties attaching to the nature of civilization which will not yield to any attempt at reform*" (p. 11; my italics). (Recall Freud's [1905b] claim that "there is no general and final solution of the conflict" [p. 234].)

Having spent most of his life studying the normal and patholog-ical vicissitudes of sexuality, Freud turns at last, in this essay, to the serious study of aggression that was foreshadowed in parts of "Thoughts for the Times on War and Death," "Beyond the Plea-sure Principle," "The Ego and the Id," and "The Economic Problem of Masochism." Humanity's inclination to aggression is declared to be an "original, self-subsisting instinctual disposition" that "con-stitutes *the greatest impediment to civilization*" (p. 122; my italics). Under "aggression" Freud includes the tendency of people to "ex-ploit [their neighbor's] capacity for work without compensation, to use him sexually without his consent, to seize his possessions, to humiliate him, to cause him pain, to torture and to kill him" (p. 111).

The device that civilization uses to inhibit the aggressiveness that would otherwise unravel it is of course the superego. As Freud elaborates on the process of inhibition (which carries us much beyond his earlier work on the ontogenesis of the moral agency), one begins to wonder if the cure is not as crippling as the illness.[7]

The individual's aggression is leashed by introjection and taken over by a part of the ego—the superego— "which sets itself against the rest of the ego . . . and is ready to put into action the same harsh aggressiveness that the ego would have liked to satisfy upon other, extraneous individuals." Civilization disarms the "individual's dangerous desire for aggression" by "setting up an agency to watch over it, like a garrison in a conquered city" (pp. 123–124).

There are two stages in the construction of the garrison. The first is the small child's fear of external authority, of losing the parent's love or receiving his punishment. A child, or a person who remains in this state of mind, conforms not in order to avoid a "sense of guilt," which cannot properly be said to exist at this point, but out of "social anxiety"—fear of the consequences of being caught. "Present-day society has to reckon in general with this state of mind" (p. 125).

In the second stage the authority is internalized. That represents, as Freud (1927b) suggested earlier, a great advance for civilization: The individual's conformity to culture's imperatives is now relatively independent of external coercion. For the individual, however, it is a mixed blessing: "The distinction . . . between doing something bad and wishing to do it disappears entirely, since nothing can be hidden from the super-ego, not even thoguht" (p. 125). This subjects the socialized person to a terrible irony: "The more virtuous a man is, the more severe and distrustful [the superego's] behavior, so that ultimately it is precisely those people who have carried saintliness furthest who reproach themselves with the worst sinfulness." "Virtue" thus "forfeits some of its promised reward." "Moreover, when saints call themselves sinners, they are not so wrong, considering the temptations to instinctual satisfaction to which they are exposed in a specially high degree—since, as is well known, temptations are merely increased by constant frustration, whereas an occasional satisfaction of them causes them to diminish, at least for the time being [a classic Stoic idea]" (pp. 125–126).

To recapitulate, in the first stage, when one has only to fear the external authority, if one renounces an antisocial temptation one is "quits with the authority and no guilt should remain." But with the erection of the superego the sense of guilt remains in spite of the renunciation: "A threatened external unhappiness—loss of love and punishment on the part of the external authority—has been exchanged for a permanent internal unhappiness, for the tension of the sense of guilt. . . . Every renunciation of instinct now becomes a dynamic source of conscience and every fresh renunciation increases the latter's severity and intolerance" (p. 127).

There are hence five sources of the aggressiveness of the enculturated individual's superego: (1) that deriving from the actual aggressiveness of the parent with whom he identifies, (2) that devolving from the aggression which the individual has himself projected onto the parent and reinternalized, (3) that deriving from the external authority's injunction that the individual renounce his aggressiveness, (4) that related to the instinctual defusion that occurs in the identification process, and (5) that which "must be developed in the child against the authority which prevents him from having his first, but none the less his most important satisfactions, whatever the kind of instinctual deprivation that is demanded of him" (p. 129).

As if these sources of the socialized individual's aggression and sense of guilt were not enough, Freud resurrects the parricide hypothesis. The introjected aggressiveness and the sense of guilt over the murderous deed are asserted to be transmitted perennially from generation to generation: "Whether one has killed one's father or has abstained from doing so is not really the decisive thing. One is bound to feel guilty in either case" (p. 132).

To this add yet two more complicating factors. First, according to Freud's (1920, 1923c) hypotheses of the death instinct, which he never abandoned, all aggression is originally directed against oneself. If the individual is to survive, he must externalize a measure of this. In short, the internalization of the aggression that society demands of him is actually a reinternalization. The individual and society are thus subject to the paradox that, if the former is to survive, he must externalize his aggression, while if the latter is to flourish, it must induce him to internalize it.

Second, civilization obeys an "internal erotic impulse which causes human beings to unite in a closely knit group," which it can only achieve by promoting the aforementioned factors that eventuate in "an ever increasing reinforcement of the sense of guilt" (p. 133). This leads to what Freud terms the "final conclusion" of his essay: "*The sense of guilt [is] the most important problem in the development of civilization. . . . the price we pay for our advance in civilization is a loss of happiness through a heightening of the sense of guilt"* (p. 134; my italics).

But the battle between Eros, pushing individuals to bind them-selves into ever larger aggregates, and the aggressive instinct is hard-ly the only front in the war between culture and "counterculture." There is also a conflict within the economics of Eros itself, between "egoistic" and "altruistic" libido: "The two urges, the one toward personal happiness and the other towards union with other human beings, must struggle with each other in every individual; and so, also *the two processes of individual and of cultural development must stand in hostile opposition to each other and mutually dispute the ground"* (p. 141; my italics).

It almost seems, Freud wryly observes, "as if the creation of a great human community would be most successful if no attention had to be paid to the happiness of the individual" (p. 140). And here he repeats his earlier reproaches that civilization, in the severity of its demands, troubles itself too little about whether the individual is psychologically capable of adhering to them and how they affect his happiness. Freud guards himself "against the enthusiastic prejudice which holds that our civilization is the most precious thing we possess . . . and that its path will necessarily lead to heights of un-imagined perfection" (p. 144). Professing to lack "the courage to rise up before my fellow men as a prophet" (p. 145), he nevertheless seems to acknowledge that he is one in the consulting room and would perhaps like to become one outside it as well:

> We are often obliged, for therapeutic purposes, to oppose the super-ego, and we endeavor to lower its demands. . . . Exactly the same objections can be made against the ethical demands of the cultural super-ego. . . . [Further investigation might lead us to] the diagnosis that, under the influence of cultural urges, some civilizations, or some epochs of civilization—possibly the whole of mankind—have be-come neurotic [from which might ensue] . . . therapeutic recommen-dations which could lay claim to great practical interest" [pp. 143–144].

Such sentiments appear to put not only sexuality (egoistic, al-truistic, sensual, and aim-inhibited libido) and aggression—the cen-tral concerns of traditional morality—under Freud's therapeutic banner, but the culture which fashioned and manages that morality itself. "A triumph of the therapeutic" indeed.

The overall tone of *Civilization and Its Discontents,* Freud's most profound statement on ethics and social theory, is pessi- mistic—or, if one prefers, "realistic." His conclusion that "the fateful question for the human species" is "whether and to what extent their cultural development will succeed in mastering the disturbance of their communal life by the human instinct of aggres- sion and self-destruction" (p. 145) has particular poignancy for the nuclear age. Freud's thesis that man's aggression is an "original and self-subsisting dispositon," his diagnosis of the problematic nature of culture's means of controlling it, and his suggestion that groups maintain their cohesion in part by externalizing their aggression toward outgroups and neighboring societies (p. 114) do not bode well for the future. "Eros will make an effort to assert himself in the struggle with his equally immortal adversary [aggression and self- destruction]. But who can foresee with what success and with what result?" (p. 145).

FREUD'S ETHIC

How can one charecterize Freud's ethic itself?Although Freud wrote continually on matters central to what has traditionally been considered the "moral sphere," he offered few explicit definitions of ethics or morality (terms he tended to use interchangeably). Among these are: "What is moral [consists in] a sense of justice and consid- eration for one's fellow men [and] in discomfort at making others suffer or taking advantage of them" (Freud to Putnam, 8 July 1915, in Hale, 1971, p. 189); "ethics [is] a kind of highway code for traffic among mankind" (Freud to Pfister, 24 February 1928, in Meng and E. Freud, 1963, p. 123); "those [ideas] which deal with the relations of human beings to one another are comprised under the heading of ethics" (1930, p. 142); "ethics is . . . a therapeutic attempt to . . . get rid of the greatest hindrance to civilization—namely the constitutional inclination of human beings to be aggressive toward one another" (1930, p. 142); "ethics is a limitation of instinct" (1939, p. 118); "a moral man is one who reacts to temptation as soon as he feels it in his heart, without yielding to it . . . *the essence of morality is renunciation,* for the moral conduct of human life is of practical human interest" (1928, p. 177; my italics).

Ethics, Freud (1928) makes plain in his response to Reik's crit-icism of his dissection of Dostoevsky's moral fiber, is a matter of "objective social assessment"—of the interpersonal consequences of one's *actions* and *renunciations*—more than of a "subjective psycho-logical view" (p. 196). Although he was not indifferent to motive and inner attitude as criteria for ethical assessment, it was his pre-eminent emphasis on *deeds* (including renunciations) rather than inner states that is the decisive line of cleavage between his and much of Christian morality. For this reason Freud was able to con-sider the "excellent citizen and Philistine" as morally superior to Dostoevsky, even though the former's morality might have been, as Reik suggested, due only to his "dull sensibility . . . and lack of imagination" (in Freud, 1928, p. 196n), while the latter was con-tinually involved in titanic internal moral struggles.[8] All the same, Freud was obviously as aware as any theological ethicist that the wish is mother to the deed.

I think it clear, moreover, that although Freud never exempted every aspect and manifestation of sexuality from the ethical sphere, for him the moral doman was primarily concerned with aggression and egoism. Had he lived to see today's new twist on the Victorian split between sensuality and affection—with the former often pre-dominant and the latter subject to suppression, repression, or dis-placement—and the aggression it often brings forth, he might have restored to the domain of ethics some of the libidinal territory he had wrested from it. Recall, in this regard, that Freud was con-cerned to free sensual libido from its chains to unconscious in-cestuous object representations not so that it could be acted on indiscriminately, but so that it could be fused with affection (or aim-inhibited libido) and directed toward a fellow being in current reality.

On whether ethical principles can be derived from psycho-analytic data and theorems—the fact–value issue that has pervaded ethics for centuries—Freud is divided. In places (1921b, p. 270; Freud to Pfister, 24 February 1928, in Meng and E. Freud, 1963, p. 123) he explicitly rejects the idea that ethical principles are deriva-ble from psychoanalytic investigation. Elsewhere (1933) he suggests that moral values may ultimately follow from scientific (among which he includes psychological) facts: "Science is content to inves-tigate and establish the facts, though it is true that from its applica-tion rules and advice are derived on the conduct of life. In some circumstances these are the same as those offered by religion; but, when this is so, the reasons for them are different" (p. 162).

One thing is clear: Freud consistently opposed any attempt to place psychoanalysis at the service of an existing ethical system, as his letters to Pfister and Putnam abundantly testify. He declared psychoanalysis to be "ethically neutral" (1921b, p. 270). In some respects, when one considers the scientific investigative approach of psychoanalysis, Freud seems correct in doing so. And yet one wonders how he can seriously and consistently maintain the value neutrality of psychoanalysis when some of his writings (such as *Jokes*, "'Civilized' Sexual Morality," "The Future of an Illusion," and *Civilization and Its Discontents*) scrutinize and pronounce upon what has for centuries been included in the ethical domain, and when he subjects morality itself to psychological dissection. Indeed, Rieff (1959) hardly exaggerates when he asserts that "all the issues which psychoanalysis treats—the health and sickness of the will, the emotions, the responsibilities of private living, the coercions of culture—belong to the moral life" (p. 300). Nor is it easy to maintain that the therapeutic aims of psychoanalysis are entirely value free (see Hartmann, 1960); this is especially true when one turns to the ego psychologists and "neo-Freudians." Furthermore, we now recognize that the line between "facts" and "values" is not so sharp as it once appeared to be. One must distinguish between data—the *relatively* uncontaminated product of sensory or instrumental perception—and facts—the meaningful organization of those data within the framework of a theory and set of questions; data, in science in general and in the psychological and social sciences in particular, invariably appear in the context of an interpretation, and the latter, just as invariably, implies a set of theoretical commitments that might itself be considered a species of value.

On whether psychoanalysis might contribute to the practical, lived morality of the individual Freud was also divided. In a letter to Putnam he explicitly opposes the Socratic idea that all vice proceeds from ignorance or madness, and adds: "The unworthiness of human beings, including the analysts, always has impressed me deeply, but why should analyzed men and women in fact be better. Analysis makes for integration but does not of itself make for goodness" (7 June 1915, in Hale, 1971, p. 188). In other places Freud expresses different sentiments: "That psycho-analysis has not made the analysts themselves better, nobler, or of stronger character remains a disappointment for me" (Freud to Putnam, 13 November 1913 in Hale, 1971, pp. 163–164). And in the *Introductory Lectures on Psycho-Analysis* (1915–1917) he puts forward the Socratic idea he opposed in the letter to Putnam: "We tell ourselves that anyone who has succeeded in educating himself to truth about himself is permanently defended against the danger of immorality, even though his standard of morality may differ in some respect from that which is customary in society" (p. 434).

A more balanced point of view, to some extent reconciling the contradictions in these passages, appears in two letters to Putnam:

> Our art consists in making it possible for people to be moral and to deal with their wishes philosophically. Sublimation, that is striving toward higher goals, is of course one of the best means of overcoming the urgency of the drives. But one can consider doing this only after psycho-analytic work has lifted their repressions. . . . Whoever is capable of sublimation will turn to it inevitably as soon as he is free of his neurosis. Those who are not capable of this at least will become more natural and more honest [14 May 1911, in Hale, 1971, pp. 121–122].

> The great ethical element in psycho-analytic work is truth and again truth and this should suffice for most people. Courage and truth are of what they are mostly deficient [30 March 1914, in Hale, 1971, p. 171].

As for the desiderata implicit and explicit in Freud's ethic, theoretical and applied, we might enumerate the following: What Rieff terms the "ethic of honesty"; a Stoic–Epicurean notion of balance between self-expression and fulfillment on the one hand and self-restraint and renunciation on the other; governance of one's life by the reality principle; adaptation—the optimal fit between a well-equilibrated psyche and its environment; empowering the ego in its negotiations with id, superego, and external reality; the independence of ethical principles from religious foundations; an increased tolerance for certain aspects of self and others (especially regarding the private fantasy and sexual lives) and for a more understanding approach to certain types of human frailty and disability (particularly that related to psychopathology and to various universal and enduring psychological features of humankind); a premium on individuation, independence, and autonomy; strong allegiance to Eros (particularly as manifested in altruistic, aim-inhibited libido and in ties based on mutual identifications) in the war against Thanatos; an emphasis on the value of sublimation and work to the individual and society; "endur[ance] with resignation" (1927b, p. 50) of that which cannot be changed; and emphasis (with the exception of his equation of Eros with *caritas*) on "prudential" (prudence, wisdom, justice, and fortitude) rather than Christian (faith, hope, and char-ity) values.

Since many of these have already been addressed, I shall limit my elaborations to four items: the ethic of honesty; the reality principle, adaptation, and the ego; the value of sublimation and work; and Freud's morality and attitudes toward moralizing as expressed in his personal life.

Freud's (1907b) essay on the sexual enlightenment of children, wherein he accuses society of prevarication and dishonesty, adum-brates the ethic of honesty that becomes explicit in a number of places: "The great ethical element in psychoanalytic work is truth and again truth" (Freud to Putnam, 30 March 1914, in Hale, 1971, p. 171); "analysis is founded on complete candour. Financial cir-cumstances, for instance, are discussed with equal detail and openess; things are said that are kept back from every fellow cit-izen . . . this obligation to candour puts a grave moral responsibility on the analyst as well" (1926, p. 207); "the analytic relationship is based on a love of truth—that is, on a recognition of reality . . . it precludes any kind of sham or deceit" (1937, p. 248). For Wortis he equated "character" with "honesty" and declared that that was what was mostly lacking in their time (in Wortis, 1954, p. 129).

Although Freud had in mind "honesty" in the old-fashioned, interpersonal sense (and certainly in one's relationship with one's analyst), it was primarily honesty about oneself to oneself about which he was talking. His ethic of honesty was not intended to be, as some have mistakenly concluded, an ethic of indiscriminate self-expression (verbal, instinctual, and so forth)—without regard to its consequences—in interpersonal relations in general.

The reality principle, adaptation, and the strengthening of the ego were crucial desiderata in Freud's personal and theoretical eth-ics, and difficult to consider divorced from one another. One of Freud's strongest arguments against religion, we remember, was that it was dominated by infantile wish fulfillment and the pleasure principle. Freud (1927b) advocated, by contrast, an "education to reality," which involved one's leaving the "parental house where

[one] was so warm and comfortable," going out into "hostile life," and "admit[ting] to [oneself] the full extent of [one's] helplessness and [one's] insignificance in the machinery of the universe. . ." (p. 49). While he acknowledged that this involved a certain loss of complacency, it entailed the gain of "know[ing] that one is thrown upon one's own resources . . . [and] learn[ing] to make proper use of them." And there is always the matter of science, which can increase our mastery still further. "As for the great necessities of Fate, against which there is no help, [one] will learn to endure them with resignation," as Freud endured his cancer for 16 years and worked in spite of it. "Of what use," he continues, "to them is the mirage of wide acres on the moon, whose harvest no one has ever yet seen? As honest small holders on this earth they will know how to cultivate their plot in such a way that it supports them" (p. 50). He advocates the ascription of "purely rational reasons to the pre-cepts of civilization" (p. 41).

As for the ethic of adaptation, it is closely related to the domi-nance of the reality princple and of the intrapsychic–environmental equilibrium that Freud hoped would become established through the primacy of the ego. The concept of "psychical efficiency," broached in *Three Essays* (p. 238) and closely related to sublimation (which we shall consider shortly), foreshadows the concept of adap-tation that Freud would elaborate in 1913: "The principle of avoid-ing unpleasure dominates human actions until it is replaced by the better one of adaptation to the external world" (1913b, p. 186). The work of Hartmann and others would of course carry forward the principle of adaptation as one of the five pillars of metapsychology.

Freud's emphasis on the ego remained strong throughout his later psychology:

> [The ego's] constructive function consists in interpolating between the demand made by an instinct and the action that satisfies it, the activity of thought which, after taking its bearings in the present and assessing earlier experiences, endeavors by means of experimental actions to calculate the consequences of the course of action pro-posed. In this way the ego comes to a decision on whether the attempt to obtain satisfaction is to be carried out or postponed or whether it may not be necessary for the demand by the instinct to be suppressed altogether as being dangerous [1940, p. 199].

The mechanism of therapy is thus a pact between the "analytic physician and the patient's weakened ego, basing themselves on the

real external world . . . [and] band[ing] themselves together into a
party against the enemies, the instinctual demands of the id and the
conscientious demands of the super-ego." Through insight the patient's ego is given back "its mastery over lost provinces of his
mental life" (1940, p. 173). This, again, is an ethic of balance—
declaring war on neither the demands of the instincts nor of the
superego, but on the excesses of both.

Aware that "civilization is built up upon a renunciation of instinct" (1930, p. 97) and that at the same time a certain remissiveness is in the best interest of the equilibrium of both the
individual and society, Freud was a great proponent of sublimation,
which was in some respects "a way out" (1914, p. 95) of the inhibition–expression dilemma, by which the demands of the culturally
induced ego ideal could be met without involving repression and the
total frustration of the instinct: Sublimation "enables especially
strong excitations arising from particular sources of sexuality to find
an outlet and use in other fields, so that a not inconsiderable increase in psychical efficiency results from a disposition which in
itself is perilous" (1905a, p. 238).

Freud (1930) has high praise for his favorite source of sublimation—his professional and intellectual work:

> No other technique for the conduct of life attaches the individual so
> firmly to reality as laying emphasis on work; for his work at least
> gives him a secure place in a portion of reality in the human commu-
> nity. The possibility it offers of displacing a large amount of libidinal
> components, whether narcissistic, aggressive, or even erotic, on to
> professional work and on to the human relations connected with it
> lends it a value by no means second to what it enjoys as something
> indispensable to the preservation and justification of existence in
> society [p. 80n].

Turning to Freud's personal life we find a man of impeccable
morality in the traditional sense of the term. He did not transfer the
"ethically netural" analytic stance from the consulting room to the
world at large. In *The Interpretation of Dreams* there is a moralistic
tone to Freud's scrutiny of some of his dreams—the treatment of his
unconscious motive to exculpate himself from blame in the handling
of Irma's case, for instance. He was a man of strong moral passion,
quite capable of being judgmental when the situation called for it.
When Jones tried to dismiss an incivility of Jung's as a parapraxis
Freud retorted, "Gentlemen should not do such things even uncon-

sciously" (in Jones, 1955, p. 145). Freud wrote Stekel in 1924 that "I broke with you after you had deceived me on a certain occasion in a most heinous manner. . . . It was exclusively your personal qualities—usually described as character and behavior—which made collaboration with you impossible for my friends and myself" (13 January 1924, in E. Freud, 1960, pp. 347–348).

He once advised a colleague against taking on a patient whom Freud thought a "scoundrel" (in Roazen, 1975, p. 147), and as-serted that he could not imagine bringing himself "to delve into the psychical mechanisms of a hysteria in anyone who struck me as low minded and repellant, and who, on closer acquaintance, would not be capable of arousing human sympathy. . ." (Breuer and Freud, 1893–1895, p. 165). He did not withhold judgment on Dostoevsky's moral fiber, nor did he refrain from telling Pfister that most people depart lamentably from his own "high ideal" (9 October 1918, in Meng and E. Freud, 1963, pp. 62–63).

Although he restored the erotic life of many a sexually anesthetic person, he held a decidedly purintanical attitude toward his own sexuality. It bears repeating that he considered sensuality without affection a degrading state of affairs and opined that Christian val-ues had a positive effect on what he viewed as the too purely sensual love of antiquity. There is ample evidence that, although possessed of high powers of enjoyment, he gave productive work priority over the pursuit of pleasure. He assisted friends and rela-tives in financial need and, we now know, contributed to the main-tenance of at least one of his patients—the Wolf Man. As Pfister (29 October 1918 in Meng and Freud, 1963, p. 63) said of him, judged only by his ethics, and not by his creed, "A better Christian there never was. . . ." Plainly Freud "was very far," as Hartmann (1960) says, "from being a moral nihilist" (p. 16).

DETERMINISM, FREEDOM, AND ETHICS

No consideration of Freud as ethicist can shirk descent into the maelstrom of determinism and free will. If philosophy is, as Barzun (1983) puts its, following "second thoughts . . . with athletic for-titude" (p. 109), then we must be at our most philosophical in the face of this most ambiguous of ambiguities in Freud's ethical thought. Although the ethicists of classical antiquity paid the matter short shrift, Judeo-Christian and secular Western ethicists have generally considered it central to considerations of morality.

The literature is large, tedious, and ambiguous. Students of the determinism-free will issue may be divided roughly into three camps: (1) those such as Hobbes [(1651)], Locke [(1690)], and Hume [(1777)] who espouse the universality of causality, and reason that this disentails the possibility of free will—defined as non-necessitated choosing, as the standing before options either or any of which the agent is actually capable of selecting; (2) those such as James (1890, 1897) and Collingwood (1946, 1972) who cleave to the universality of causation, but deny that this disallows free will—i.e., they argue that, at least in the sphere of human psychology, not all causes necessitate; and (3) those such as Oakeshott (1933), Marrou (1966), and, in the philosophy of psychoanalysis, Schafer (1976, 1978) who deny the validity of the causal principle in psychological and historical affairs and hence claim to have side-stepped the controversy.

Freud occupied, alternatively, and never, I believe, with conscious acknowledgment of the fact, the first two positions. And he did so in both his professional and personal life.

The first position is perhaps best captured in the *Introductory Lectures on Psycho-Analysis* (1915–1917), wherein Freud equates the "deeply rooted faith in undetermined psychical events" with "free will," and argues that both are "unscientific and must yield to the demands of a determinism whose rule extends over mental life" (p. 106). Earlier in the same work Freud takes to task the libertarian "counterfactual"—that is, the idea that the agent is ever in a position to say, after an action, that he "could have done otherwise."

> Imagine that someone had undertaken the chemical analysis of a certain substance and had arrived at a particular weight for one component of it—so and so many milligrammes. Certain inferences could be drawn from this weight. Now do you suppose that it would ever occur to a chemist to criticize those inferences on the ground that the isolated substance might equally have had some other weight? Everyone will bow before the fact that this was the weight and none other and will confidently draw his further inferences from it. But when you are faced with the psychical fact that a particular thing occurred to the mind of the person questioned, you will not allow the fact's validity: something else might have occurred to him! [pp. 48–49].

To deny that validity would indeed, as Freud surmised, place the free association method in jeopardy, at least if that method is understood to lead to causal information.

The second position is exemplifed by statements such as "[we analyze homosexuality so that the patient might be enabled] to choose whether he wished to abandon the path that is abandoned by society" (1920, p. 151), and "analysis does not set out to make pathological reactions impossible, but to give the patient's ego *freedom* to decide one way or the other" (1923e, p. 50n). Ambiguous statements, but perhaps suggestive of some measure of belief in free will, include Freud's numerous disquisitions (1925b, p. 238; 1926, p. 95; 1930, p. 79; 1933, pp. 76–79; 1940, p. 198) on the deliberating and controlling "higher functions" of the ego, and passages such as the following (which seems to allow for what Hartmann would come to call "conscious volition" alongside, and in some respects independent of unconscious determination):

> According to our analyses it is not necessary to dispute the right to the feeling of conviction of having a free will. If the distinction between conscious and unconscious motivation is taken into account, our feeling of conviction informs us that conscious motivation does not extend to all our motor decisions. *De minimas non curat lex.* But what is thus left free by the one side receives its motivation from the other side, from the unconscious; and in this way determination in the psychical sphere is still carried out without any gaps [1901, p. 254].[9]

Consider also the following remark, which appears to allow some limited range of operation to free will: "*Very rarely* does the complexity of a human character, driven hither and thither by dynamic forces, submit to a *choice* between simple alternatives, as our antiquated morality would have us believe" (Freud, 1900, p. 621; my italics).

Before turning to the ethical implications of any position on the matter, it is necessary to go into more general aspects of the free will–determinism problem. Many of these I have addressed at length in a recent book (1985a). There I marshal a number of arguments for the universal applicability of the principle of causation to human historical and psychological affairs, including its parsimony, superior explanatory power, and internal consistency; its continuity with the established explanatory tradition in science and the scholarly disciplines; its predictive power; and the fruitfulness of inter-ventions based on deterministic formulations. On the other hand, I acknowledge cogent objections that have been leveled against uni-versal determinism, including its inferential, nonempirical nature; its segmentation of the temporally continuous flow of reality into frozen instants that are then denominated "causes" and "effects"; the often elliptical character of cause–effect propositions; and cer-tain problems inherent in the mode of identification of causes.[10] In the monograph I explicate the concept of purposive, meaningful, and intersectional multicausality that I contend has been native to psychoanalysis all along, and remain agnostic on the sort of pos-sibility permitted in a deterministic universe (Wallace, 1985a, pp. 247–253; see Wallace, 1985b for a sequel).[11]

Even those scientists and scholars who cleave to the universality of causation—and they constitute the majority—must acknowledge that causation is in the nature of an axiom. The best 20th century students of the topic—Russell (1929), Nagel (1969), Pap (1962), Popper (1965), Von Wright (1972), Bunge (1979), and Taylor (1967)—agree that there is not now, and may never be, any decisive logico-empirical proof of the concept (to say nothing of those such as Heisenberg who deny the validity of determinism altogether). And the "proof" of the deterministic hypothesis in the social sciences, where one often finds the most vociferous avowals of it, is largely anecdotal, inferential, and retrospective—the prospective studies and controlled experimentation of the natural sciences are conspic-uously lacking. The *Geisteswissenschaften* have further to contend with the fact that the relationship between hermeneutics and causality is far from elucidated. In fine, it is *patterns* and *meaningful and productive continuity* that investigators are concerned to identi-fy, demonstrate, and reconstruct; and those principles (causal or otherwise) that are used to make them intelligible reflect in-terpretive commitments.

Pivotal to any consideration of the relationship between deter-minism and ethics are the concepts of "responsibility" and "evalua-tion." Both determinists and libertarians, from the time of Kant right on through Berlin (1954), Strawson (1971), Hospers (1958), and Koestler (1967), have generally considered the thesis of univer-sal determinism to be incompatible with moral accountability, inso-far as the latter entails notions of praise and blame; philosophers, as Frankfurt (1969) notes, have almost unanimously held that a person is "morally responsible for what he has done only if he could have done otherwise" (p. 829). If unconscious psychobiological processes and history determine one's motives, if one's constitutional endow-ment and early environment are not freely chosen, if one's thoughts, feelings, and desires begin unconsciously, and if one's personality structure and situation invariably necessitate one's choices, then, it is argued, one cannot be held praise- or blameworthy in the tradi-tional moral sense. Freud himself would seem to have concurred: "Ethics, disregarding the fact that such differences [in human be-havior] are determined, classifies [them] as 'good' or 'bad'" (1930, p. 111). As with other facets of the determinism–free will contro-versy, each position involves its interpretive commitments. For ex-ample, there is no decisive test, after an action has transpired, of whether it might have been otherwise, of whether (to state what is really at issue) the agent, at the instant before his action, possessed the genuine capacity to choose one way or the other. Determinists and libertarians each make their assumptions—the determinists' "if you could have done otherwise you would have" countering the libertarians' "I could have chosen differently had I wished to—and it was within my power to do so."

On the matter of responsibility both libertarians and determinists hold persons responsible—but on different grounds. The former hold people responsible on the ground that they possess free choice and hence could have acted differently, in any given situation, from the way they actually did. The latter base responsibility on the concept of intersectional and mediate causation—i.e., that each in-dividual is part of those interactions which have determined him, and that his personality structure is the proximate cause of his behavior ("causal responsibility"). Determinists contend that it is only because the individual's behaviors are determined by his per-sonality structure—rather than being purely whimsical or arbi-trary—and because he is self-determining in certain relatively en-during ways that reward, punishment, and education can affect his behavior. And, at the interpersonal level, the notion that persons can, through their actions, participate in the causing of distress and untoward reactions in others is considered indispensable to society's regulation of the conduct of its members.

Nevertheless, this purely deterministic conception of responsibil-ity, while logically permitting both reward and punishment, is un-likely to satisfy the traditional moralist. If every decision and action—and not merely externally compelled or psychopathological ones—is always necessitated, then our moral discourse, as well as much of our everyday language and mode of viewing ourselves, would have to change considerably. Furthermore, if reward and punishment lose their connotations of praise and blame, then would they be as likely to produce the desired impact on behavior? If determinism disentails praise and blame, then clearly Freud was not a consistent determinist, for we have seen that he was capable of strong moral passion.

Where an issue is as knotty (and perhaps unresolvable) as the free will–determinism controversy it seems prudent not to build our system of moral valuation on one pole or the other. When morality is viewed as a vantage point for assessing the beneficence or malefi- cence of one's intent toward and impact on others, then moral appraisal can proceed quite independently of the truth value of determinism or free will. What is then decisive is, as so many jurists have held, whether the agent was reality-oriented, appreciated the difference between right and wrong, and understood the likely con- sequences of his behavior. Whether he could have acted otherwise is beside the point.

On these matters Freud's (1925e) brief essay on the "moral re- sponsibility of the dreamer" repays serious study:

> Must one assume responsibility for the content of one's dreams? Obviously one must hold oneself responsible for the evil impulses of one's dreams. What else is one to do with them? Unless the content of the dream (rightly understood) is inspired by alien spirits, it is a part of my own being. If I seek to classify the impulses that are present in me according to social standards into good and bad, I must assume responsibility for both sorts; and *if, in defense, I say that what is unknown, unconscious and repressed in me is not my 'ego', then I shall not be basing my position upon psycho-analysis*, I shall not have accepted its conclusions—and I shall perhaps be taught better by the criticisms of my fellow-men, by the disturbances in my actions and the confusion of my feelings. *I shall perhaps learn that what I am disavowing not only 'is' in me but sometimes acts out of me as well.*
>
> Moreover, if I were to give way to my moral pride and tried to decree that for purposes of moral valuation I might disregard the evil in the id and need not make my ego responsible for it, what use would that be to me? Experience shows me that I nevertheless *do* [Freud's italics] take that responsibility, that I am somehow com- pelled to do so.

The ethical narcissism of humanity should rest content with the knowledge that the fact of distortion in dreams, as well as the existence of anxiety-dreams and punishment-dreams, afford just as clear evidence of his *moral* [Freud's italics] nature as dream-interpretation gives of the existence and strength of his *evil* [Freud's italics] nature. *If anyone is dissatisfied with this and would like to be 'better' than he was created, let him see whether he can attain anything more in life than hypocrisy or inhibition* [pp. 132–134; my italics].

CONCLUSION: SOME ADDITIONAL DIMENSIONS OF FREUD'S IMPACT ON ETHICS

Throughout this essay I have been concerned primarily to let Freud's multifaceted approach to ethics speak for itself. Freud's ambiguity and apparent inconsistency on many of the issues, particularly in regard to remissions and interdicts, is as much an accurate reflection of the complexities, ironies, and paradoxes built into the topic as of any confusion or ambivalence on Freud's part.

As a scientist and medical man he was convinced of the need to soften the interdicts. As a civilized intellectual he was aware of the need for structure, inhibitions, sublimations, and imperatives. He was, as Rieff (1959) asserts, "ambivalent toward repressive culture: its major critic and yet defender of its necessity" (p. 323). Rieff (1959), of all writers, has most accurately captured that ambivalence:

> To make delicacy of feeling, not the lack of it, the problem of our health discloses how near the Freudian psychology drifts to a sophisticated primitivism. . . . For reasons of libidinal economy, some of the heavier investments in culture have to be written off . . . [p. 311].

> . . . if moral rules come only from cultures which legislate deviously for their own advantage, against the freedom of the individual, how can any part of conduct be taken for granted? If every limit can be seen as a limitation of personality, the question with which we may confront every opportunity is: After all, why not? While Freud never committed himself, the antinomian implications are there. And those who have interpreted Freud as advocating for reasons of health, sexual freedom—promiscuity rather than the strain of fidelity, adultery rather than neurosis—have caught the hint, if not the intent, of his psychoanalysis. . . . If Freud takes sides against culture, it is only for therapeutic purposes. He believed no more in

instinct than in culture; for his day and age he sought only to correct the imbalance between these two main categories of the moral life. . . . He wrote no briefs for the pleasure principle. Rather he exhibited its futility. It is toward the reality principle that Freud turns us, toward the sober business of living and with no nonsense about its goodness or ease [p. 324].

Freud disdained permissiveness as much as asceticism; both falsely resolved the essential dualism between mind and flesh that produces the misery of the human condition. What man suffers from finally is no more the supremacy of spirit over flesh than of flesh over spirit; it *is the dualism that hurts* [p. 343, my italics; see also 1966].

Hartmann (1960), as well, acknowledges the antinomian aspects of Freud's thought, but derides as a popular misperception the no-tion that "deep interpretation, the broad range of communication, unlimited self-revelation, widest permissiveness, the discarding of every consideration which stands in the way of full psychological understanding . . . the avoidance of what we consider moral judge-ment" are "the only 'right' ways" to deal with interpersonal rela-tions in general (pp. 74–75). That *Weltanschauung* or ethic results, he asserts (and I firmly believe he is correct), from an inappropriate displacement of the analyst's attitude toward the analysand in the consulting room to the world at large. When it occurs in a person who is actually undergoing analysis, it would have to be termed a transference phenomenon. In short, Hartmann views analysis as technique rather than ethic, and puzzles over "why, in our culture, many other people who have not been in analysis themselves find it so easy to adopt these technical codes in the place of moral princi-ples" (p. 75).

That Freud has been popularly misconstrued as champion and prophet of the sexually, aggressively, and narcissistically permissive society owes, I believe, to four factors: (1) the tendency to ignore the cultural–historical context in which he wrote; (2) failure to distinguish between "repression" and "suppression"; (3) failure to read Freud's corpus as a whole: the use of passages out of context that appear to support a particular philosophy; and (4) lack of recog-nition that the "ethic of honesty" is a tool that can be used in the service of morality, but that it carries no moral content with it— that it is a means, not an end in itself.

I have already elaborated on the first point, and need not belabor it here. I wish merely to suggest that the members of our "sexually liberated" society are, by and large, no freer of sexual repression than were our Victorian ancestors. The repressed sexual and aggressive impulses of the oedipal constellation remain, by and large, as repressed as before. It is, rather, their *conscious derivative fantasies* that are now more likely to be acted out rather than suppressed or sublimated.

Second, and related to the above, is the failure of Freud's popularizers to understand the difference between "repression" and "suppression." The former is an unconscious and automatic process that prevents the ego from exercising its judgment and that may lead to a variety of often pathological compromise formations. The latter is a quite *conscious* decision based on the ego's assessment of adaptation (in its relationship to instinctual and moral agencies and to external reality) to forgo, postpone, or sublimate an erotic, aggressive, or egoistic satisfaction. Misunderstanding of this distinction has led libertine prophets such as Norman O. Brown and Norman Mailer (who proclaimed that had he not stabbed his wife he would have internalized his aggression and become cancerous) to conclude from the repression theory of neurosis that any self-restraint is unhealthy.

From numerous quotations throughout this essay it is clear that Freud's aim was to replace repression with a conscious, prudent, and thoughtful costs/benefits analysis of one's instinctual strivings, which would then lead to the satisfaction of some and the suppression and sublimation of others. Freud recognized that a certain distance between fantasy and action is necessary to civilization: "Between the image and the act is the ordained space of actual existence. In that space everything human finds its history and grows up" (Rieff, 1959, p. 387). It is repression, and not suppression and sublimation, that makes people "sick." And even here I do not believe that Freud was arguing that all repression is maladaptive. One must remember that a good many adaptive characteristics are the result of *unconscious* sublimation, reaction formation, repression, and compromise formation. Furthermore, Freud (1910) was aware that there are some individuals in whom repression, and even psychopathology, "may be the least of the evils possible in the circumstances . . . [for otherwise they] would rapidly succumb or would cause a mischief greater than their own neurotic illness" (p. 150).

Third, many of those who have mistaken Freud as a proponent of a sexually, aggressively, and narcissistically permissive society have done so precisely because they have failed to appreciate his corpus as a whole, and the overwhelming message of balance that comes through the periodic extremes. Picking and choosing Freud's more remissive texts and tearing them from their subtle and sophisticated contexts (the secular equivalent of the fundamentalist's "proof texting"), advocates of indiscriminate self-expression then invoke Freud as their prophet. Although Freud must, on the basis of some of his more extremely antinomian statements, be held partly responsible for what others have done with his ideas and for the emergence of recent trends that I believe he would have deplored, much of the problem lies with those who have failed to rise to the demands of so complex and multifaceted a thinker. In any event, many of society's aggressively and sexually antinomian trends had begun surfacing before Freud began work. By the 1890s the interdicts had already begun to break down. Freud's work, or rather a misunderstanding of it, is not so much the cause of as the rationalization for previously existing remissive currents:

> Today we witness a powerful trend . . . toward considering morals as an unfortunate and burdensome relic of religious or metaphysical systems. . . . [Psychoanalysis] was expected to become a powerful ally in the fight to free humanity altogether from the heavy load of morality. From this point of view, such people find it easier to recognize as factual in man what has usually been called "bad" rather than what has usually been called "good." Of Freud's statement that man is not only much more immoral than he thinks but also much more moral than he knows, they would rather accept the first than the second half [Hartmann, 1960, pp. 43–44].

Fourth, Freud's ethic of honesty was not intended to be extended indiscriminately from the consulting room to the world at large, and did not constitute an endorsement of any and all varieties of self-expression. In his encomium of honesty in "The Sexual Enlightenment of Children" (1907b) Freud included instructing them "in the moral obligations which are attached to the actual satisfaction of the instinct" (p. 138).

As I have suggested, honesty in the analytic framework primarily means honesty to oneself and one's analyst, not indiscriminate self-relevation to others. It is common knowledge that "honesty" often serves to rationalize the expression of hostile or demeaning sentiments to others. Although Freud favored honesty and deplored

deception in interpersonal relations in general, he was aware that a
certain amount of "cultural hypocrisy" is necessary for the maintenance of civilization (1915, pp. 284–285). Honesty is a tool for self-
scrutiny; it does not specify the content of one's moral system. It is
an indispensable instrument for the realization of one's moral strivings—a means, not an end: "As a purely explanatory and scientific
ideal, honesty has no content. . . . [after] a calm and neutral appraisal of all the demanding elements of a life situation, still, the
freedom to choose must end in choice. Here, at the critical moment,
the Freudian ethic of honesty ceases to be helpful" (Rieff, 1959, p.
32). The ethic of honesty, moreover, can be turned against one's (or
culture's) moral demand system in a cynical, debunking,
Nietzschean fashion : "Since my humanitariansim and animal-
loving are reaction formations to my infantile sadism, it would be
dishonest of me to continue them."

Let me turn now to the impact of Freud's concept of adaptation
on the ethical sphere and to the question of whether psychoanalysis
can furnish us with moral imperatives, issues that I believe are
intimately intertwined. Rieff (1959), although recognizing the value
of the psychoanalytic emphasis on individual adaptation, points out
the asocial twist this can sometimes take in producing "pedants of
the inner life" rather than "virtuosi" of the "outer" one (p. 299):
"His newly acquired health entails a self-concern that takes prece-
dence over social concern and encourages an attitude of ironic insight toward all that is not self. Thus the psychoanalyzed man is
inwardly alienated even if he is often outwardly reconciled, for he is
no longer defined essentially by his social relations" (p. 330).

The popularizations of the clinical psychoanalytic *summum
bonum* of adaptation, as expressed in a variety of newer therapies,
self-help paperbacks, newspaper columns, and so forth, "teach
mostly," Rieff (1959) asserts, "the character virtues of resignation
and adjustment . . . [and the] ethics of 'living on a twenty-four
hour basis' " (p. 299). "Psychological man," for whom Rieff considers Freud partly responsible, is "anti-heroic, shrewd, carefully
counting his satisfactions and dissatisfactions, studying unprofitable
commitments as the sins most to be avoided . . . liv[ing] by the ideal
of insight" rather than the ideal "right" of "religious man" or
"might" of "economic man" (p. 356).

The psychoanalytically sophisticated philosopher Hospers (1959)
raises questions as well about adaptation as the goal of psycho-

analytic therapy, at least if it is understood in the popular sense as "adjustment": "The first question is, Adjusted to what? To twentieth-century civilization as it now exists? I confess that I can think of few things more ghastly" (p. 351). While acknowledging that the concept of adaptation takes account of the needs of the environment as well as of the individual and includes "the ideal of a person doing constructive work and making some contribution to society," Hospers asserts that it is not the ideal of the "*extremely* noble leader of mankind" (p. 353). These latter, he says, citing Socrates, Christ, and Gandhi, are not drawn from the ranks of the adjusted: "A really great degree of moral fervor, such as is required to shock mankind into a new kind of awareness in a world where moral insights quickly become fossilized, plus the tremendously strong motivation that is required to stir lethargic humanity and to face possible calumny and persecution and death—these things do not seem to be found among the 'adjusted' " (p. 353).

Although Freud did not explicitly endorse an ethic of "adjustment" (and certainly did not live his life in accord with one), I believe that Rieff and Hospers are correct in asserting that it is at least implicit in some of his writing. I also believe that it has been carried much farther than Freud would have desired by his latter-day redactors. But one must remember that Freud also broached the idea that whole cultures may become psychopathological. If that be the case and if, as Hospers, Lasch (1978), and many others imply, today's society is a "sick" one, then would one call "adjustment" to the society adaptation?

On the other hand, one must recognize that while it is true that the analytic procedure entails an increased concern with self, that is not its ultimate end; it is rather the temporary means to the patient's release from his neurosis. And one could argue that it is the neurotic process rather than analysis that makes the patient self-centered, that cuts him off from the real world and the people in it. Similarly, much that is popularly styled "selfish," "narcissistic," or "prideful" behavior is in reality a reaction to an underlying sense of worthlessness, and diminishes with the restoration of self-esteem. It has been my impression that many people are less, rather than more, egoistic following dynamic treatment. In such matters it is essential to distinguish healthy from pathological narcissism, a degree of the former being prerequisite to mature object relations (including altruism and mutuality) and social productivity.

As to whether adaptation might become the decisive criterion for moral evaluation, Hartmann (1960) replied in the negative:

> One can, on principle, verify whether moral behavior of a certain kind is biologically useful; whether it has or has not survival value for the individual or for society (but, considering what we know about the genesis of moral valuations, it would be absurd to expect that only what has survival value for individual or species would actually be called "good," or that everything called "evil" must have the opposite effect); whether it is social or antisocial; whether or not it contributes to happiness. . . . At any rate, in all these cases the appointment of happiness, or biological advantage, or any utilitarian aim, as a supreme moral value is still the expression of an empirically subjective attitude. It cannot be deduced from any data of biology, or of social science, or of any other science [p. 66].

"*No scientific psychology,*" Hartmann continued, "*even if it were perfected beyond what it is today, could take the place of personal responsibility in these matters*" (p. 102; my italics). Recall that Freud tended to agree.

Nevertheless, although adaptation may never itself become the primary or sole desideratum for moral evaluation (and for the evaluation of moral demand systems), it appears that it must play some role in such an appraisal. By the standards of adaptation, as implicit and explicit in Freud's psychological and sociocultural writings, contemporary remissiveness—on principle—with regard to sexual, aggressive, and egoistic trends (to the point that it often amounts to a new "moral imperative") would be considered undesirable. In the psychopathological sphere Freud taught us that the sexual provocativeness of a parent can prove quite as deleterious to the child's subsequent sexual functioning, and can lead to quite as severe an unconscious sense of guilt, as can prudery and heavy-handed repression.

Freud believed that some quiescence of libido, and its aim-inhibited diversion in the latency period, was essential to the enculturation of children. And yet we witness in the media and the growing sexualization of interpersonal relations a society that seems bent on denying its children just such a libidinal moratorium. Freud's ideal of health—genital sexuality—was a state of fusion of sensual and aim-inhibited libidinal currents toward a member of the opposite sex. He would not have applauded social mores that invite people to use one another as sexual part objects, a usage that manifests, I might add, as much aggression as libido. (Indeed, and every psychoanalytic social theorist would do well to ponder the meaning of this, the acting out of sexual fantasies seems to be increasing *pari passu* with the acting out of aggressive fantasies, as demonstrated on television and in the movies, and in the rising incidence of marital infidelity, divorce, promiscuity, and teenage pregnancy, and in the increased rate of violent crime.)

In Freud's cultural writings there is clear warrant for the necessity of some degree of restraint of aggression, sexuality, and narcissism: "It is impossible to overlook the extent to which civilization is built up upon a renunciation of instinct. . ." (1930, p. 95). This is the case not only because of the previously discussed socially disruptive effects of the indiscriminate release of such impulses, but because a certain amount of sublimation (aim-inhibited libido) and capacity for identification with others is necessary to the maintenance of social cohesion. (The "coeducational army," I am told by military psychiatrists, is relearning the truth of Freud's teachings about the divisive effects of unsublimated sexuality on groups; group therapists have known it for years.)

I have already touched on many aspects of the positive impact of Freud's theory and therapy on what most would subsume under morality. As Hartmann and Freud emphasize, morality and mental health do not necessarily go hand in hand. But if moral inadequacy is due to neurotic causes, then successful dynamic treatment might remedy it. The strengthening of the ego, the diminution of the harsh and archaic qualities of the superego, and the heightened awareness of one's moral values and their dynamic significance which result from analysis can make for a more consistent and integrated moral code. Broadened awareness can lead to a broadened sense of responsibility, the avoidance of easy rationalizations, and a more subtle form of self-control. The current demand to base moral evaluations on more complete psychological knowledge is, moreover, as Hartmann asserts, a legacy of Freud. And awareness that there are antisocial motives in all of us, that our moral capacities are largely shaped by early constitutional–environmental factors beyond our control, and that conscious moral positions are often a function of (and rationalizations for) unconscious defensive or expressive (including aggressive) trends helps diminish one species of what many consider immorality: intolerance and self-righteousness.

Unquestionably Freud is our most profound and complex psychological analyst of the moral sense. In this lies both his positive and negative impact on the ethical sphere—one's calculation of the balance depends largely on one's own understanding of ethics and the moral task. Nothing, to echo Hartmann, can "take the place of personal responsibility in these matters."

Notes

1. In regard to the pleasure principle and its relationship to behavior in general and moral behavior in particular, Freud was very likely influenced by Bentham (perhaps through reading Mill, if not Bentham himself): "Nature hath placed mankind under the governance of two sovereign masters, pain and pleasure. It is for them alone to point out what we ought to do, as well to determine what we shall do. On the one hand the standard of right and wrong on the other the chain of cause and effect are fastened to their throne" (Bentham, quoted in Abelson and Nielson, 1967, p. 81).

2. According to Rieff (1966): "To help us distinguish between guilt on the one hand and a sense of guilt on the other, between responsibility for an offense committed and fantasies about offenses intended or merely imagined seems a moral as well as a therapeutic aim. . . . [Nevertheless, Freud's] ambition to exhaust the sense of guilt by clinical exposure of all details may be dangerous, as he himself recognized, to a culture that is on the defensive. If a self-trained casuist gets along better by resolving his guilt into a sense of guilt, then he is the healthier for that resolution. This is a vulgar and popular misinterpretation of Freud; but there is something about the presuppositions of psychoanalytic therapy that encourages just such misinterpretations" (pp. 57–58).

3. Analysts, Hartmann (1960) asserts, "do not expect an analyzed person to have no guilt feelings (we consider the capacity to experience guilt an entirely normal characteristic of human experience). But we expect that his guilt reactions will be more clearly in line with the integrated parts of his personality, with his authentic moral codes, and with the reality situations" (p. 90).

4. In his considerations of the relationship between sensuality and affection Freud generally (e.g., 1905a, p. 200; 1921a, p. 111) considers the former to be the older and the latter to be its aim-inhibited derivative, although in 1912 he declares the affectionate current to be the older of the two (p. 180).

5. This counterbalances Freud's (1921a, 1927b, 1930) somewhat elitist notions about the crucial role of the strong, wise, and prudent leader in social cohesion and his concomitant picture of the masses as governed by the primary process and characterized by laziness and lack of self-restraint.

6. Freud was well aware that maintenance of his balance required what might be termed "moral mithridatism." Thus Freud (1922b) applauded the latitude given the wife's desire to attract and the husband's desire to make sexual conquests by allowing some degree of flirtatiousness, which functioned, in effect, as a "safety valve" to render "innocuous" the "inevitable tendency to unfaithfulness." The desire kindled in such dalliances then found satisfaction "in some kind of return to faithfulness to the original object" (p. 224).

7. While Freud is generally interdictive in regard to aggression, as opposed to his pleas for relaxation in the area of sexuality, he could be remissive as well.

"Thoughts for the Times on War and Death," as Rieff (1959, p. 311) observes, gives at least mild endorsement to the idea that violence could be a useful cathartic to an over-refined society.

8. Contrast this, for example, with the stance of C. S. Lewis (1952), a represen-tative lay theologian: "When a man who has been perverted from his youth and taught that cruelty is the right thing, does some tiny little kindness, or refrains from some cruelty he might have committed, and thereby, perhaps, risks being sneered at by his companions, he may, in God's eyes, be doing more than you and I would do if we give up life itself for a friend" (p. 85).

9. The philosopher and psychoanalyst Hanly (1979, pp. 224–227) has noted that a similar ambivalence and ambiguity pervades the analytic literature: Glover, Rycroft, Winnicott, and Kohut are among the many who have implicitly or ex-plictly espoused some version of free will alongside determinism. "Ego psychology and the structural theory have been used to formulate an ambiguous concept of psychic determinism that allows the ego some kind of freedom of choice" (p. 225n). Elsewhere (1985a) I have pointed out that the positions of Knight (1946) and Brierly (1951) exemplify further this ambiguity (pp. 248–249n). There may be some validity to the charge of Schafer and others that structural theory has spawned a multitude of intrapsychic homunculi that become endowed with the free will that is no longer permitted to the whole person. Consider Freud's numer-ous anthropomorphisms in elaborating on the intersystemic relations of the psyche.

10. To these might be added the tautological character of many of the arguments for determinism: Causation is taken as the only legitimate connecting principle, the only manner of expressing a meaningful relationship between events or of intelligi-bly characterizing a line of development; any plausible or demonstrable relationship between events or characterization of development is then declared to support the necessity for the principle of causality and to refute any alternative explanatory system.

11. After this essay entered page proofs, I completed an attempt at a determin-istic resolution of the free will and ethics issue. See Wallace (in press).

References

Abelson, R., & K. Nielsen (1967), History of ethics. In: *Encyclopedia of Philosophy*, ed. P. Edwards. Vol. 2. New York: Macmillan, pp. 81–117.

Ackerknecht, E. (1943), *Medicine and Ethnology*. Baltimore: Johns Hopkins Uni-versity Press, 1971.

Barzun, J. (1983), *A Stroll with William James*. New York: Harper & Row.

Berlin, I. (1954), *Historical Inevitability*. Oxford: Oxford University Press.

Breuer, J., & Freud, S. (1893–1895), *Studies on Hysteria. Standard Edition, 2*. London: Hogarth Press, 1955.

Buber, M. (1965), *The Knowledge of Man*. New York: Harper & Row.

Bunge, M. (1979), *Causality and Modern Science*. New York: Dover.

Collingwood, R. (1946), *The Idea of History*. Oxford: Oxford University Press.

―――― (1972), *Essay on Metaphysics*. Chicago: Gateway.

Frankfurt, H. (1969), Alternate possibilities and moral responsibility. *J. Philosophy,* 65:829–839.

Freud, E. L., Ed. (1960), *Letters of Sigmund Freud,* trans. T. Stern & J. Stern. New York: Basic Books, 1975.

Freud, S. (1892–1899), Extracts from the Fliess papers. *Standard Edition,* 1:173–280. London: Hogarth Press, 1966.

—— (1895), *Project for a Scientific Psychology. Standard Edition,* 1:281–387. London: Hogarth Press, 1966.

—— (1900), *The Interpretation of Dreams. Standard Edition,* 4 & 5 London: Hogarth Press, 1953.

—— (1901), *The Psychopathology of Everyday Life. Standard Edition,* 6. London: Hogarth Press, 1960.

—— (1905a), *Three Essays on the Theory of Sexuality. Standard Edition,* 7:130–245. London: Hogarth Press, 1953.

—— (1905b), *Jokes and Their Relation to the Unconscious. Standard Edition,* 8. London: Hogarth Press, 1960.

—— (1906), Psycho-analysis and the establishment of the facts in legal proceedings. *Standard Edition,* 9:103–114. London: Hogarth Press, 1959.

—— (1907a), Obsessive actions and religious practices. *Standard Edition,* 9:117–127. London: Hogarth Press, 1959.

—— (1907b), The sexual enlightenment of children. *Standard Edition,* 9:131–139. London: Hogarth Press, 1959.

—— (1908a), Character and anal erotism. *Standard Edition,* 9:167–175. London: Hogarth Press, 1959.

—— (1908b), 'Civilized' sexual morality and modern nervous illness. *Standard Edition,* 9:177–204. London: Hogarth Press, 1959.

—— (1909a), *Analysis of a Phobia in a Five-Year-Old Boy. Standard Edition,* 10:5–149. London: Hogarth Press, 1955.

—— (1909b), *Notes upon a Case of Obsessional Neurosis. Standard Edition,* 10:155–318. London: Hogarth Press, 1955.

—— (1909c), Five lectures on psycho-analysis. *Standard Edition,* 11:1–55. London: Hogarth Press, 1957.

—— (1910), Future prospects of psycho-analytic therapy. *Standard Edition,* 11:139–151. London: Hogarth Press, 1957.

—— (1912), On the universal tendency to debasement in the sphere of love. *Standard Edition,* 11:177–190. London: Hogarth Press, 1957.

—— (1913a), *Totem and Taboo. Standard Edition,* 13:1–161. London: Hogarth Press, 1958.

—— (1913b), The claims of psycho-analysis to scientific interest. *Standard Edition,* 13:165–190. London: Hogarth Press, 1959.

—— (1914), On narcissism: An introduction. *Standard Edition,* 14:73–102. London: Hogarth Press, 1957.

—— (1915), Thoughts for the times on war and death. *Standard Edition,* 14:275–300. London: Hogarth Press, 1957.

—— (1916), Some character types met with in psycho-analytic work. *Standard Edition,* 14:309–333.

—— (1915–1917), *Introductory Lectures on Psycho-Analysis. Standard Edition,* 15 & 16. London: Hogarth Press, 1961, 1963.

_____ (1917), Mourning and melancholia. *Standard Edition*, 14:243–258. London: Hogarth Press, 1955.

_____ (1920), Beyond the pleasure principle. *Standard Edition*, 18:7–64. London: Hogarth Press, 1955.

_____ (1921a), Group psychology and the analysis of the ego. *Standard Edition*, 18:69–143. London: Hogarth Press, 1961.

_____ (1921b), Preface to J. J. Putnam's "Addresses on Psychoanalysis." *Standard Edition*, 18:269–270. London: Hogarth Press, 1961.

_____ (1923a), Josef Popper-Lynkeus and the theory of dreams. *Standard Edition*, 19:259–263. London: Hogarth Press, 1959.

_____ (1923b), A short account of psycho-analysis. *Standard Edition*, 19:189–209. London: Hogarth Press, 1961.

_____ (1923c), The ego and the id. *Standard Edition*, 19:12–66. London: Hogarth Press, 1961.

_____ (1923d), Two encyclopedia articles on psycho-analysis. *Standard Edition*, 18:233–259. London: Hogarth Press, 1955.

_____ (1924), The economic problem of masochism. *Standard Edition*, 19:159–170. London: Hogarth Press, 1961.

_____ (1925a), An autobiographical study. *Standard Edition*, 20:7–74. London: Hogarth Press, 1959.

_____ (1925b), Negation. *Standard Edition*, 19:233–239. London: Hogarth Press, 1961.

_____ (1925c), The resistances to psycho-analysis. *Standard Edition*, 19:211–224. London: Hogarth Press, 1959.

_____ (1925d), Some psychical consequences of the anatomical distinction between the sexes. *Standard Edition*, 19:248–258. London: Hogarth Press, 1961.

_____ (1925e), Some additional notes on dream-interpretation as a whole. *Standard Edition*, 19:123–138. London: Hogarth Press, 1961.

_____ (1926), The question of lay analysis. *Standard Edition*, 20:177–250. London: Hogarth Press, 1959.

_____ (1927a), Postscript to "The question of lay analysis." *Standard Edition*, 20:251–258. London: Hogarth Press, 1959.

_____ (1927b), The future of an illusion. *Standard Edition*, 21:5–56. London: Hogarth Press, 1961.

_____ (1928), Dostoevsky and parricide. *Standard Edition*, 21:177–194. London: Hogarth Press, 1961.

_____ (1930), *Civilization and Its Discontents*. *Standard Edition*, 21:64–145. London: Hogarth Press, 1961.

_____ (1933), *New Introductory Lectures on Psycho-Analysis*. *Standard Edition*, 20:5–182. London: Hogarth Press, 1964.

_____ (1935), Postscript to "An autobiographical study." *Standard Edition*, 22:5–182. London: Hogarth Press, 1964.

_____ (1937), Analysis terminable and interminable. *Standard Edition*, 23:216–253. London: Hogarth Press, 1964.

_____ (1939), *Moses and Monotheism*. *Standard Edition*, 23:1–137. London: Hogarth Press, 1964.

_____ (1940), An outline of psycho-analysis. *Standard Edition*, 23:144–207. London: Hogarth Press, 1964.

Hale, N., Ed. (1971), *James Jackson Putnam and Psychoanalysis: Letters between Putnam and Sigmund Freud, Ernest Jones, William James, Sandor Ferenczi, and Morton Prince, 1887–1917*. Cambridge, Mass.: Harvard University Press.

Hartmann, H. (1960), *Psychoanalysis and Moral Values*. New York: International Universities Press.

Hobbes, T. (1651), *Leviathan*. New York: Collier, 1962.

Hospers, J. (1958), What means this freedom? In: *Determinism and Freedom in the Age of Modern Science*, ed. S. Hook. New York: Macmillan, pp. 126–142.

——— (1959), Philosophy and psychoanalysis. In: *Psychoanalysis, Scientific method, and Philosophy*, ed. S. Hook. New York: New York University Press, pp. 336–357.

Hume, D. (1777), *A Treatise on Human Nature*. New York: Collier, 1962.

James, W. (1890), *Principles of Psychology*, 2 vols. New York: Henry Holt.

——— (1897), *The Will to Believe and Other Essays in Popular Philosophy*. New York: Dover, 1956.

Jones, E. (1955), *The Life and Work of Sigmund Freud*, Vol. 2. New York: Basic Books.

——— (1957), *The Life and Work of Sigmund Freud*, Vol. 3. New York: Basic Books.

Koestler, A. (1967), *The Ghost in the Machine*, New York: Random House.

Küng, H. (1979), *Freud and the Problem of God*. New Haven: Yale University Press.

Lasch, C. (1978), *The Culture of Narcissism*. New York: W. W. Norton.

Lewis, C. S. (1952), *Mere Christianity*. New York: Macmillan.

Locke, J. (1690), An essay concerning human understanding. In: *The Empiricists*, ed. R. Taylor, Garden City, N.Y.: Dolphin Books, 1961, pp. 17–133.

Marrou, H. (1966), *Meaning in History*. Baltimore : Helicon Press.

Meng, H., & Freud, E. L., Eds. (1963), *Psychoanalysis and Faith: The Letters of Sigmund Freud and Oskar Pfister*, trans. E. Mosbacher. New York: Basic Books.

Mowrer, O. H. (1950), The problem of anxiety. In: *Learning Theory and Personality Dynamics*. New York: Ronald Press, pp. 531–561.

Nagel, E. (1969), Determinism in history. In : *Ideas in History*, Vol. 2, ed. R. Nash. New York. E. P. Dutton, pp. 319–350.

Nunberg, H., & Federn, E., Eds. (1962–1975), *Minutes of the Vienna Psycho-Analytic Society*, 4 vols., trans. H. Nunberg, E. Federn, & M. Nunberg. New York: International Universities Press.

Oakeshott, M. (1933), *Experience and Its Modes*. Cambridge: Cambridge University Press.

Pap, A. (1962), *An Introduction to the Philosophy of Science*. New York: Free Press.

Popper, K. (1965). *The Logic of Scientific Discovery*. New York: Harper.

Rieff, P. (1959), *Freud: The Mind of the Moralist*, 3rd ed. Chicago: University of Chicago Press, 1979.

——— (1966), *The Triumph of the Therapeutic: Uses of Faith after Freud*. New York: Harper & Row, 1968.

Roazen, P. (1975), *Freud and His followers*. New York: Knopf.

Russell, B. (1929), *Mysticism and Logic*. New York: Norton.

Schafer, R. (1976), *A New Language for Psychoanalysis*. New Haven: Yale University Press.

———— (1978), *Language and Insight*. New Haven: Yale University Press.

Strawson, P. (1971), Freedom and resentment. In: *Free Will*, ed. G. Watson. Oxford: Oxford University Press, 1982, pp. 59–80.

Taylor, R. (1967), Causation. In : *The Encyclopedia of Philosophy*, Vol. 2, ed. P. Edwards. New York: Macmillan, pp. 56–66.

Tillich, P. (1952), *The Courage to Be*. New Haven: Yale University Press.

Von Wright, G. H. (1972), *Causality and Determinism*. New York: New York University Press.

Wallace, E. (1977), The development of Freud's ideas on social cohesion. *Psychiatry*, 40:232–244.

———— (1983), *Freud and Anthropology: A History and Reappraisal*. New York: International Universities Press.

———— (1984), Freud and religion: A history and reappraisal. *The Psychoanalytic Study of Society*, 10: 113–161. Hillsdale, N.J.: Analytic Press.

———— (1985a), *Historiography and Causation in Psychoanalysis*. Hillsdale, N.J.: Analytic Press.

———— (in press), Determinism, possibility, and ethics. *J. Amer. Psychoanal. Assn.*

Wortis, J. (1954), *Fragments of an Analysis with Sigmund Freud*. New York: Simon & Schuster.

Barry Silverstein ————————————————————

"Now Comes A Sad Story":
Freud's Lost Metapsychological Papers

Psychoanalysis is my creation.
—Freud, "On the History of the Psycho-Analytic Movement"

According to Ernest Jones, on March 15, 1915, Freud began writing a series of twelve essays on metapsychology that he intended to incorporate in a book which he would publish at the end of World War I (Jones, 1955, p. 185; Strachey, 1957, p. 105). In less than seven weeks Freud completed five essays: "Instincts and Their Vicissitudes," "Repression," "The Unconscious," "The Meta-psychological Supplement to the Theory of Dreams," and "Mourn-ing and Melancholia." During the next six weeks he wrote five additional papers: "Consciousness," "Anxiety," "Conversion Hys-teria," "Obsessional Neurosis," and a "General Synthesis of the Transference Neuroses," and by early August Freud had completed all twelve essays of the series (Jones, 1955, pp. 185–186). Only the first five papers were published, however—the first three in 1915, the last two in 1917.

The author is grateful for the critical comments received at a presentation of an earlier version of this paper to the Section on Psychiatric History, New York Hospital–Cornell Medical Center, November, 1983. Mr. David Joseph provided valuable bibliographic assistance, Dr. Paul Stepansky offered insightful editorial suggestions, and Mr. Steven Silverstein provided a helpful critical reading.

143

"Now comes a sad story," according to Jones: "None of the last seven essays were ever published, nor have their manuscripts sur-vived . . . . I can't understand now why none of us asked him after the war what had become of them. And why did he destroy them?" (1955, p. 186). Jones also states that the "only single allusion" to the twelve essays in any of Freud's correspondence after 1915 is to be found in a 1917 letter to Abraham. In fact, however, Freud made several references to his collection of metapsychological essays in his correspondence with Lou Andreas-Salomé between 1915 and 1919, and in one postwar exchange Andreas-Salomé did indeed ask him what had happened to the unpublished essays. Freud responded impatiently to her query, denying that he had completed the collec-tion of essays, in apparent contradiction of his earlier admission to her that "the book is just finished except for the necessary revision caused by the arranging and fitting in of the individual essays" (Freud to Andreas-Salomé, 30 July 1915, in Pfeiffer, 1972, p. 32).

In this paper I shall review the references to the proposed book of essays in the currently available Freud correspondence. That review will be the starting point for a consideration of several questions: Why did Freud write the twelve essays in 1915; why did he publish only five of them, three in 1915 and two in 1917; and why did he not publish the complete collection after the end of World War I?

THE CORRESPONDENCE

Freud may have first suggested that he was working on a compre-hensive statement of his metapsychology in a letter he wrote to Andreas-Salomé on November 25, 1914. After commenting on how the war had negatively affected the Wednesday evening meetings of the Vienna Psychoanalytic Society, Freud told her: "I am working in private at certain matters which are wide in scope and also perhaps rich in content" (in Pfeiffer, 1972, p. 21).

On December 11, 1914, Freud wrote Abraham: "After some good results, my own work has plunged into deep darkness . . . My way of working used to be different; I used to wait for an idea to come to me. Now I go out to meet it, and I do not know whether I find it any more quickly because of that." On December 21, 1914, Freud reported to Abraham: "I might manage a theory of neuroses with chapters on the vicissitudes of the instincts, repression and the unconscious if my working energy does not finally succumb to my depressed mood" (in H. Abraham and E. Freud, 1965, pp. 204–205, 206).

On January 10, 1915, Freud wrote to Ludwig Binswanger: "I am alternatively productive and morose . . . Occasionally I work on a kind of exercise book of psychoanalytic theories, but it doesn't make much headway" (in Binswanger, 1957, p. 58). Two months later, on March 4, 1915, Freud told Abraham: "I have decided to publish three chapters of my germinating summary (instincts, repressions, the unconscious) in three successive numbers of the *Zeitschrift*" (in H. Abraham and E. Freud, 1965, p. 213).

On March 15, 1915, Freud related to Abraham: "When I have finished this letter, I shall begin drafting *Instincts and Their Vicissitudes.*" Almost two weeks later, on March 27, he told Abraham: "I am working slowly and steadily on the papers for *Imago* and the *Zeitschrift*" (in H. Abraham and E. Freud, 1965, pp. 214–215).

Five days later, on April 1, 1915, Freud reported to Binswager that he was preparing "a characterization of the unconscious that is intended to make it intelligible. Also an elucidation of melancholia that traces it to narcissism" (in Binswanger, 1957, p. 59). On that same day he wrote to Andreas-Salomé: "You know that I concern myself with the particular, and wait for the general to emerge of itself. And so I find my views on narcissim very useful in investigating melancholia and other hitherto obscure conditions. The next numbers of the *Journal* will contain a kind of psychological synthesis of various ideas of mine under three headings: Instincts and their Vicissitudes—Repression—The Unconscious; incomplete, like everything I do, but not without some new content. The essay on the Unconscious in particular will contain a new definition of the term, which is really tantamount to a restatement" (in Pfeiffer, 1972, p. 28).

According to Jones, Freud wrote to Sandor Ferenczi three days later (April 4, 1915) and told him he had completed the essays "Instincts and Their Vicissitudes" and "Repression." On April 23, 1915, Freud again reported his progress to Ferenczi, announcing that he had completed the essay, "The Unconscious," which he said was his favorite (Jones, 1955, p. 185).

About two weeks later, on May 4, 1915, Freud told Abraham: "My work is now taking shape. I have finished five papers: that on Instincts and their Vicissitudes, which is rather dry, but is essential as an introduction and is justified by those that follow, then those on Repression and the Unconscious, the 'Metapsychological Sup-

plement to the Theory of Dreams' and 'Mourning and Melancholia.' The first four are to appear in the new series of the
Zeitschrift, and all the rest I am keeping for myself. If the war lasts
long enough, I hope to get together about a dozen such papers and in
quieter times to offer them to a nonunderstanding world under the
title of 'Introductory Papers on Metapsychology.' I think that on the
whole it will represent an advance. The manner and level will be
that of the seventh chapter of the *Interpretation of Dreams*" (in H.
Abraham and E. Freud, 1965, p. 221).

Freud continued to work at a rapid pace. According to Jones, he
wrote five more essays in the next six weeks, although two of them,
"Consciousness" and "Anxiety," still required a little revision. On
June 21, 1915, Freud wrote to Ferenczi that he had just completed
the essay on "Conversion Hysteria" and that he was ready to write
one on the "Obsessional Neurosis," to be followed by a "General
Synthesis of the Transference Neuroses." Nine days later, on June
30, 1915, Freud reported to Jones that the twelve essays of the series
were "almost finished" (Jones, 1955, pp. 185–186), and three days
afterward, on July 3, 1915, he told Abraham: "Today I have already
reached the middle of the eleventh of the proposed twelve papers"
(in H. Abraham and E. Freud, 1965, p. 225).

Five days later, on July 8, 1915, Freud wrote to James Jackson
Putnam: "For me an all embracing synthesis never has been the
important issue. Certainty, rather, always has been worth the sacrifice of everything else . . . I am taking advantage of this holiday to
complete a volume of twelve psychological essays" (in Hale, 1971,
p. 190). Three weeks thereafter, Freud told Andreas-Salomé: "The
product of these months will probably take the form of a book
consisting of twelve essays, beginning with one on instincts and
their vicissitudes. But I seem to remember that I have already told
you about this. The book is just finished except for the necessary
revision caused by the arranging and fitting in of the individual
essays . . . I so rarely feel the need for synthesis. The unity of this
world seems to me so self-evident as not to need emphasis. What
interests me is the separation and breaking up into its component
parts of what would otherwise revert to an inchoate mass . . . In
short, I am of course an analyst, and believe that synthesis offers no
obstacles once analysis has been achieved" (in Pfeiffer, 1972, p. 32).

Two days later, on August 1, 1915, Freud wrote to Abraham:
"Since I have been here I have finished my twelve papers, they are
war-time atrocities, like a lot of other things. Several, including that

on consciousness, still require thorough revision" (in H. Abraham and E. Freud, 1965, p. 228). And, according to Jones, eight days thereafter, on August 9, 1915, Freud wrote to Ferenczi that the twelve essays were completely finished (Jones, 1955, p. 186).

Freud did not appear eager to publish the book of essays immediately. On November 7, 1915, Andreas-Salomé asked him: "I am right in thinking, am I not, that the book announced by you will come out before the individual sections have all appeared in the *Journal*, since this would take a long time in these days?" Freud replied on November 9, 1915: "The new collection, from which the article on the Unconscious is now appearing in the *Journal*, will, as you correctly surmise, not be continued there. But I do not know whether the book will be published any earlier on that account. I will send the *Lectures* first and give myself time for the final editing of some of the twelve essays. All these works suffer from the lack of good cheer in which I wrote them and from their function as a kind of sedative" (in Pfeiffer, 1972, pp. 33, 35).

More than a month later, on December 17, 1915, Freud wrote to Binswanger: ". . . I've got several things ready for publication when the war ends. Among these is a series of essays, the first of which you have seen in the *Zeitschrift*. All in all, twelve are almost completed. They will be entitled "Introduction to Metapsychology" (Binswanger, 1957, p. 62).

After 1915 Freud made few further references to his book of twelve essays. In a letter to Freud on April 1, 1916, Abraham praised his paper on the unconscious which had been published in the *Zeitschrift*, and expressed regret that such an exceptionally important piece of work should have had to appear in wartime, when it could not attract the attention it deserved. Abraham continued: "But I take it that the whole series will appear in book form as soon as the war is over?" (in H. Abraham and E. Freud, 1965, pp. 233–234). The next letters written by Freud to Abraham as they appear in their collected correspondence contain no reply from Frued to Abraham's query about the book of twelve essays. A few of Freud's letters to Abraham were lost owing to wartime conditions, however, so it is possible that Freud did write an answer to Abraham's question which Abraham never received (H. Abraham and E. Freud, 1965, p. vii).

Despite Jones' claim that the only single allusion Freud made to his book of twelve essays after 1915, in any of his correspondence, came in a letter to Abraham of November 11, 1917 (Jones, 1955, p.

186), Freud clearly made several references to the volume in letters to Andreas-Salomé after 1915. On May 21, 1916, Andreas-Salomé wrote Freud concerning a book of her own which Freud thought she already had sent to the printer. She told him that her book was not yet finished, and continued: "And since your book is about to appear, I will in any case wait for its publication, so that I shall not have read only the four essays in the *Journal* before finishing my own." Four days later, on May 25, 1916, Freud replied: "I beg you not to postpone it and not to wait for my book to appear first. My book consisting of twelve essays of this kind cannot be published before the end of the war, and who knows how long after that ardently longed-for date? Spans of life are unpredictable and I would so much like to be able to have read your contribution before it is too late" (in Pfeiffer, 1972, pp. 44–45).

On June 30, 1916, Andreas-Salomé replied to Freud: "The main thing, however, was that I was very sad at the news that your new book will not appear till the end of the war. How can we all wait so long, when we know that it is all finished and ready?" Freud responded two weeks later, on July 14, 1916: "I object to the calm announcement in your letter that your book is to be delayed, while you lament the unavoidable delay of mine. I see things the other way round: I am not at all curious about my book, but very much so about yours" (in Pfeiffer, 1972, pp. 46, 48).

Andreas-Salomé apparently kept hoping that Freud would eventually publish his book. A year later, on June 14, 1917, she asked Freud: ". . . and when shall we see at last the rest of your Metapsychology following on the first four sections? We do need them so much" (in Pfeiffer, 1972, p. 57). The immediately following letters from Freud to Andreas-Salomé in their published correspondence offer no answer to her question.

In 1917, Freud decided to publish two more of his metapsychological essays in the *Zeitschrift*. On November 11, 1917, he wrote to Abraham: "At any rate I behave as if we were faced with the end of all things, and in the last few days, I have got ready for publication in the *Zeitschrift* two papers of the 'metapsychological' series ('Supplements to the Theory of Dreams,' 'Mourning and Melancholia'). I originally intended to use these and other papers, with some that have already appeared ('Instincts and their Vicissitudes', 'Repression', 'The Unconscious'), for a book. But this is not the time for it" (in H. Abraham and E. Freud, 1965, p. 261).

After she received the issue of the *Zeitschrift* containing the two newly published metapsychological papers, Andreas-Salomé wrote to Freud on June 20, 1918: "Almost at the same time as your letter, there arrived the new number, containing the two further sections—which I had almost given up hope of receiving—of the still unprinted *Metapsychology*. In consequence, I have been carrying on an almost uninterrupted conversation with you, even though I did not mean it to reach your ears quite yet. What joy these long-awaited chapters have given me! It is true that they break off at a point where the tension becomes so great that one cannot help asking for more: it will come soon, won't it?" Freud replied on July 1, 1918: "I am writing to you today only to beg you not to expect anything of mine in the next number of the *Journal*. For the time being there is nothing more to come. Not only the normal weariness at the end of a working year, but also other signs oblige me to hold back until I am more in the mood for it" (in Pfeiffer, 1972, pp. 80–81, 82).

Eight months later, on March 9, 1919, Freud asked Andreas-Salomé if she did not have a short work on the unconscious ready for publication. On March 18, 1919, Andreas-Salomé replied that her little book no longer seemed to her to be good enough since its publication in parts, and she was not inclined to publish it. "But now I am going to turn the tables on you," she continued, asking: "What has happened to the *Metapsychology* now that the printed chapters have been included in the fourth volume of the *Neurosenlehre*? What has happened to the other ones which were already finished?" About two weeks later, on April 2, 1919, Freud responded: "I must make a vigorous protest against your riposte. What has happened to my *Metapsychology*? In the first place, it has not yet been written. The systematic working through of material is not possible for me; the fragmentary nature of my experiences and the sporadic character of my insights do not permit it. But if I still have ten years to live and remain capable of work in this period, do not die of starvation, or meet a violent end, nor am too severely afflicted by the misery of my family or of the world around me—a bit too much to ask—then I promise to make further contributions to it. A first example of this will be found in an essay of mine entitled *Beyond the Pleasure Principle*, concerning which I look forward to a detailed critical-synthetic appreciation from you" (in Pfeiffer, 1972, pp. 93–95).

Andreas-Salomé made one more plea to Freud on August 25, 1919: "I cannot reconcile myself to the fact that the Meta-psychology has not yet been published in book form, because you wrote a few years ago as if it were already finished and had only not been printed because of the war and as if you only needed to make some editorial alterations" (in Pfeiffer, 1972, p. 100). Freud said nothing more about it.

ANTECEDENTS OF THE METAPSYCHOLOGY PROJECT

To gain insight into Freud's conflicted unwillingness to publish the metapsychology papers of the war years in book form, we must consider briefly some of Freud's personal traits as they became man-ifest in his relationships to his disciples. We must also look at devel-opments in the psychoanalytic movement in the years immediately preceding this "sad story." Specifically, we must consider the degree to which Freud's bursts of theoretical creativity, and his attitude toward metapsychology in particular, were conditioned by certain personal, theoretical, and institutional needs occasioned by the de-fections of Adler and Jung.

Sporadic Inspiration

Freud characterized his theoretical productivity as marked by occasional intuitive insights and a decided preference for analysis over synthesis (Mahony, 1982, pp. 109–111). As we have seen, he protested to Andreas-Salomé in 1919 that the "systematic working through of material" was not possible for him; the "fragmentary nature" of his experiences and the "sporadic character" of his in-sights did not permit it. We also observed Freud telling Andreas-Salomé, in 1915, that he concerned himself with the particular, and waited for "the general to emerge of itself"; later that year he told Putnam that he rarely felt the need for synthesis—certainty was worth the sacrifice of everything else. Nevertheless, Freud did feel moved to synthesize his metapsychology in 1915. Why?

We may gain some insight into Freud's frame of mind in 1915 by recalling that he had told Abraham in December 1914 that his way of working used to be different; he used to wait for an idea to come to him, now he went out to meet it. From this it would appear that Freud was not moved by some spontaneous, intuitive insight to synthesize his metapsychology as he entered 1915; other factors seemed to have forced that on him. Freud told Jung on December 17, 1911: "Often it seems, I can go for a long while without feeling the need to clarify an obscure point, and then one day I am compelled by the pressure of facts or by the influence of someone else's ideas" (in McGuire, 1974, p. 472). In 1915, Freud appeared to be compelled to struggle with metapsychology less by the force of a natural creative rhythm than by a confluence of internal and external pressures related to the defections of Adler and Jung.

The loss of Adler in 1911, and Jung in 1914, as members of the psychoanalytic community, and their full emergence as rival theorists with alternative viewpoints, constituted the external pressure on Freud to try to achieve clarity and synthesis in his metapsychology, even while he may have felt little intrinsic need to do so. In this regard, the observations recorded by Andreas-Salomé in her journal entry of February 12–13, 1913 are pertinent. Commenting on the friction between Freud and Tausk which she had observed in the Vienna Psychoanalytic Society she noted: "It is also clear that any independence around Freud, especially when it is marked by aggression and display of temperament, worries him and wounds him quite automatically in his noble egoism as investigator, forcing him to premature discussion, and so forth. The value to analysis of an independent mind can only be established in the future, and that must result in probably unavoidable battles of the present. Certain it is that for Freud it is all an annoyance and that he longs in his heart for the peace of undisturbed research which he enjoyed until 1905—until the founding of his school" (Andreas-Salomé, 1964, pp. 97–98).

According to Jones, by late 1913 Freud had become increasingly annoyed at Adler, who had left his fold, and Jung, who was still the President of the International Psychoanalytic Association, for what he called "sailing under false colors" (Jones, 1955, p. 362). That is, in spite of their theoretical deviations from basic Freudian positions, they still called their work psychoanalysis, thus causing confusion in the minds of those outside the field. Freud insisted that the founder of psychoanalysis must be the person best qualified to decide what was psychoanalysis and what was not. Therefore, he felt compelled to take some active step to defend his work. He took the offensive and wrote "On Narcissism" (1914b) and "On the History of the Psychoanalytic Movement" (1914c), to which we shall return below. These works only served as prolegomena to the larger work he would attempt in 1915, the book consisting of twelve metapsychological essays.

Freud as Group Leader

Freud's need to go on the offensive against Adler and Jung from late 1913 on becomes more comprehensible in the context of his anxiety to ensure the survival and acceptance of his theories. In this regard, let us briefly review the chronology of Freud's changing relationships to his disciples up to this point. In the early years of the psychoanalytic movement, Freud's conception of discipleship was never quite the same as that of Adler and Jung (Stepansky, 1976, 1983). Freud wanted disciples who would accept his views and promulgate them, rather than generating original conceptions that could constitute alternative explanatory systems. In 1903, Freud welcomed Adler into the new Wednesday Evening Psychological Society—which evolved into the Vienna Psychoanalytic Society—because Adler was a reputable physician and Freud desperately craved medical acceptance of his psychoanalytic doctrines. Even though Adler had presented his own nonpsychoanalytic medical views at the Vienna Society meetings for several years, it was not until 1910, when the distinctiveness of his theoretical viewpoint crystallized, and when he emerged as a rival authority figure within the group, that Freud's opinion of him changed: A political asset became a political liability (Stepansky, 1983, pp. 110–113). In 1911, Freud told the Vienna Society that he regarded Adler's theories as incompatible with psychoanalysis, and Adler, who was the Society's president, soon resigned, along with several other members (Nunberg and Federn, 1974, pp. 145–151, 281).

Freud's altered view of Adler's value to the psychoanalytic movement in 1910 was related to his hope that in Jung, a Zurich gentile with ties to institutional psychiatry, he had found a proper successor with the best prospects of forming ties between psychoanalysis and the world of general science (Stepansky, 1983, p. 110). Thus, Freud's anxiety about the future of psychoanalysis in 1910 led him to alienate his Viennese followers (including Adler) by championing Jung's election as president of the newly founded International Psychoanalytic Association (Wittels, 1924, p. 140; Stekel, 1950, pp. 128–129; Jones, 1955, pp. 69–70; Stepansky, 1976, pp. 237–239). Adler's value to the movement decreased as Jung's increased.

Although Freud believed he had found a proper successor in Jung, Jung had been forthright in telling him since their correspondence began in 1906 that he could not accept all of his views; he increasingly expressed reservations concerning childhood sexuality and the sexual etiology of the neuroses, as Freud understood them (Stepansky, 1976). Nevertheless, Freud's view of Jung as a political asset for his movement allowed him to be tolerant of Jung's dissent, just as for some time he had tolerated Adler's nonpsychoanalytic views. By 1913, however, when Jung had become a significant alternative theorist, Freud was prepared, if only reluctantly, to see him leave the fold. In April 1914, Jung resigned his presidency of the International Psychoanalytic Association.

Freud's readiness to separate from Jung was influenced by the formation in 1913 of a secret committee that was to ensure the future development of psychoanalysis, and defend it against criticism after Freud's death. The international committee consisted of Abraham, Ferenczi, Jones, Rank, and Sachs (Jones, 1955, pp. 152–155). All these men were proper disciples, content with the roles of elaborating Freud's discoveries and applying psychoanalysis in their clinical practices. Freud responded to Jones's suggestion for the creation of such a committee in August 1912 by telling him: "I daresay it would make living and dying easier for me if I knew of such an association existing to watch over my creation" (Jones, 1955, p. 153). Just as Adler's value to Freud decreased when he pinned all his hopes on Jung, so Jung's value diminished with the creation of the secret committee. After his disenchantment with Jung, Freud never again relied on one special successor; instead he fell back upon the members of the committee, who collectively might ensure the institutional success of psychoanalysis.

By late 1913, with his secret committee behind him, Freud was driven to focus on the real theoretical differences between himself, Adler, and Jung. He had been accepting of, or at least tolerant of, many theoretical differences with Adler and Jung during the time when he regarded them as political assets for the psychoanalytic movement. Now that neither was a part of a movement under Freud's control, he felt compelled to dissociate his views from theirs and to assert the superiority of his conceptions over those of his rivals.

The Shadow of Death

We can gain further insight into Freud's anxiety for the fate of his creation, and his struggle to put his metapsychology in order in 1915, by considering certain inner pressures Freud had to cope with: his "old age complex" and his fear of impending death. Freud appeared to take seriously the prediction that he would die between May 1917 and May 1918 (perhaps a legacy of his relationship with Fliess and the latter's bio-rhythm numerology). On April 16, 1909, he wrote to Jung: "Some years ago I discovered within me the conviction that I would die between the ages of 61 and 62, which then struck me as a long time away. (Today it is only eight years off)" (in McGuire, 1974, p. 219). In 1910, Freud told Ferenczi that he had believed "for a long time" that he had to die in February 1918 (10 January 1910, in Jones, 1955, p. 392). In 1907, Freud warned Jung, his newly found disciple, to expect harsh opposition to psychoanalysis, but assured him: ". . . just let five or ten years pass and the analysis of 'aliquis', which today is not regarded as cogent, will have become cogent, though nothing in it will have changed . . . you will live to see the day, though I may not" (27 May, 1907, in McGuire, 1974, p. 54).

Given Freud's fear that he would die between the ages of 61 and 62, we can understand why he appeared to see himself as an old man in his early fifties. On February 2, 1910, he told Jung: "I am resigned to being old and no longer even think continually of growing old" (in McGuire, 1974, p. 292). Freud was then only 53 years old. On April 27, 1911, when he was not yet 55 years of age, Freud wrote to Jung of his anger at Putnam for writing "Freud is no longer a young man": "You see, it's my 'old age complex'. . . !" Freud exclaimed (in McGuire, 1974, p. 419). That same year Freud wrote a piece on name forgetting, related to his "old age complex," which he incorporated in the edition of the *Psychopathology of Everyday Life* that appeared in 1912. There he stated: "I know I don't much like to think about *growing* old, and I have strange reactions when I'm reminded of it" (1912, p. 31).

On April 14, 1912, Freud wrote to Binswanger, who had just had a malignant tumor removed: "I, an old man, who will have no right to complain if his life ends in a few years (and I have decided not to complain) am particularly pained when one of my flowering young men—one of those who were supposed to continue my own life—tells me that he has become uncertain of his life" (in Binswanger, 1957, p. 39). In 1914, when he was 58, Freud described himself as follows: "But in fact you have grown old . . . you are on the eve of your sixtieth birthday, and your physical feelings, as well as your mirror, show unmistakably how far your life's candle is burnt down" (1914d, p. 241).

Freud's "strange reactions" to growing old would appear to have been related to a fear of death; that fear of death may have been related in turn to his oedipal fantasy that death symbolized a longed-for union with the mother (Mahony, 1982, pp. 207–208). In the 1911 letter to Jung he wrote: "You see, it's my 'old-age complex', whose erotic basis is known to you" (in McGuire, 1974, p. 419). Perhaps that erotic basis is revealed in "The Theme of the Three Caskets," which Freud wrote in 1912 shortly after visiting Binswanger, who was facing a dim prognosis after surgery, and shortly after his 77-year-old mother had been ill (Schur, 1972, p. 274). It was also only five years before Freud's predicted death year. He wrote of "the three forms taken by the figure of the mother in the course of a man's life—the mother herself, the beloved one who is chosen after her pattern, and lastly the Mother Earth who receives him once more. But it is in vain that an old man yearns for the love of woman as he had it first from his mother; the third of the Fates alone, the silent Goddess of Death, will take him into her arms" (1913b, p. 301).

It is well known that Freud fainted in Jung's presence in Munich in November 1912. According to Jones, "his first words as he was coming to were strange: 'How sweet it must be to die'—another indication that the idea of dying had some esoteric meaning for him" (Freud to Jones, 8 December 1912, in Jones, 1953, p. 317). In explaining this incident to Jones a few weeks later, Freud connected it with previous similar experiences with Fliess; with his current displeasure with Jung; and with "some piece of unruly homosexual feeling at the root of the matter" (Jones, 1953, p. 317). Shortly thereafter, he wrote to Binswanger: "Repressed feelings, this time directed against Jung, as previously against a predecessor of his, naturally play the main part" (1 January 1913, in Binswanger, 1957, p. 49). Schur (1972, pp. 266–271) suggests that many of Freud's deepest conflicts had been stirred up at this time (latent homosex-uality, death wishes against a rival, survivor guilt), and that the fainting spell defensively took him away from it all. Suffice it to point out here that one of the unpleasant facts Freud momentarily escaped by fainting was that he had lost his successor once and for all; Jung would not fulfill that mission for him. His comment "How sweet it must be to die" may indeed have been partially rooted in his fantasy of death as union with the mother. But an additional basis for that enigmatic statement may be found in his relationship with Jung, and in particular, in a developing fantasy Freud would project into his writing of *Totem and Taboo* during 1912–1913, when he and Jung were becoming increasingly estranged. In sum: Although his sons would not defer to his authority and wished to replace him, in death he would triumph over them, for after his death his author-ity, and his truth, would be internalized by his repentent disciples, who would then honor his memory.

Freud completed the first of the essays of which *Totem and Taboo* is comprised in January 1912, and the final part in May 1913 (Jones, 1955, pp. 352–354). The work may be read, on one level, as an allegory of Freud, his disciples, and the psychoanalytic movement (Ostow, 1977, pp. 169–172). Although the primal father is mur-dered by his sons, his short-run defeat prepares the way for his long-run victory in consolidating his control over the guilty sons. It seems likely that, in Freud's imagination, his death became a prerequisite for the inhibition of the ambitious struggle to beget heretical doc-trines and dethrone the father that he perceived among his fol-lowers. After his death, in Freud's fantasy, and even if it took more than one generation, he would become the totem god of succeeding generations of psychoanalysts: They would call themselves Freudi-ans, revere him, and function in an orderly organization, united in their acceptance of his doctrines. Thus death, for Freud, would bring his disputes with his disciples to a desired end. In death he would return to a blissful womb, and eventually become incorporat-ed as the undisputed godhead of a unified psychoanalytic move-ment. How sweet that would be!

On July 21, 1911, when he still had hopes that Jung would be his successor, Freud hinted at the fantasy that his immortality would be achieved by death and resurrection through incorporation by Jung. Freud explained an incident of name forgetting that had aroused associations with the words *young* and *old,* and *young* with *Jung,* by telling Jung: "It is the old mythological motif: the old god wants to be sacrificed and rise again rejuvenated in the new one. I hope that you will fare better than I have and not just copy me" (in McGuire, 1974, p. 436). When Binswanger told Freud that he was writing an essay entitled "The Significance of Freud for Clinical Psychiatry," Freud responded on November 23, 1911: "A generation must die before the next one can heed your admonitions. . ." (in Binswanger, 1957, pp. 35, 37).

As Freud's relationship with Jung first developed, he hoped that his psychoanalytic doctrines would survive his death, and find greater acceptance after his death, because Jung would preach them and win more converts than he could. As Freud came increasingly to see Jung as a rival theorist, however, and feared that separation from him might become necessary, his fantasy of immortality through Jung shifted in the direction of being murdered by Jung and incorporated by him. Such a murder and incorporation fantasy con-tained elements of projected aggression, but it was also a vehicle for a merger of two males, which might have been an expression of "some piece of unruly homosexual feeling." According to Jung, Freud's fear that Jung harbored death wishes toward him was a common element in two incidents in which Freud fainted in Jung's presence, one in 1909 (Jones, 1955, p. 54), and the one in 1912 discussed above (Jung, 1963, pp. 156–157). What was a fear in 1909 had developed into a primal-father-murder-and-incorporation fantasy by 1912–1913.

By 1914, Freud's death and resurrection fantasy had evolved beyond incorporation by Jung and his generation. It would perhaps take some time after his death before his truth was accepted, and perhaps it would only be by future generations that he was properly honored. He would become immortal nevertheless, because eventually, inevitably, he would be *rediscovered* as the original dis-coverer of psychoanalytic truth. Thus, in "On the History of the Psychoanalytic Movement" (1914c), Freud embellished his personal myth by retrospectively portraying his thinking during the 1890s, his period of great discovery, in these words: "I pictured the future as follows: —I should probably succeed in maintaining myself by means of the therapeutic success of the new procedure, but science would ignore me entirely during my lifetime; some decades later, someone else would infallibly come upon the same things—for which the time was not now ripe—would achieve recognition for them and bring me honor as a forerunner whose failure had been inevitable" (p. 22). Freud's creation, then, would survive him without Jung's help, and he would triumph posthumously over Adler and Jung through rediscovery. Before he died in 1918, however, he had to be sure to leave behind a precise statement of his truth—the proof that he got there first—to be rediscovered by the next visionaries who travelled down the right path. Thus, he felt internally driven to create the book of metapsychological essays in 1915, to leave his theoretical statement in good order before he died, both as an immediate rallying point for his secret committee and as a kind of archaeological dicovery for later generations.

Rival Texts

Freud began working on *Totem and Taboo* in the summer of 1911 (Jones, 1955, pp. 350–351). For some time Jung already had been investigating the literature on mythology and comparative religion, and Freud had in hand a manuscript of the first part of Jung's essay *Transformations and Symbols of the Libido* (McGuire, 1974, pp. 438–439). These two texts were being written somewhat in parallel (Wallace, 1983, pp. 105–108). Freud told Jung on August 20, 1911: "I have been working in a field where you will be surprised to meet me," and Jung replied, ". . . let my 'Transformations and Symbols of the Libido' unleash your associations and/or fantasies" (29 August 1911, in McGuire, 1974, pp. 438–439).

By April 1912, Jung was telling Freud that he regarded "incest primarily as a fantasy problem," and by May he told him: "The incest taboo does not correspond with the specific value of incest . . . incest is forbidden *not because it is desired* but because the free-floating anxiety regressively reactivates infantile material . . . (as though incest had been, or might have been desired)" (27 April 1912 and 17 May 1912 in McGuire, 1974, pp. 502, 505). Freud responded on May 23, 1912: "In the libido question, I finally see at what point your conception differs from mine. (I am referring of course to incest, but I am thinking of your heralded modifications of the concept of the libido). . . . I own a strong antipathy towards your innovation. It has two sources. First, the regressive character of the innovation. . . . Secondly, because of a disastrous similarity to a theorem of Adler's. . . . He said the incest libido is 'arranged'; i.e., the neurotic has no desire at all for his mother. . . . Now this still strikes me as fanciful, based on utter incomprehension of the unconscious" (in McGuire, 1974, p. 507).

It is very likely that by April 1912, Freud's awareness of Jung's desexualizing trend led him to write not just a parallel, but a rival text. If Jung (as well as Adler) was denying the role of Freud's libidinous Oedipus complex in culture, then Freud would emphasize it even more, both as a psychological and historical factor (Wallace, 1983, p. 106). If Jung was dealing with incest primarily as a "fantasy problem," then Freud would demonstrate that it actually existed in human prehistory—and that this provided the basis for the real existence of incestuous desires in individual childhoods.

In 1913, Freud was acutely aware that the publication of *Totem and Taboo* would separate Jung's work from his own. He told Ferenczi on May 13, 1913: "In the dispute with Zurich it comes at the right time to divide us as an acid does a salt"; two weeks later, however, he displayed a fear of really losing Jung: "Jung is crazy, but I don't really want a split; I should prefer him to leave on his own accord. Perhaps my *Totem* work will hasten the break against my will" (27 May 1913, in Jones, 1955, p. 354).

Moses and Joshua

A brief consideration of some father–son transference factors in the Freud–Jung relationship will clarify the nature of this uneasy alliance and the extent to which Freud was deeply affected by the official loss of Jung in 1914. There are some similarities between Freud's relationship to Jung and his previous relationships to Breuer and Fliess. The relationship to Jung, however, differed in an important way: In the earlier relationships Freud played something of the role of a son to initially overidealized father figures, whereas, with Jung, it was the middle-aged Freud who functioned as an oedipal father, while the younger man, Jung, related to him as an idealized father figure (Alexander, 1982; Gedo, 1983, pp. 229–263).

Jung introduced an element of idealization and homosexual eroticism into the relationship from the start. On October 28, 1907, he wrote to Freud: "Actually—and I confess this to you with a struggle—I have a boundless admiration for you both as a man and a researcher . . . my veneration for you has something of the character of a 'religious' crush. Though it does not really bother me, I still feel it is disgusting and ridiculous because of its undeniable erotic under-tone. This abominable feeling comes from the fact that as a boy I was the victim of a sexual assault by a man I once worshipped" (in McGuire, 1974, p. 95). Two weeks later Freud replied: ". . . a transference on a religious basis would strike me as most disastrous; it could end only in apostasy . . . I shall do my best to show you that I am unfit to be an object of worship" (15 November 1907, in McGuire, 1974, p. 98).

On February 17, 1908, Freud alluded to a homosexual overtone in his estrangement from Fliess, and told Jung: "The paranoid form is probably conditioned by restriction to the homosexual compo-nent. . . . My one-time friend Fliess developed a dreadful case of paranoia after throwing off his affection for me." Jung replied: "The reference to Fliess—surely not accidental—and your relationship with him impels me to ask you to let me enjoy your friendship not as one between equals but as that of father and son" (20 February 1908, in McGuire, 1974, pp. 121–122). Both men appeared to be afraid of homoerotic attractions and repercussions.

Since Jung pleaded to be treated as a son by idealized father Freud, let us consider how Jung recalled his relationship with his actual father, a Protestant minister. Starting with recollections of his early childhood, Jung (1963) reported: "At that time, too, there arose in me profound doubts about everything my father said. . . . Later, when I was eighteen years old, I had many discussions with my father . . . But our discussions invariably came to an unsatisfac-tory end. They irritated him, and saddened him. 'Oh nonsense,' he was in the habit of saying, 'you always want to think. One ought not to think, but believe.' I would think, 'no, one must experience and know,' but I would say, 'give me this belief,' where upon he would shrug and turn resignedly away" (pp. 42–43).

Jung transferred much of his view of the father as one who tried to stop his son from thinking independently, and who sought to impose dogma on him, to his relationship to Freud. At the start of that relationship, Jung told Freud on December 4, 1906 of his reluc-tance to accept Freud's views on faith: "If I confine myself to ad-vocating the bare minimum, this is simply because I can advocate only as much as I myself have unquestionably experienced, and that in comparison with your experience is naturally very little." Freud then fed into Jung's transference by asking him, as his father had, to accept his doctrine on faith. He replied: "I am delighted with your promise [a promise Jung never made] to trust me for the present in matters where your experience does not yet enable you to make up your own mind—though of course only until it does enable you to do so" (6 December 1906, in McGuire, 1974, pp. 10, 13).

Freud, behaving as an oedipal father, praised Jung on January 1, 1907 as "the ablest helper to have joined me thus far" (in McGuire, 1974, p. 17). On April 7, 1907, he told Jung: "You have inspired me with confidence for the future . . . I could hope for no one better than yourself . . . to continue and complete my work" (in McGuire, 1974, p. 27). By August 13, 1908, Freud the father had delegated a *mission* to Jung the son: "My selfish purpose, which I frankly confess is to persuade you to continue and complete my work by applying to psychoses what I have begun with neuroses. With your strong and independent character, with your Germanic blood which enables you to command the sympathies of the public more readily than I, you seem to be better fitted than anyone else I know to carry out this mission" (in McGuire, 1974, p. 168).

Freud's expectation that Jung would be his successor was at a high point in January 1909 when he told him: "We certainly are getting ahead; if I am Moses, then you are Joshua and will take possession of the promised land of psychiatry, which I shall only be able to glimpse from afar" (17 January 1909, in McGuire, 1974, pp. 196–197).

While Freud denied that he wanted to be an object of worship, he nevertheless increasingly demanded filial piety from Jung inasmuch as he expected him to accept his fundamental theoretical positions on authority, and delegated to him the mission to be his successor. While Jung asked Freud to be a godlike father—one worthy of worship—he nevertheless feared the loss of his individuality if he allowed himself to merge too much with Freud, and his already developed heretical tendency was exacerbated by Freud's fatherly attempts to make him believe by the weight of his authority. Thus, each was repeatedly disappointed by the other.

On April 16, 1909, Freud expressed his disappointment with Jung: "It is strange that on the very same evening when I formally adopted you as eldest son and annointed you—*in the lands of the unbelievers* [italicized in Latin in the original]—as my successor and crown prince, you should have divested me of my paternal dignity, which divesting seems to have given you as much pleasure as I, on the contrary, derived from the investiture of your person" (in McGuire, 1974, p. 218).

By December 1909, Freud's attitude to Jung had become quite ambivalent: He still hoped Jung would be his successor, but he feared Jung would destroy his work and set up his own doctrines instead. He wrote to Jung: "Your notion that after my retirement from the ranks my errors may come to be worshiped as relics amused me a good deal, but I don't believe it. I believe on the contrary that the younger men will demolish everything in my heritage that is not absolutely solid as fast as they can. . . . Since you are likely to play a prominent part in this work of liquidation, I shall try to place cer-tain of my endangered ideas in your safekeeping" (19 December 1909, in McGuire 1974, p. 277). In 1915, when Freud saw Jung as trying to "liquidate" his basic doctrines—rather than keeping them safe—he struggled to produce his book of metapsychological essays to make his positions as solid as possible, before it was too late.

By March 1912, when they were working on their rival texts, Jung responded to Freud's criticism that he was not doing a good job administering the psychoanalytic movement when Freud depended on him to do so: ". . . can it be that you mistrust me? . . . Of course I have opinions which are not yours about the ultimate truths of psychoanalysis—though even this is not certain. . . ." And, in a manner reminiscent of Jung's challenge to his father to "give me this belief," he went on: "I am ready at any time to adapt my opinions to the judgment of someone who knows better, and always have been. I would never have sided with you in the first place had not heresy run in my blood" (3 March 1912, in McGuire, 1974, p. 491).

After the fainting spell in Munich, Freud wrote to Jung on November 29, 1912 that such an occurrence was "a bit of neurosis that I ought really to look into." Jung's reply suggests that he sensed Freud might be entertaining a wish to die, but also that this wish was at the heart of his fear that Jung wished to murder him. Jung responded: "My very best thanks for one passage in your letter where you speak of a 'bit of neurosis' you haven't got rid of. This 'bit' should, in my opinion, be taken very seriously indeed because, as experience shows, it leads 'to the semblance of a voluntary death' [in Latin in the original]. I have suffered from this bit in my dealings with you. . ." (3 December 1912, in McGuire, 1974, pp. 524, 525).

On December 18, 1912, Jung made it clear that he no longer could play the role of "son" for Freud: "You go around sniffing out all the symptomatic actions in your vicinity, thus reducing everyone to the level of sons and daughters who blushingly admit the existence of their faults. Meanwhile you remain on top as the father, sitting pretty. . . . If ever you should rid yourself entirely of your complexes and stop playing the father to your sons . . . then I will mend my ways and at one stroke uproot the vice of being in two minds about you." Freud responded on January 3, 1913: "It is a convention among us analysts that none of us need feel ashamed of his own bit of neurosis. But one who while behaving abnormally keeps shouting that he is normal gives ground for the suspicion that he lacks insight into his illness. Accordingly, I propose that we abandon our personal relations entirely" (in McGuire, 1974, pp. 535, 539).

On April 11, 1913, Jung wrote to Sabina Spielrein expressing his feelings about his lost relationship to Freud: "He wants to give me love, while I want understanding. I want to be a friend on an equal footing, while he wants to have me as a son. For that reason he ascribes to a complex everything I do that does not fit the framework of his life" (in Carotenuto, 1982, p. 184). Thus Jung, who entered the relationship with Freud pleading to be accepted as a son, left the relationship demanding to be treated as an equal.

Freud felt betrayed by his wayward Joshua; instead of being a proper spiritual son who would honor and defend the work of his father, Jung wished, in Freud's eyes, to push the father aside so he could violate Freud's work in furtherance of his own ambitions. In May 1914, Freud sent a draft of "On the History of the Psychoanalytic Movement" to Jones. Jones objected to one phrase which apparently Freud later deleted: "this characteristic in Jung—his inclination ruthlessly to push aside someone who stands in his way" (Jones to Freud, 18 May 1914, in Brome, 1983, p. 107).

Psychoanalysis as "Woman"

Another analogy between Freud as a group leader and the mythical primal father of his imagination will shed further light on his inner needs and the tensions in the psychoanalytic movement that led to the writing of the 1915 metapsychological essays. If the primal father enjoyed exclusive possession of the females in his group, then Freud jealously guarded his theory from violation by his male disciples as if that theory were his woman (Ostow, 1977, p. 170; Mahony, 1982, p. 214). Even before writing *Totem and Taboo*, Freud gave evidence that he regarded psychoanalysis not only as his child, his creation, but also as something feminine. We can see this in a letter to Jung written on February 2, 1910. Preparing for the Nuremberg Congress Freud told Jung: "For the Congress I now have the following: you on the development of psychoanalysis . . . me on the prospects for psychoanalysis, a happy combination since you represent the lady's future and I her past" (in McGuire, 1974, p. 292).

We see the image of his theory as feminine in other correspondence of Freud's. After he had decided that Adler had become a liability to the movement, he wrote to Pfister on February 26, 1911 of the changes he was orchestrating in the Vienna Psychoanalytic Society: "Wednesday I am letting myself be elected president . . . Adler's theories were departing too far from the right path, and it was time to make a stand against them . . . and I am in the process of carrying out on him the revenge of the offended goddess Libido" (in Meng and E. Freud, 1963, p. 48). On March 3, 1911, he told Jung: "Since the day before yesterday, I have been chairman of the Vienna group. It had become impossible to go on with Adler . . . I now feel that I must avenge the offended goddess Libido, and I mean to be more careful from now on that heresy does not occupy too much space in the *Zentralblatt* (in McGuire, 1974, pp. 399–400).

In addition to defending his theory as woman, Freud was involved in real conflicts with Adler and Jung over the "possession" of certain female followers: Andreas-Salomé and Spielrein. In 1912 Andreas-Salomé informed Freud that, as well as attending meetings of his Vienna Psychoanalytic Society, she was going to attend the meetings of the new group that had formed around the defector Adler. Freud responded as follows: "Since you have informed me of your plan to attend Adler's evening group, I am taking the liberty, unasked, to say a few words to you by way of orientation in this disagreeable state of affairs. . . . We have been forced to stop all intercourse between Adler's splinter group and our own association, and our medical guests are also requested to choose which of the two they will visit. . . . It is not my purpose, my dear lady, to enforce such limitations in your case. I only request of you that with due regard for the situation you make use of an artificial psychic split, so to speak, and make no mention there of your role here and vice versa" (4 November 1912, in Andreas-Salomé, 1964, pp. 40–41). In 1917, three years after he had altered his metapsychology by revising the instinct theory in "On Narcissism," Freud wrote to Andreas-Salomé with reference to his concept of narcissistic libido: "Without this, I feel, you too might have slipped away from me to the system-builders, to Jung or even more to Adler" (13 July 1917, Pfeiffer, 1972, p. 61).

Spielrein became a member of the Vienna Psychoanalytic Society in 1912, and Freud knew that she and Jung had been intimate for several years (Carotenuto, 1982, pp. 41, 91–121). Jung resigned as president of the International Psychoanalytic Society on May 20, 1914, and about that time, possibly shortly before, Spielrein wrote to Freud: "Everyone knows that I declare myself an adherent to the Freudian Society, and J. cannot forgive me for this. Nothing to be done!" Freud replied on June 12, 1914: "There will be a warm welcome for you if you stay with us here, but then you will have to recognize the enemy over there" (in Carotenuto, 1982, pp. 112, 123, 226n). Now Freud had her!

We can see a precedent for Freud's rivalry with his disciples over women in his earlier relationship to his mentor Breuer, with whom he had also developed theoretical differences. This is revealed in his "Irma" dream of 1895. When Abraham asked him on 8 January 1908 whether certain symbols in the dream pointed to a syphilitic infection in the patient, Freud responded the following day: "Syphilis is *not* the subject-matter of the examples you refer to. Sexual megalomania is hidden behind it, the three women, Mathilde, Sophie and Anna, are my daughters' three god-mothers, and I have them all" (in H. Abraham and E. Freud, 1965, pp. 18, 20). Freud named his three daughters Mathilde, Sophie, and Anna, and in this way came imaginatively to "possess" three women who represented the "property" of Breuer, namely, Breuer's wife Mathilde, and Breuer's patients, Sophie Paneth and Anna Lichtheim, the latter also being a sister of Breuer's son-in-law (Swales, 1983, pp. 24n–25n). The "Irma" dream occurred when Freud was angry at Breuer's unwillingness to accept his claim that all neuroses were sexual in origin. Freud had also been a recipient of monetary assistance from

Breuer, and he had been financially in debt to the husband of Sophie and the father of Anna (Hartman, 1983, pp. 569–580).[2] Thus, we see Freud's longstanding tendency imaginatively to turn his rela-tionships to men into battles over the "possession" of women.[3]

In Freud's mind psychoanalysis was his woman; therefore, only he had the right to fertilize her. His disciplines could admire her and bring her gifts, but she belonged to Freud. Any attempts by fol-lowers to suggest alternative or contrary theoretical formulations were viewed by him as attempts to take his place as the only rightful fertilizer of psychoanalysis: His disciples could extend and apply his theory, but they should not try to impregnate the lady. Freud would regard offspring produced by the fertilization of psychoanalysis by disciples as illegitimate children. He felt called upon to defend his lady from the assults made on her by ambitious disciples; he had to keep her *pure* and avenge her against those who sought to dishonor her. Such motives were among the determinants of his struggle to produce a book of metapsychological essays in 1915.

Such thinking on Freud's part was probably intensified by his awareness of certain features of the relationship between Spielrein and Jung. Spielrein fantasized about bearing Jung a child she would name Siegfried (Carotenuto, 1982, pp. 13, 21, 48, 77). This child would bridge the gap between her being Jewish and Jung's being Aryan. Spielrein told Freud on June 20, 1909 that "it was Wagner who planted the demon in my soul. . ." (in Carotenuto, 1982, p. 107). The allusion to Wagner is to the point that Siegfried was the son of Sigmund, an allusion that neither Freud nor Jung could have missed. Thus, as well as bringing together a Jew and an Aryan, Siegfried would be a symbol of the union of Freud and Jung: Freud would be the spiritual father, Jung the biological father. Thus, Freud and Jung would come together in Spielrein, an idea that could arouse latent homosexual feelings and anxiety. Siegfried could also represent a union of Freud's and Jung's thoughts, an illegitimate child for both of them.

On August 28, 1913, after Freud had learned that Spielrein had married and become pregnant he wrote her: "I can hardly bare to listen when you continue to enthuse about your old love and past dreams, and count on an ally in the marvelous little stranger. I am, as you know, cured of the last shred of my predilection for the Aryan cause, and would like to take it that if the child turns out to be a boy he will develop into a stalwart Zionist. . . . We are and remain Jews. The others will only exploit us and will never understand or appreciate us" (in Carotenuto, 1982, pp. 120–121).

For the Sake of a Cause

Just before writing his 1914 essays "On Narcissism" and "On the History of the Psychoanalytic Movement" in which he would challenge Adler and Jung directly, Freud composed "The Moses of Michelangelo." The essay was written during the last week of 1913 and finished on New Years Day 1914 (Jones, 1955, p. 366). In it Freud strengthened his identification with Moses, this time the Moses betrayed by followers who had abandoned the God he had shown them and returned to worshipping idols. The situation paralleled Freud's in relation to the dissension within his movement, highlighted by Adler's defection, and exacerbated by Jung's "betrayal" of the cause. Both Freud and Moses had to struggle to control the rage they felt toward those who had shown themselves to be unworthy of the gifts their leaders had bestowed on them (Jones, 1955, pp. 366–367).

We can get a good sense of how Freud felt at the start of 1914 by observing the feelings he attributed to Michelangelo's Moses. The statue shows Moses holding the stone tablets containing the Ten Commandments while he watches his followers worshipping the idol they constructed while he was away receiving God's laws for them. According to Freud (1914a):

> What we see before us is not the inception of a violent action but the remains of a movement that has already taken place. In his first transport of fury, Moses desired to act, to spring up and take vengeance and forget the Tables; but he has overcome the temptation, and he will now remain seated and still, in his frozen wrath and in his pain mingled with contempt [p. 229].

Moses does not smash the tablets. According to Freud, Michelangelo

> does not let Moses break them in his wrath, but makes him be influenced by the danger that they will be broken and makes him calm that wrath, or at any rate prevent it from becoming an act . . . the giant frame with its tremendous physical power becomes only a

concrete expression of the highest mental achievement that is possible in a man, that of struggling successfully against an inward passion for the sake of a cause to which he has devoted himself [p. 229].

Like Moses, Freud had to control the rage he felt toward Adler and Jung. He could not deny the rage, but he could channel it constructively in defense of his cause. Rather than abandon psychoanalysis and leave the field in the hands of Adler and Jung, Freud would write two works that differentiated his viewpoint from theirs and demonstrated the superiority of the views of the master over those of his wayward disciples. His narcissism and history papers accomplished that mission for the short run. Before he died, however, Freud felt the need to codify all of his psychoanalytic doctrines in a final, definitive synthetic statement. As the Jews had their Ten Commandments and their Torah, so the psychoanalytic movement would have its Book of Metapsychology, consisting of the twelve essays Freud would write in 1915.[4]

Libido: "The Offended Goddess"

In the first three months of 1914 Freud constructively channelled his anger at Adler and Jung into the writing of the theoretical essay "On Narcissism" (1914b) (Jones, 1955, p. 362). In the essay "the offended goddess Libido" was defended against the doctrines of Adler and Jung, both of whom had rejected Freud's emphasis on sexual motivations—Adler by stressing his concept of "masculine protest," Jung by professing a nonsexual libido. If Adler was developing a psychology of the ego without a sexual organic foundation, and if Jung rejected childhood sexuality, the sexual nature of the Oedipus complex, and the sexual etiology of schizophrenia or the psychoneuroses, then Freud would emphasize sexual libido even more by arguing that sexual functions and self-preservative ego functions could be traced back to a common source of energy.

Challenging Jung's account of schizophrenia, Freud argued that in the early stages of development the same energy powered the sexual and ego drives (p. 76). Furthermore: "We are bound to suppose that a unity comparable to the ego cannot exist in the individual from the start; the ego has to be developed. The autoerotic instincts, however, are there from the very first" (pp. 76–77).

In children we find an original direction of libido toward the self or ego, from which some is later directed outward toward objects, but which fundamentally persists (p. 75). There is a relatively fixed quantity of libido available to the individual at any particular moment, so the more libido the individual directs toward objects, the less is invested in his own ego, and vice versa (p. 76). "Narcissistic libido" and "object libido" are thus inversely related. A phase of self-love in which one is self-absorbed and overestimates the importance of the self may be a normal feature of human development (p. 75). Contrary to Jung, then, schizophrenia has a libidinous base in that the schizophrenic has returned to an earlier state by directing toward his own ego the libido he has withdrawn from the external world (pp. 74–75).

If there is no unity "comparable to the ego" in the individual from the start, and if the development of the ego proceeds from "a differentiation of libido into a kind which is proper to the ego and one which is attached to objects" (p. 77), then Freud had a basis for arguing that Adler's "masculine protest" must be traceable to the threat of castration, which injured the child's original sense of narcissistic well-being: "Psychoanalytic research has from the very beginning recognized the existence and importance of the 'masculine protest', but it has regarded it, in opposition to Adler, as narcissistic in nature and derived from the castration complex" (p. 92). In addition, if the history of the development of the individual is inseparable from the dynamics of narcissism and libidinal conflict, then Freud's conception of narcissism located the conflict within the person, and ultimately within the ego itself, whereas Freud saw Adler's concept of "masculine protest" as locating the conflict between the ego and the other, and therefore as presupposing the originally constituted, unified ego he challenged (Weber, 1982, p. 17).

Freud had defended the "offended goddess," but in that defense he had weakened his long-professed instinct theory which had assumed qualitatively different energies at the roots of sexual and ego drives. Now it appeared there was only one group of drives, all energized by libido. While the narcissism essay provided a constructive outlet for Freud's rage at Adler and Jung, and while it separated his viewpoint from theirs, his conception of psychic conflict still required a mental structure that was attuned to reality and that could oppose the sexual drive by means of its own source of energy. Perhaps this theoretical fuzziness was on Freud's mind when on April 6, 1914 he wrote to Abraham: "Your acceptance of my 'Narcissism' affected me deeply and binds us still more closely together. I have a strong feeling of its serious inadequacy" (in H. Abraham and E. Freud, 1965, pp. 170–171). Freud had written "On Narcissism" more because of the pressure of "someone else's ideas" than because of the pressure of facts. Had he not had to respond to Adler and Jung, he might not have revised his instinct theory in 1914 in a manner that did not satisfy him.

"A Good Clobbering"

Almost simultaneously with the writing of "On Narcissism," Freud composed the avowedly polemical essay "On the History of the Psychoanalytic Movement" (1914c) (Jones, 1955, p. 362). In the first paragraph Freud declared his patriarchal right to define what legitimately constituted psychoanalysis: "Psychoanalysis is my creation!" he exclaimed (p. 7). The third section of the work contained a lengthy attack on the dissenting views of Adler and Jung (pp. 48–66).

Even though Freud had broken off personal relations with Jung when he began writing the "History," his wayward disciple was still president of the International Psychoanalytic Association. Freud wrote to Andreas-Salomé on January 12, 1914: "I am busy writing contributions to the history of the psychoanalytical movement for our *Jahrbuch* and expect that this statement of mine will put an end to all compromises and bring about the desired rupture" (in Pfeiffer, 1972, p. 16). On that same day Freud told Ferenczi that he was "fuming with rage" while writing the "History" (Jones, 1955, p. 304). Thus, one of Freud's intentions in writing the essay was to force Jung to resign from the post into which Freud had pushed him in 1910. Although for some months he had been waiting reluctantly for Jung to leave on his own accord, Freud now was ready to give him a push. In April 1914, before the "History" appeared, Jung resigned his position as president (McGuire, 1974, p. 551).

Although he no longer was president, Jung and some Zurich followers were still members of the International Psychoanalytic

Association. Thus, after the publication of the "History" in June 1914, Freud wrote to Abraham: "So the bombshell has now burst, we shall soon discover with what effect. . . . I am not sure they will respond to the blandishments bestowed upon them by resigning" (25 June 1914, in H. Abraham and E. Freud, 1965, p. 181). Four days later, in discussing the "History" with Andreas-Salomé, Freud told her that in it he "intentionally gave everyone a good clobbering" (in Pfeiffer, 1972, p. 17).

In August 1914, just before the outbreak of World War I, Jung announced his withdrawal from the International Association, and Freud learned that the Zurich contingent probably would not come to the next Congress (Jones, 1955, p. 150; H. Abraham and E. Freud, 1965, p. 185). Freud responded to the news by telling Abraham: "So we are at last rid of them, the brutal, sanctimonious Jung and his disciples" (26 July 1914 in H. Abraham and E. Freud, 1965, p. 186).

Thus, by August 1914 the "Narcissism" and "History" essays had accomplished their purpose. Freud had defended his libido theory, albeit with works he regarded as seriously inadequate. He had given his enemies a "good clobbering" and eliminated the Zurich dissenters from the ranks of the International Association. Even with his secret committee in place, however, all was not in order, inasmuch as Freud believed his life would end in February 1918. The "serious inadequacy" of the "Narcissism" essay rendered it unworthy of being his last theoretical statement. It could only be a prolegomenon to a more definitive statement, one fit to be a theoretical last will and testament that would stand against Adler and Jung, and that future generations would revere. Therefore, on November 25, 1914, Freud revealed to Andreas-Salomé: "I am working in private at certain matters which are wide in scope and also perhaps rich in content. After two months of inability to work my interest seems liberated again, and I feel very clearly that my mind has had a thorough rest" (in Pfeiffer, 1972, p. 21). Thus, even though he now felt somewhat depressed by the outbreak of the war in August, and even though worn out by his institutional war with Jung, which had ended in the same month, by late November Freud had summoned up enough energy to struggle once more with metapsychology—this time to ensure his ultimate triumph, and his rightful place in the history of science.

WRITING THE METAPSYCHOLOGY SERIES

A review of the antecedents of the metapsychology project has revealed that, by the end of 1914, a convergence of professional and personal anxieties impelled Freud to plan the series of essays that would constitute his summary statement. The professional anxieties were the residue of his failed collaborations with Adler and Jung; they embodied his concern lest those ambitious wayward disciples appropriate the "psychoanalytic" appellation that should be applied only to that which was truly Freud's creation. The personal anxieties centered around his belief, possibly dating from his involvement with Fliess and his bio-rhythm numerology, that he would die early in the predicted year 1918, compounded by the increasing hardships in living brought about by World War I. Out of the confluence of the political requirements of the psychoanalytic movement, Freud's idiosyncrasies, and his personal belief that his days were numbered came the resolve to formulate summary statements on a number of metapsychological issues.

"Extraordinary Discipline"

On April 23, 1915, when he was deeply involved in the writing of his metapsychological essays, Freud characterized his creative outbursts as anal explosive activity. He wrote to Ferenczi: "My productivity probably has to do with the enormous improvement in the activity of my bowels. I will leave it open whether I owe this to a mechanical factor, the hardness of the present-day bread, or to a psychical one, the changed relationship to money that is forced on us. At all events the war has already meant a loss to me of 40,000 Kronen [$8,104.00]" (Jones, 1955, p. 183). The war had reduced the flow of patients, leaving Freud more time than he might have had otherwise for writing; his diminished income and the personal and familial hardships brought on by the war had left him morose and in need of a creative distraction from daily cares. These factors added impetus to his channelling of energies into the writing of the metapsychology papers, but the initial motivations for his book of essays, as outlined above, had developed independently of the outbreak of the war and its sequelae, and would have driven him in that direction even if the war had not occurred.

The driven quality of Freud's productivity may be appreciated in light of the remarkable fact that it took him only three weeks to write "Instincts and Their Vicissitudes" (1915a) and "Repression" (1915b), and only another two weeks to write "The Unconscious" (1915c) (Jones, 1955, p. 185). These essays required intense mental concentration, discipline, and complexity of thought. Holt (1982) has observed: "I calculated that it would take me a full week merely to *copy* these three papers in longhand—the way Freud always wrote—writing as many hours a day as I could stand" (p. 9).

Even though Freud wrote the metapsychological essays driven by the demons discussed above, his creative outpouring did not burst spontaneously forth. Going against his intuitive grain, Freud forced himself in an extraordinary display of self-discipline to do what he had to do, for his cause and for history. On December 11, 1914, as he struggled with metapsychology, he told Abraham: "After some good results, my own work has plunged into deep darkness; I go on because one cannot remain without 'something to do' . . . but often without enthusiasm and with only slight expectation of solving the very difficult problems. My way of working used to be different; I used to wait for an idea to come to me. Now I go out to meet it, and I do not know whether I find it any more quickly because of that" (in H. Abraham and E. Freud, 1965, pp. 204–205).

As we have seen from the correspondence quoted above, and according to Jones (1955, p. 185), Freud actually started to write the metapsychology papers on March 15, 1915, and had completed twelve essays by early August. A comment Freud made to Jung on December 17, 1911, while he was struggling with *Totem and Taboo,* seems appropriately to characterize his feeling as he wrestled so productively with metapsychology in 1915: "I can see from the difficulties I encounter in this work that I was not cut out for inductive investigation, that my whole make-up is intuitive, and that in setting out to establish the purely empirical science of psy-choanalysis I subjected myself to an extraordinary discipline" (in McGuire, 1974, p. 472).

Why Metapsychology?

Before we consider the product of Freud's 1915 burst of creativity, let us consider the importance of metapsychology for him, above and beyond his battles with Adler and Jung. Freud

(1917a) stated in a footnote to one of the published metapsychology papers, "A Metapsychological Supplement to the Theory of Dreams": "This paper and the following one are derived from a collection which I originally intended to publish in book form under the title 'Preliminaries to a Metapsychology' . . . The intention of the series is to clarify and carry deeper the theoretical assumptions on which a psychoanalytic system could be founded" (p. 222n). Freud had long been concerned that psychoanalysis be recognized as a science, and in his own mind a theory of mental life had to meet certain criteria before he could be satisfied that the approach was scientific. In his metapsychological writings, Freud tried to build a foundation for all of psychoanalysis that was properly scientific by his own standards. According to Freud's criteria, Adler's and Jung's systems failed to be adequate sciences of mental life.

It is important to note that from as early as 1886 Freud worked with certain basic assumptions in this area (Silverstein, 1985). For Freud, the mental and the physical were distinctly different phe-nomena, and each had to be studied by methods appropriate to the nature of the phenomenon under investigation: Physical phenomena should be studied by the methods of physical science, mental phe-nomena by introspective methods. Even though he did not know how it occurred, Freud believed that mind and body interacted. Therefore, mental life had an organic foundation in bodily pro-cesses, and a properly scientific theory of psychic functioning had to start by specifying that organic foundation. By 1895, Freud had come to believe that sexuality—the body's production of sexual substances and their impact on the nervous system—was the fore-most organic foundation for psychic functioning. That functioning was conceived as beginning when bodily needs—particularly those created by organic sexual process—became represented in the men-tal realm on a symbolic level. Thus Freud could insist to Jung on April 19, 1908: "In the sexual processes we have the indispensable 'organic foundation' without which a medical man can only feel ill at ease in the life of the psyche" (in McGuire, 1974, pp. 140–141).

From Freud's point of view, an appreciation of the sexual organic basis of mental life was a criterion for a full scientific understanding of psychic conflict, the unconscious, repression, and the psycho-neuroses. Adler's and Jung's failure to accept Freud's "indispensable 'organic foundation,'" and their assertion of alternative organic foundations—Adler's organ inferiority, oversensitivity, and compensatory strivings, and Jung's nonsexual libido and phylogenetic archetypes—made their positions inadequate bases for a science of mental life, in Freud's view.

In struggling with metapsychology in 1915, Freud was attempt' ing, before it was too late, to clarify and integrate his understanding of the scientific foundation for a theory of mental life. He believed that his creation, psychoanalysis, was the only psychological system that accurately portrayed the depths of psychic functioning, and that fully recognized its primary organic foundation in sexuality. Only Freud could spell out this truth in detail, and he would leave it as his legacy to a nonunderstanding world.

PUBLISHING THE METAPSYCHOLOGY SERIES

Did Freud Really Intend to Publish?

Freud wrote the essays as a kind of theoretical will and testa' ment: He was driven to set down on paper before he left the world early in 1918 the basic principles that could serve as the foundation for a scientific psychoanalytic system. But after drafting the essays in a fever pitch in 1915—and believing that he still had through 1917 before he was embraced by the "silent Goddess of Death"— Freud cooled down and became increasingly disenchanted with the final product, particularly with those essays about which he had had serious reservations even when he first wrote them. The three papers Freud decided to publish quickly, on instincts, repression, and the unconscious, were those which he believed presented the most essential elements of the foundation for a system properly called "psychoanalysis" and which clearly set his views apart from those of Adler and Jung.

Freud's declaration that he would publish all of the essays in book form after the war probably was a true expression of his inten' tions when he first said it. When Freud told Abraham on May 4, 1915, "If the war lasts long enough, I hope to get together about a dozen such papers and in quieter times to offer them to a nonunder' standing world under the title of 'Introductory Papers on Meta' psychology'" (in H. Abraham and E. Freud, 1965, p. 221), he was indicating two things: that he was using the extra time he had because of the war to write the book and that he did not believe the war would last very long. In May 1915, then, Freud saw wartime as conducive to writing the book, peacetime as conducive to publishing it. By August 1915, however, when he finished the essays, the end of the war was not yet in sight. Since that was necessary for his work to receive the attention and international recognition it deserved, the time was not yet ripe to publish the book. He could publish immediately those essays most necessary to combat Adler's and Jung's misappropriation of the "psychoanalytic" appellation, and then take some time to review and revise the rest before making a final commitment.

The continuation of the war through the summer of 1915 negatively affected Freud's attitude toward the collection of metapsychological essays he was writing, as can be seen from his statement to Abraham at the time he completed the series, August 1, 1915: "Since I have been here I have finished my twelve papers, they are war-time atrocities, like a lot of other things. Several, including that on consciousness, still require thorough revision" (in H. Abraham and E. Freud, 1965, p. 228). On November 9, 1915, Freud told Andreas-Salomé that all these works suffered "from the lack of good cheer" in which he wrote them, and "from their function as a kind of sedative" (in Pfeiffer, 1972, p. 35). When Freud described the collection of metapsychology essays as "war-time atrocities," it may not only have been because they were written during the war; it may also have been because they were the product of warfare within the psychoanalytic movement. And if the essays were written with a "lack of good cheer," it was not only because war-time conditions had made living hard, but also because Freud was compelled to write them in a personal race with death. Finally, just as father Freud lived in fear for the fate of his creation, so he lived in fear for the fate of his sons in the army: In the letter in which he called his essays "war-time atrocities," Freud also told Abraham that his son Ernst should have left for Galicia the day before, and his son Martin had been through some severe fighting, with a bullet grazing his right arm and another going through his cap.

The war continued into 1917, Freud's predicted final year. On November 11, 1917, Freud told Abraham that he occasionally felt doubtful whether he would live to see the end of the war. "At any rate," Freud continued, "I behave as if we were faced with the end of all things, and in the last few days, I have got ready for publication in the *Zeitschrift* two papers of the 'metapsychological' series ('Supplements to the Theory of Dreams,' 'Mourning and Melancholia'). I originally intended to use these and other papers, with some that have already appeared . . . for a book. But this is not the time for it" (in H. Abraham and E. Freud, 1965, p. 261). In 1917 Freud appeared genuinely doubtful that he would live much longer.[5] He also feared that publication of psychoanalytic journals might stop because of the continuing war. Given these concerns, he selected two more essays in which he had some confidence, and which would help him advance in the war against Adler and Jung, and published them in his psychoanalytic journal while it still was possible to do so.

Freud claimed that it was not the time to publish all of the essays in book form for several reasons. First, he probably still was unhappy with the content of the remaining unpublished essays, having not yet solved the theoretical problems he confronted in those essays to his own satisfaction. Second, the war was still on and wartime conditions would prevent his book from receiving the type of reception for which he hoped. Third, Freud's less technical *Introductory Lectures on Psycho-Analysis* were being published in 1916 and 1917, so that there would exist some kind of comprehensive statement of that which constituted "psychoanalysis" if he now died, even if some theoretical inconsistencies had not yet been remedied and some obscure points not yet clarified.

There is still another reason why Freud may have held back publication of the essays in book form in 1917. Since the book constituted a theoretical last will and testament, not publishing it might have served as a counterphobic device, such that if it did not appear, perhaps he would not have had to die as predicted. Since he did not publish it in 1917, and was still living in 1918, why press his luck and publish it in 1919, when the war was over? If Freud could believe in numerological death predictions, then perhaps he could also believe, on an emotional level, that not publishing the book helped keep him alive.

As more time went by since the first drafting of the essays, and as he survived both February 1918 and the war, Freud had an opportunity to reflect on the inadequacy of some of the already published essays, as well as the unpublished ones. With an apparent new lease on life, he could produce new theoretical works that would correct the problems he had found in his old publications.

Why Publish the First Five Essays?

As is well known, Freud first published his theory of mental functioning in Chapter Seven of *The Interpretation of Dreams* (1900). In the five metapsychological essays published in 1915 and 1917, he tried to expand upon and correlate systematically several theorems scattered over that chapter related to the dynamic, topographic, and economic points of view. In fact, in "The Unconscious" (1915c), Freud stated: "I propose that when we have succeeded in describing a psychical process in its dynamic, topographical and economic aspects, we should speak of it as a *metapsychological* presentation" (p. 181).

It is not possible here to provide a comprehensive survey of the *specific* theoretical statements and advances found in the five published essays. Let us focus instead on certain features of the essays insofar as they provide clues as to Freud's motivation for publishing them, and their function in relation to their antecedents.

"Instincts and Their Vicissitudes" (1915a) served to continue Freud's defense of the "goddess Libido" begun in "On Narcissism." In it he made explicit the distinctly Freudian (as opposed to Adlerian or Jungian) conception of the function of the mind. For Freud, the mental apparatus served a biological purpose: the mastering of stimuli. The stimuli which most required mastering were those which emanated continually from the interior of the body— related to the special chemistry of the sexual function. The aim of mental functioning was to diminish the amount of excitation to which the organism was subjected (pp. 120–121, 124–125).

Freud then argued that a dualistic theory of the instincts was provisionally justified, and reiterated his old point of view that the opposing forces could be conceptualized as ego or self-preservative instincts and sexual instincts (p. 124). All the same, he was apparently not very satisfied with this classification because he had not cleared up the muddle created by the "Narcissism" essay: Were both the sexual instincts and the opposed ego instincts libidinal in origin, or were there ego instincts other than libidinal ones, and if so, what was their nature?

The issue of aggression—which had played a prominent part in Adler's psychology—bedeviled Freud when he wrote and then pondered his metapsychological essays. This was so for several reasons: He needed to respond to Adler's theoretical challenge; the destruc tiveness of the war had forced him to give greater acknowledgment to human aggression; and he suffered considerable guilt and conflict over his own aggressive propensities—from his infantile death wishes toward a younger brother through his adult death wishes toward a whole host of succeeding "revenants" (Schur, 1972, pp. 153–198, 225–272; Stepansky, 1977, pp. 159–164). Freud saw Adler as proposing a special "aggressive instinct," as opposed to his own view that all instincts were a priori "aggressive in pursuing their ends" (Stepansky, 1983, p. 187). Thus, if Freud stressed in his "Instincts" essay that all instincts were characterized by pressure—"the amount of force or the measure of the demand for work which it represents" (p. 122), then it seemed pointless to isolate one conceptually self-contained aggressive instinct, as Freud believed Adler had done.

In pursuing his study of the instincts related to the vicissitudes of libido, Freud offered an analysis of the transformation of love into hate (p. 133). He did so to offer an example of how the "content" of an instinct might be changed into its opposite. Now Freud spoke of an aggressive, hating ego that was not simply the concomitant of childish egoism: "Hating, too, originally characterized the relation of the ego to the alien external world" (p. 136) in response to unpleasurable stimuli. Hate "always remains in an intimate relation with the self-preservative instincts" (p. 139), as an expression of the pain reaction instigated by objects. Here we see Freud for the first time tentatively approaching the equation of aggression with health (Stepansky, 1977, p. 149). He now allowed for some innate aggressiveness in a manner consistent with his libido theory, and in contradistinction to his understanding of Adler's nonlibidinal position.

Freud published the "Instincts" essay quickly because it continued the defense of the "goddess Libido" initiated in the "Narcissism" essay, and because it strategically opened up a place for aggression (as a normal factor) in the psychoanalytic world view. He strengthened the role of aggression in his theory when, in 1917, after living through two more years of war, he finally published "Mourning and Melancholia" (1917b). In this essay, probably somewhat revised since first drafted in 1915, Freud sought to demonstrate the clinical usefulness of his narcissism concept for the analysis of a psychotic condition—pathological depression. He further emphasized an aggressive componenet of the ego instincts. Just as the ego originally "hated" an environment that aroused tension, now Freud argued that even in the context of pathological depression, aggression might be seen as a higher, ego-syntonic function that could be therapeutic for a person suffering from the loss of a highly libidinally cathected object (p. 257; Stepansky, 1977, pp. 150–153). Thus, while coping with anger over personal losses of disciples, patients, and income, Freud used the "Instincts" and "Mourning" essays as platforms on which he obliquely confronted "hate" and justified it as a purposeful, ego-syntonic necessity, and as a manifestation of a potential for "healthy" aggression.

The second essay published in 1915, "Repression" (1915b), began where the "Instincts" paper left off. Freud started by pointing out that one of the vicissitudes an instinctual impulse may undergo is to meet with resistances that seek to make it inoperative (p. 146). Without referring to Adler or Jung, Freud used this paper to advance his unique view of the dynamics of mental life. The Freudian view started from the premise that psychic functioning inevitably was based on conflict. Freud wanted it understood that the truly psychoanalytic view of the conflict inherent in mental life did not start with the struggle to be on top (Adler), or the struggle to individuate (Jung); rather, the conflict at the heart of mental life was the struggle to deny the psychic representative of the sexual instinct entrance into consciousness, when the resulting unpleasure would outweigh the possibility of pleasure (pp. 147, 151–153). In this essay, Freud tried to correlate the dynamics of psychic conflict with economic considerations—force and counterforce—and with topographic and developmental considerations concerning the cleavage that develops between conscious and unconscious mental activity. These correlated considerations were the bedrock of any system properly called "psychoanalysis," which appellation should not be applied to any system not built upon such a foundation. Freud argued that these metapsychological theorems were necessary for an understanding of mental life in general, and of the psychoneuroses in particular (pp. 152–158).

The third metapsychological essay published in 1915, "The Unconscious" (1915c), was the longest of the series and Freud's favorite. In it he expanded on the topographic point of view introduced in 1900, and correlated more specifically than he had before the dynamic and economic aspects of repression with topographic considerations. Again, without mentioning Adler, who he felt had overlooked the depths of the psyche while focusing on surface (ego) phenomena, and Jung, who he felt had failed to appreciate the true organic base of the unconscious, Freud stressed the view he wanted associated with the psychoanalytic label: "The nucleus of the Ucs. consists of instinctual representatives which seek to discharge their cathexis; that is to say, it consists of wishful impulses" (p. 186). He also described the different qualities he attributed to psychic functioning according to whether the functioning was truly unconscious, or merely preconscious (pp. 186–189).

The final published essay, "A Metapsychological Supplement to the Theory of Dreams" (1917a), correlated the dream theory introduced in 1900 with the dynamic, topographic, and economic points of view to a greater extent than had been done before. As the title implied, it supplemented the earlier presentation by demonstrating the power of Freud's metapsychological theorems to illuminate normal, as well as pathological, psychic functioning.

Why Not Publish the Rest?

We can never know for certain why Freud decided not to publish any of the remaining essays of the metapsychology series. Based on their titles, however, we can offer an educated guess concerning some of them. Several of the essays forced Freud to wrestle with the enigma of consciousness and the problem of mind–body interaction, issues that had perplexed him throughout his career. He probably pursued some ideas related to the mind–body dilemma as far as he could in trying to clarify obscure theoretical issues, but found no solution that satisfied him. This probably occurred in relation to the essays "Consciousness," "Anxiety," and "Conversion Hysteria."

We know that Freud was not happy with the consciousness essay from the start. When on August 1, 1915, he told Abraham that he had completed all twelve essays, and called them "war-time atrocities," he also told him: "Several, including that on consciousness, still require thorough revision." In "The Unconscious" (1915c), Freud repeatedly recognized the need to answer questions about the nature of consciousness and the mode of functioning of the system Cs., but always postponed the discussion for a later time, probably intending to deal with the issues in the unpublished "Consciousness" essay. Thus he postponed consideration of the higher system (p. 188), the preconditions for becoming conscious (p. 191), and the relations between the systems Cs. and Pcs. (pp. 192, 203). In "A Metapsychological Supplement to the Theory of Dreams" (1917a), he postponed consideration of the qualitative aspects of consciousness and the functioning of the system Cs. as a perceptual system (p. 232). He also admitted that he could not explain how the system Cs. performed the function of orienting the individual to the world by discriminating between what is internal and what is external: "We can say nothing more precise on this point, for we know too little as yet of the nature and mode of operation of the system Cs." (p. 233). Freud's failure to publish his "Consciousness" essay probably reflected his failure to resolve the problems associated with consciousness that he had reserved for that essay. His invocation of structural theory after the war eased his dilemma somewhat because, instead of stressing topographic distinctions between conscious and unconscious, he changed the language of discourse and emphasized the distinction between the controlling ego and the id.

A brief review of some of Freud's statements relating to the problems of consciousness and mind–body interaction suggest that he never worked out satisfactory explanations for them. As early as 1888, Freud was forced to grapple with consciousness and mind–body interaction in an article entitled *"Gehirn"* (The Brain). He distinguished between mechanical brain processes, which might be investigated empirically, and certain states of the conscious mind over and above these mechanical occurrences, not completely determined by them, but interactive with them. "Although the mechanical process is not understood," "Freud (1888) stated, "it is the actual presence of this coupling of material changes of conditions in the brain with changes in the state of the conscious mind which makes the brain a center of psychic activity. Although the essence of this coupling is incomprehensible to us, it is not haphazard, and on the basis of combinations of experiences of the outer senses on the one hand and introspection on the other we can determine something about the laws which govern this coupling" (p. 691).

In the 1895 *Project for a Scientific Psychology* Freud tried the gambit of considering consciousness as the subjective side of the functioning of only one of three hypothetical neuronal systems, the Omega (perceptual) system, but admitted: "No attempt, of course, can be made to explain how it is that excitatory processes in the perceptual neurones bring consciousness along with them" (p. 311). Five years later, in *The Interpretation of Dreams* (1900), when Freud introduced his topographic model of the mind, he took the position that "ideas, thoughts and psychical structures in general must never be regarded as localized in organic elements of the nervous system but rather, as one might say, *between* them, where resistances and facilitations provide the corresponding correlates" (p. 611). And, in his final metapsychological statement, "An Outline of Psycho-Analysis" (1940), Freud stated: "We know two kinds of things about what we call our psyche (or mental life): firstly, its bodily organ and scene of action, the brain (or nervous system) and, on the other hand, our acts of consciousness, which are immediate data and cannot be further explained by any sort of description. Everything that lies between is unknown to us, and the data do not include any direct relations between these two terminal points of our knowledge. If it existed, it would at the most afford an exact localization of the processes of consciousness and would give us no help toward understanding them" (pp. 144–145).

The unpublished essay "Conversion Hysteria" must have forced Freud to wrestle with the issue of possible modes of interaction between mind and body, since the concept of conversion implied the influence of mental processes on bodily functions through the direction of libido into somatic pathways. That concept also intruded on Freud's conflicted relationship to Adler, whose notion of organ inferiority imputed relationships between specific psychic events and specific organic defects. This nonlibidinal approach to the determination of psychic functioning and neurosis had been a thorn in Freud's side for many years (Nunberg and Federn, 1974, p. 146; Stepansky, 1983, pp. 51–54). Nevertheless, he was unable to come up with a satisfactory explanation for the mechanism by which a psychic process can produce a somatic effect. This can be seen in remarks he made before and after 1915. He wrote of "the leap from a mental process to a somantic innervation—hysterical conversion—which can never be fully comprehensible to us" (1909, p. 157), and of "the puzzling leap from the mental to the physical" (1916–1917, p. 258). Although he spoke in 1912 of "paths leading from the unconscious into the somatic" (Nunberg and Federn, 1975, p. 34), which affect the innervation of organs, he did not clarify in writing how it was possible to cross the boundary from psyche to soma.

The unpublished essay "Anxiety" found Freud at a theoretical impasse that was only surmounted through the invocation of structural theory after the war. Since 1896 he had held the view that anxiety essentially was a toxic state, related to the excitant action on the nervous system of an endogenously produced sexual chemical, which should be regulated through sexual intercourse (in Bonaparte, A. Freud, and Kris, 1954, pp. 159, 161). He assumed that anxiety was transformed or converted libido that had not been discharged properly; this assumption, however, begged the question of what process or mechanism transformed the libido into anxiety, a question he could not answer to his own satisfaction. He finally broke the theoretical impasse several years later when he weakened the close connection between libido and anxiety. With his structural theory, Freud (1926, pp. 160–163) made the ego the seat of anxiety, and the function of anxiety the signalling of danger.

Theoretical Aftermath

After the war Freud returned to his metapsychology, and particularly addressed himself to what he had come to regard as the shortcomings of the metapsychological essays he had published in haste in 1915. A number of statements from metapsychological works written in the few years following the end of the war illustrate how his thinking had evolved, such that by 1919 his 1915 essays had to be superseded by new works.

On April 4, 1919, when Freud told Andreas-Salomé that his metapsychology had "not yet been written," he also told her that he would "make further contributions to it. A first example of this will be found in an essay of mine entitled *Beyond the Pleasure Principle* . . ." (in Pfeiffer, 1972, p. 95). In that work Freud (1920) explicitly recognized the confusion he had caused in "On Narcissism," and which he had left unresolved in "Instincts and Their Vicissitudes," when he weakened his dualistic conception of instincts by assigning a libidinous origin to ego instincts. Now he offered a way out of the dilemma:

> If the self-preservative instincts too are of a libidinal nature, are there perhaps no other instincts whatever but the libidinal ones? At all events there are none other visible. But in that case we shall after all be driven to agree with the critics who suspected from the first that psycho-analysis explains *everything* by sexuality, or with innovators like Jung who, making a hasty judgement, have used the word 'libido' to mean instinctual forces in general . . . Our views have from

the very first been dualistic, and today they are even more definitely dualistic than before—now that we describe the opposition as being, not between ego instincts and sexual instincts but between life instincts and death instincts. Jung's libido theory is on the contrary *monistic;* the fact that he has called his one instinctual force 'libido' is bound to cause confusion, but need not affect us otherwise [pp. 52–53].

After the war, then, Freud revised his instinct theory to reestablish a distinct dualism. In so doing, he continued to defend the "goddess libido," particularly against Jung, while trying to salvage that dualism from his apparent reduction of all instincts to libido in his earlier defenses of 1914 and 1915. Moreover, the new concept of a death instinct allowed Freud to elevate aggression to the status of a driving force, and thus to respond to the continuing influence of Adler and the war. Freud could now explain a great deal of outwardly directed aggression—independent of sexual impulses and outside the realm of self-preservation—as a derivative of the death instinct, without having to hypothesize a conceptually self-contained, intrinsic aggressive instinct (see Stepansky, 1977).

Freud came to recognize that a weakness of his presentations in "Repression" and "The Unconscious" lay in certain limitations of the topographic approach, particularly in regard to repression: Since the repressing forces and the repressed content were both dynamically unconscious, some way of distinguishing between them seemed to be called for. His solution to the problem was his structural theory. According to Freud (1923):

> We have come upon something in the ego itself which is also unconscious, which behaves exactly like the repressed—that is, which produces powerful effects without itself being conscious and which requires special work before it can be made conscious . . . we land in endless obscurities and difficulties if we keep to our habitual forms of expression and try, for instance, to derive neuroses from a conflict between the conscious and the unconscious. We shall have to substitute for this antithesis another . . . the antithesis between the coherent ego and the repressed which is split off from it [p. 17].

The structural theory located the drives, whose representations suffered repression, in the id, and assigned the function of repression to the controlling structure, the ego. By 1919, when he was writing "Beyond the Pleasure Principle" (1920), Freud already realized that it had become necessary to "correct a shortcoming in our terminology. We shall avoid a lack of clarity if we make our contrast not between the conscious and the unconscious but between the coherent *ego* and the *repressed*" (p. 19).

Finally, in revising his view of the unconscious, and creating the concept of the superego, Freud was continuing the battle with Jung begun in *Totem and Taboo*. The superego was something in the unconscious that was not repressed, but also not part of the repressing ego. The superego represented an archaic, transpersonal inheritance, and contained the "higher" values of the personality. Unlike Jung's archetypes, however, Freud's superego was "the heir of the Oedipus complex," and thus it was also "the expression of the most powerful impulses and the most important libidinal vicissitudes of the id" (1923, p. 36).

> Psycho-analysis has been reproached time after time with ignoring the higher, moral, supra-personal side of human nature. The reproach is doubly unjust, both historically and methodologically. . . . So long as we had to concern ourselves with the study of what is repressed in mental life, there was no need for us to share in any agitated apprehensions as to the whereabouts of the higher side of man. But now that we have embarked upon the analysis of the ego we can give an answer to all those whose moral sense has been shocked and who have complained that there must surely be a higher nature in man: 'Very true', we can say, 'and here we have that higher nature, in this ego ideal or super-ego, the representative of our relations to our parents. When we were little children we knew these higher natures, we admired them and feared them; and took them into ourselves' [1923, pp. 35–36].

For Freud, how regrettable it was that his "adopted son" Jung had not properly incorporated his spiritual father, but had instead acted out patricidal rebellion against him.

GRANDSON OF THE *PROJECT*

Freud's first attempt to write a comprehensive metapsychological statement was his *Project for a Scientific Psychology*, which he never published. If Chapter Seven of *The Interpretation of Dreams* can be called the "son of the *Project*," then the book of twelve essays Freud attempted to write in 1915 might be considered its "grandson." Besides the fact that both the *Project* and the book of essays represented Freud's attempts at synthesizing his metapsychological con-

cepts as best he could at a given time, there are some striking similarities in the theoretical impasses he came up against in both
works, and in the manner in which they were produced. Both were
written at a very rapid pace, and in writing each Freud struggled to
clarify obscure theoretical points that had bedeviled him. After
completing each he cooled down and, upon careful examination of
the product of his feverish spurt of creativity, felt unhappy with the
result, and was unwilling to commit the entirety to publication.
After mailing the two notebooks to Fliess that we know today as
the *Project,* Freud told him on November 29, 1895: "I no longer
understand the state of mind in which I concocted the psychology; I
cannot conceive how I came to inflict it on you. I think you are too
polite; it seems to me to have been a kind of aberration" (in Bonaparte, A. Freud, and Kris, 1954, p. 134). How similar this statement is to the one Freud made to Abraham in 1915 when he told
him, upon having completed all twelve essays, "they are war-time
atrocities."

Fliess apparently encouraged Freud to publish the ideas contained in the *Project,* and Freud responded in a manner similar to
that in which he responded to Abraham's and Andreas-Salomé's
inquiries about his plans to publish his book of essays. On December
8, 1895, Freud wrote Fliess: "Do you really mean that I should
attract attention to these stutterings by a preliminary article? I think
it would be better to keep it to ourselves until we see whether
anything comes of it" (in Bonaparte, A. Freud, and Kris, 1954, p.
137).

We have seen how the enigma of consciousness bedeviled Freud
in 1915 and 1917, such that he apparently decided not to publish
the "Consciousness" essay. One of the reasons was that he could
not explain the qualitative aspect of consciousness, i.e., how consciousness distinguishes between what is internal and what is external. The same question haunted him in writing the *Project,* and his
failure to come up with a satisfactory answer probably was a significant factor in determining his decision not to publish it. Before
actually writing the *Project,* Freud already was working out the
concepts contained therein, and on August 16, 1895 he told Fliess:
"This psychology is really an incubus—skittles and mushroom-
hunting are certainly much healthier pastimes. All I was trying to
do was to explain defense, but I found myself explaining something
from the very heart of nature. I found myself wrestling with the

problems of quality, sleep, memory—in short, the whole of psychology. Now I want to hear no more of it" (in Bonaparte, A. Freud,
and Kris, 1954, p. 123). After he sent the *Project* to Fliess, Freud
still struggled to improve his explanation of the qualitative aspect of
consciousness. On January 1, 1896 he told Fliess that he had a
better explanation of consciousness than the one in the notebooks
he had sent him, based on a reorganization of the location of his
hypothetical neuronal systems first described in the *Project* (in Bonaparte, Freud, and Kris, 1954, pp. 141–144). Freud soon gave up
trying to explain consciousness with reference to neuronal functioning, however, and adopted the topographic approach stressing psychic locality of functions, divorced from any consideration of anatomical locality, which he published in *The Interpretation of Dreams*
(1900, pp. 536, 611).

Just as Freud came to feel uneasy about his 1915 explanation of
repression, which eventually required the invocation of structural
theory after the war, so the explanation of repression bedeviled him
when he wrote the *Project*. When Freud sent the *Project* to Fliess he
told him: "Now for my two notebooks. I wrote them in one breath
since my return, and they contain little that will be new to you. I
have a third notebook, dealing with the psychopathology of repression, which I am not ready to send you yet, because it only takes the
subject to a certain point. From that point I had to start from scratch
again, and I have been alternately proud and happy and abashed and
miserable, until now, after an excess of mental torment, I just apa-
thetically tell myself that it does not hang together yet and perhaps
never will. What does not hang together yet is not the mechanism—I could be patient about that—but the explanation of repression, clinical knowledge of which has incidentally made great
strides" (8 October 1895, in Bonaparte, A. Freud, and Kris, 1954,
pp. 125–126).

Similarities can also be found in the antecedents of both the
Project and the book of twelve essays. In both cases, Freud wrote in
reaction to rivals. In the case of the *Project,* the rival was Breuer.
Freud's rivalry with Breuer came to a head when they could not
agree on the point of view to be taken in their joint publication
Studies on Hysteria (Breuer and Freud, 1893–1895). Freud told
Fliess in 1892 that his and Breuer's preliminary communication was
going to appear, but "it has meant a long battle with my collab-

orator" (18 December 1892, in Bonaparte, A. Freud, and Kris, 1954, pp. 63–64). Before the book appeared, Freud told Fliess on June 22, 1894: "The book with Breuer will include five case histories, a chapter by him—from which I dissociate myself—on the theories of hysteria (summarizing and critical), and one by me on therapy which I have not started yet. . ." (in Bonaparte, A. Freud, and Kris, 1954, p. 95). Breuer and Freud disagreed over the principal mechanism of hysterical symptom formation and the significance of sexual ideas in that etiology. Breuer argued that hysterical symptoms derived from hypnoid mental states, and that sexual ideas played a role when their affect overstimulated the nervous system and contributed to mental dissociation, Freud contended that the primary factor in symptom formation was defense against incompatible sexual ideas, with the ideas becoming pathogenic because they were repressed and their split-off affect was channeled into somatic innervation. On November 8, 1895, Freud told Fliess: "Not long ago Breuer made a big speech to the physicians' society about me, putting himself forward as a convert to belief in sexual etiology. When I thanked him privately for this he spoiled my pleasure by saying: 'But all the same I *don't* believe it!' Can you make head or tail of that? I cannot" (in Bonaparte, A. Freud, and Kris, 1954, p. 134).

The *Project* was the theoretical chapter Freud would have liked to have seen included in *Studies on Hysteria* (Silverstein, 1985). It might be said that he wrote it to defend the embryonic "goddess Libido"! In the *Project* Freud made sexual stimuli arising from within the body the primary driving force sustaining all psychic activity. This was the forerunner of his concept of the sexual instinct and its vicissitudes. He wrote the *Project* because he was withdrawing his libido from Breuer, and because its writing helped him vent his aggression against Breuer. He wrote the *Project* as he was transferring libido to Fliess, and seeking to win an ally in his war with Breuer. After the emotional venting obtained through the writing, Freud cooled off and had second thoughts about his work—he might well have called it a "war-time atrocity."

In defending his sexual views against the doubting Breuer, Freud may have come to believe that Breuer had blinded himself to a complete acceptance of sexual etiology because he could not afford to face the sexual attraction developed in his treatment of Anna O. In defending the "goddess Libido" against Jung, Freud may have

come to believe that Jung had likewise blinded himself to the primacy of sexuality because he could not examine objectively his
involvement with Spielrein, nor consider the implications of his
homosexual rape experience as a boy. Thus, in each case, Freud
could blame events in the life of his rivals for determining a defensive unwillingness on their part to see the truth he presented them.

Finally, Freud's rivalries with Breuer, Jung, and Adler all contained elements of Freud's "sexual megalomania." As we have observed, Freud admitted to Abraham that his Irma dream involved
his taking sexual possessim of women associated with Breuer. We
have also seen Freud motivated to take "possession" of Spielrein
from Jung, and to keep Andreas-Salomé from slipping away to
Adler. Thus, the rivalry for "possession" of women in Freud's mind
probably played a part in stimulating the combative bursts of energy
required for the production of both the *Project* and the book of
twelve metapsychological essays.

CONCLUSIONS

By the time Freud met Adler and Jung he believed that he had
discovered a great truth; his writing, whether in case histories or in
metapsychological statements, was intended to prove that truth to
doubters through persuasive rhetoric.[6] He believed, moreover, that
his discoveries should make him immortal, even if his generation
threw up great resistances to the truth he showed them. As he
became middle-aged, his drive to be immortal began to take prece-
dence over all: It colored his relationships to colleagues, and drove
him into bursts of theoretical creativity. Psychoanalysis was his creation and his cause, and his perception of colleagues was shaped by
considerations of their usefulness to the cause. Spurts of theoretical
synthesis were conditioned by the need to defend his truth and
advance the cause in the face of dangerous rivals. From such considerations the 1915 book of twelve metapsychological essays was
born, and ultimately died.

Freud was mortal, and as such his drive for immortality could
override his scientific and clinical objectivity. And yet Freud was no
ordinary mortal; in pursuit of his immortality he created works of
genius, of extraordinary richness and complexity, among which are
surely the surviving metapsychology papers of 1915. If the attention

we are paying to those works is any indication, Freud indeed achieved immortality through his writing.

By late 1914, a convergence of professional and personal anxieties impelled him to plan a series of essays that would serve as his theoretical last will and testament. The personal anxieties centered around his belief that he had only a few years left to live. His professional anxieties centered around his fear that the ambitious Adler and Jung would rob him of his immortality by appropriating the psychoanalytic appellation for their dissenting viewpoints. Out of this confluence of personal and professional anxieties, fed by his idiosyncracies, Freud produced a book of twelve essays. The essays suffered from the emotionally driven manner in which they were written, and because of the defensive purposes they served. He quickly published those most necessary as a matter of strategy to combat the heresies of Adler and Jung. As he held on to the rest, his sense of the inadequacy of the published, as well as the unpublished, essays increased. After surviving the time of his predicted death, and the war, he believed that his theoretical thinking had advanced so far that, rather than publish his twelve essays as a whole, he had to publish entirely new works that largely superseded the product of his expulsive creativity of 1915. So ends the "sad story."

Notes ————————————————————————

1. On January 8, 1900, Freud did tell Fliess: "I do not count on recognition, at any rate in my lifetime" (in Bonaparte, A. Freud, and Kris, 1954, p. 307.

2. It should be noted that Sophie and Anna were both widows. After telling Abraham that in the dream "I have them all," Freud wrote: "There would be one simple therapy for widowhood, of course" (in H. Abraham and E. Freud, 1965, p. 20). The therapy Freud was referring to was sexual intercourse, consistent with his thesis, developed in 1894, that regulation of sexual chemistry through uninter- rupted intercourse was necessary to prevent neuroses (Bonaparte, A. Freud, and Kris, 1954, pp. 86–94). Thus, in the dream Freud wished to possess all of the women sexually, including Mathilde Breuer, who was not a widow but the wife of a rival.

3. Freud had one important hobby, his passion for collecting antiquities. He began to indulge this passion at least as early as 1896, when he could ill afford such luxuries, and continued to collect hundreds of antiquities over the rest of his life (Jones, 1953, pp. 329–330; 1957, p. 317). It is pertinent to note that, in 1895, Freud argued that a man's obsession with collecting some particular type of object is a substitute for his need for a multitude of conquests: "Every collector is a substitute

for Don Juan Tenorio . . . These things are erotic equivalents" (in Bonaparte, A. Freud, and Kris, 1954, p. 112).

4. It is interesting to note that Freud's identification with Moses lasted until the end of his life. In the year of his death, Freud published *Moses and Monotheism* (1939) in which we can see further analogies between the fate of Moses and his teachings and the fate of Freud and psychoanalysis (pp. 89, 122–124). In Freud's account, Moses was murdered by his people and his teachings were abandoned. In time, however, he was resurrected and his truth rediscovered through the work of the prophets. Thus, both Moses and Freud were primal fathers destined to be slain by their sons. Through resurrection—if only through rediscovery—they and their truth would live on (Sachs, 1941, p. 162). As we have seen, this is precisely the image of his fate Freud expressed in 1914 in "On the History of the Psychoanalytic Movement" (1914c, p. 22), and it constituted an essential motivation in compelling him to discipline himself to codify his metapsychology in 1915.

5. According to Jones (1955, p. 392), Fliess's calculations had given Freud only 51 years to live. After Freud lived past his 51st year (1907), he told Ferenczi in 1910 that he had believed "for a long time" that he had to die in February 1918. On the other hand, Freud told Abraham in 1915 that he regarded as a "gloomy prospect" the possibility that it might be genetically determined that he would reach, but not surpass, the age of 81½—the age at which his father and (in 1914) his half-brother Emanuel died (3 July 1915, in H. Abraham and E. Freud, 1965, p. 226).

6. While writing *Totem and Taboo*, for example, Freud told Jung on December 17, 1911: "My study of totemism and other works are not going well . . . Besides, my interest is diminished by the conviction that I am already in possession of the truths I am trying to prove" (in McGuire, 1974, p. 472).

References

Abraham, H. C., & Freud, E. L., Eds. (1965), *A Psycho-Analytic Dialogue: The Letters of Sigmund Freud and Karl Abraham, 1907–1926*, trans. B. Marsh & H. C. Abraham. New York: Basic Books.

Alexander, I. E. (1982), The Freud-Jung relationship—the other side of Oedipus and countertransference. *Amer. Psychol.*, 37:1009–1018.

Andreas-Salomé, L. (1964), *The Freud Journal*, trans S. A. Leavy. New York: Basic Books.

Binswanger, L. (1957), *Sigmund Freud: Reminiscences of a Friendship*. New York: Grune & Stratton.

Bonaparte, M., Freud, A., & Kris, E., Eds. (1954), *The Origins of Psycho-Analysis: Letters to Wilhelm Fliess, Drafts and Notes: 1887–1902*, trans E. Mosbacher & J. Strachey. New York: Basic Books.

Breuer, J., & Freud, S. (1893–1895), *Studies on Hysteria. Standard Edition*, 2. London: Hogarth Press, 1955.

Brome, V. (1983), *Ernest Jones: A Biography*. New York: Norton.

Carotenuto, A. (1982), *A Secret Symmetry: Sabina Spielrein between Jung and Freud*. New York: Pantheon.

Freud, S. (1888), *Gehirn* [The Brain]. In: *Handwörterbuch der gesamten Medizin*, Vol. 1, ed. A. Villaret. Stüttgart: Ferdinand Enke, pp. 684–697.

———— (1895), *Project for a Scientific Psychology. Standard Edition*, 1:283–397. London: Hogarth Press, 1966.

———— (1900), *The Interpretation of Dreams. Standard Edition*, 4 & 5. London: Hogarth Press, 1953.

———— (1909), *Notes upon a Case of Obsessional Neurosis. Standard Edition*, 10:153–318. London: Hogarth Press, 1955.

———— (1912), Addition to the 4th Edition of *The Psychopathology of Everyday Life. Standard Edition*, 6:30–32. London: Hogarth Press, 1960.

———— (1913a), *Totem and Taboo. Standard Edition*, 13:1–161. London: Hogarth Press, 1953.

———— (1913b), *The theme of the three caskets. Standard Edition*, 12:289–301. London: Hogarth Press, 1958.

———— (1914a), The Moses of Michelangelo. *Standard Edition*, 13:211–238.

———— (1914b), On narcissism. *Standard Edition*, 14:67–102. London: Hogarth Press, 1957.

————(1914c), On the history of the psycho-analytic movement. *Standard Edition*, 14:7–66. London: Hogarth Press, 1957.

———— (1914d), Some reflections on schoolboy psychology. *Standard Edition*, 13:241–244. London: Hogarth Press, 1953.

———— (1915a), Instincts and their vicissitudes. *Standard Edition*, 14:117–140. London: Hogarth Press, 1957.

———— (1915b), Repression. *Standard Edition*, 14:146–158. London: Hogarth Press, 1957.

———— (1915c), The unconscious. *Standard Edition*, 14:166–204. London: Hogarth Press, 1957.

———— (1915–1917), *Introductory Lectures on Psycho-Analysis. Standard Edition*, 15 & 16. London: Hogarth Press, 1961, 1963.

———— (1917a), A metapsychological supplement to the theory of dreams. *Standard Edition*, 14:222–235. London: Hogarth Press, 1957.

———— (1917b), Mourning and melancholia. *Standard Edition*, 14:243–258. London: Hogarth Press, 1957.

———— (1920), Beyond the pleasure principle. *Standard Edition*, 18:7–64. London: Hogarth Press, 1955.

———— (1923), The ego and the id. *Standard Edition*, 19:13–59. London: Hogarth Press, 1961.

———— (1926), Inhibitions, symptoms and anxiety. *Standard Edition*, 20:87–174. London: Hogarth Press, 1959.

———— (1939), *Moses and Monotheism. Standard Edition*, 23:7–137. London: Hogarth Press, 1964.

———— (1940), An outline of psycho-analysis. *Standard Edition*, 23:144–207. London: Hogarth Press, 1964.

Gedo, J. E. (1983), *Portraits of the Artist: Psychoanalysis of Creativity and Its Vicissitudes*. New York: Guilford.

Hale, N. G., Ed. (1971), *James Jackson Putnam and Psychoanalysis: Letters between Putnam and Sigmund Freud, Ernest Jones, William James, Sandor Ferenczi, and Morton Prince, 1887–1917*. Cambridge, Mass.: Harvard University Press.

Hartman, F. R. (1983), A reappraisal of the Emma episode and the specimen dream. *J. Amer. Psychoanal. Assn.*, 31:555–585.

Holt, R. R. (1982), Review of *Freud: The Man and the Cause*, by R. W. Clark. *Rev. Psychoanal. Bks.*, 1:3–13.

Jones, E. (1953), *The Life and Work of Sigmund Freud*, Vol. 1. New York: Basic Books.

——— (1955), *The Life and Work of Sigmund Freud*, Vol. 2. New York: Basic Books.

——— (1957), *The Life and Work of Sigmund Freud*, Vol. 3. New York: Basic Books.

Jung, C. G. (1963), *Memories, Dreams, Reflections*, ed. A. Jaffe. New York: Vintage, 1965.

Mahony, P. (1982), *Freud as a Writer*. New York: International Universities Press.

McGuire, W. Ed. (1974), *The Freud/Jung Letters*, trans R. Manheim & R. F. C. Hull. Princeton: Princeton University Press.

Meng, H., & Freud, E. L., Eds. (1963), *Psycho-Analysis and Faith: The Letters of Sigmund Freud and Oskar Pfister*, trans. E. Mosbacher. London: Hogarth Press.

Nunberg, H., & Federn, E., Eds. (1974), *Minutes of the Vienna Psychoanalytic Society, Vol. 3: 1910–1911*, trans. M. Nunberg. New York: International Universities Press.

Ostow, R. (1977), Autobiographical sources of Freud's social theory. *Psychiat. J. Univ. Ottawa*, 2:169–180.

Pfeiffer, E., Ed. (1972), *Sigmund Freud and Lou Andreas Salomé: Letters*, trans. W. Robson-Scott & E. Robson-Scott. New York: Harcourt Brace Jovanovich.

Sachs, H. (1941), "The Man Moses" and the man Freud. *Psychoanal. Rev.*, 28:156–162.

Schur, M. (1972), *Freud: Living and Dying*. New York: International Universities Press.

Silverstein, B. (1985), Freud's psychology and its organic foundation: Sexuality and mind-body interactionism. *Psychoanal. Rev.*, 72:203–228.

Stekel, W. (1950), *Autobiography: The Life Story of a Pioneer Psychoanalyst*. New York: Liveright.

Stepansky, P. E. (1976), The empiricist as rebel: Jung, Freud, and the burdens of discipleship. *J. Hist. Behav. Sci.*, 12:216–239.

——— (1977), *A History of Aggression in Freud*. New York: International Universities Press.

——— (1983), *In Freud's Shadow: Adler in Context*. Hillsdale, N.J.: Analytic Press.

Strachey, J. (1957), Editor's introduction to "Papers on Metapsychology." *Standard Edition*, 14:105–107. London: Hogarth Press.

Swales, P. J. (1983), Freud, Martha Bernays, and the language of flowers. Privately printed.

Wallace, E. R. (1983), *Freud and Anthropology: A History and Reappraisal*. New York: International Universities Press.

Weber, S. (1982), *The Legend of Freud*. Minneapolis: University of Minnesota Press.

Wittels, F. (1923), *Sigmund Freud: His Personality, His Teaching, and His School*, trans E. Paul & C. Paul. New York: Dodd, Mead, 1924.

Brief Contributions

Patrick J. Mahony —————————————————————

The Oral Tradition, Freud, and Psychoanalytic Writing

The mouth is the cradle of perception. —Rene Spitz

The letter kills but the breath gives life. —2 Corinthians 3:6

I write this essay with some trepidation, for the surge of modern research on the issue of oral versus written culture has still left many questions unanswered; furthermore, no appreciable treatment of the field exists anywhere in psychoanalytic literature. To start off, I accept the tenet that orality can enter into and modify the production, transmission, reception, and conservation of information,[1] in other words, that there veritably is an oral noetics. Accordingly, my general aim is to propose a vantage point, other than the usual exclusive one of written culture, from which we might appreciate certain aspects of the discovery, nature, and transmission of psychoanalysis. Due to the dearth of relevant information, in part because of the written orientation of previous psychoanalytic investigators, some of my remarks must remain tentative for the moment. I might quickly add, however, that lately two comprehensive books have appeared which have greatly advanced my thinking about oral communication—Walter Ong's *Orality and Literacy* (1982) and Paul Zumthor's *Introduction à la poésie orale* (1983)—and that anyone desiring to pursue the subject will profit from their complementary and highly suggestive bibliographies.

The main orientation of those two works will influence the direction of my presentation. Yet I am quite cognizant that an exhaustive treatment of my subject would have to consider orality in three modalities: as a congenital and constitutional factor (e.g., Charcot's strabismus as bearing on the visual theatricality of his clinical "performances"); as a factor in an individual's development and psychosexual experience (e.g., auditively pronounced primal scenes); and as a social factor proper to the means of communication. We need no prolonged reflection to realize that an analysis of the interaction between all three factors is fraught with imponderables, and this undeniable fact should serve to temper any investigative zeal for premature synthesis. Still, while concentrating on the orality of media, I shall not avoid the opportunity to touch on some synergistic considerations.

A primary orality typifies those cultures untouched by print or writing. Psychoanalysis, though, was born in what is called the Era of Second Orality, ushered in by new means of communication, such as the telephone and radio, which introduced a sensorial shift into the previous chirographic and typographic traditions. The historical impact of the development of communication media on the human sensorium has yet to be fully charted. Such a history would surely illuminate the fundamental nature of psychoanalytic terms. To be specific:

> For purposes proposed as scientific, psychoanalysis makes use of the very "proximity" senses which Freudian thought itself has advertised as prescientific and full of danger for abstract thinking. For psychoanalysis has pointed out that for the rise of civilization, taboos must be imposed on the senses providing greater bodily pleasures (touch most of all, as well as taste and smell), and more attention must be given to the more sublime (abstract, distancing) senses such as hearing and, especially, sight. The relationship of the rise of psychoanalysis to the history of the sensorium and concomitantly of the communications media certainly deserves more attention than there is room or reason to give it [in a general survey].
>
> *What we need is a phenomenology of psychoanalytic concepts* [Ong, 1967, p. 110; my italics].

Of course, in the Era of Second Orality, sensorial shifts are gradual and uneven in development. In this regard, we cannot overestimate the significance of the belated progress of psychoanalysis from the topographic model in *The Interpretation of Dreams* (1900), conceiving the psyche as a mechanical apparatus, to the structural model of "The Ego and the Id" (1923), using an organismic metaphor to describe the mind. The vocal implications of the latter were to some extent borne out subsequently in Isakower's etiological study of the superego, "On the Exceptional Position of the Auditory Sphere" (1939). Bearing the foregoing in mind, we may wonder to what degree the distorted idea of psychoanalysis rampant in certain circles—pharmacological, behavioristic, psychiatric—is based on the distrust of orality and a predilection for the visual and kinetic models current in scientific formation.

Of all disciplines arising in the contemporary period, psycho- analysis is the most preeminently oral—in terms of its treatment modality and the instruction and supervision of analytic candidates. What professional organization other than the American Psycho- analytic Association devotes a section in annual meetings to its oral history? Even within the larger history of discourse, psychoanalysis stands alone. Prior to the psychoanalytic "talking cure," there was never an enunciatory form, literary genre, or social ritual in which the four basic types of discourse (i.e., the referential, rhetorical, expressive, and aesthetic) figured saliently. Even more importantly, in the psychoanalytic setting each of these four discourses takes on new traits, whereas a certain dynamic interaction between the four discourses contributes to the uniqueness of psychoanalytic treat- ment and even comprises one genre of verification for its therapeutic success (Mahony, 1979).

Although steeped in vocalization, psychoanalysis as a discipline has yet to realize fully the intrapsychic as well as the transcultural influences of sound. It is not significant that, before birth, the human being not only swims in a "uterine music," but responds more to low-pitched than to high-pitched voices—an acoustic ad- vantage favoring a primitive paternal incorporation? (see Zumthor, 1983, p. 17). On another score, would Otto Rank have qualified his imputation of *universal* importance to birth trauma if he had known, as Margaret Mead (1964) revealed years ago, that there was a South Pacific society in which a special woman was designated to adjust immediately to the neonate's distress and to cry in unison with him? Along the same line, among the Zulus, each child is given a cradle song, composed especially for him, which is retained like a name or motto for life (Zumthor, 1983, p. 91). It is only very re- cently that an analyst, Anzieu (1979), postulated a sound image of the self which developmentally initiates the body image; quite rele- vantly, Anzieu also observed that the editors of the *Standard Edi- tion* of Freud's works did not index such capital terms as "voice," "sound," and "audition"! As I have observed elsewhere (1982), such editorial neglect would not have occurred

> if psychoanalysis had been invented in a tonal language such as Chinese or in an African language such as Khosi, which mixes words and a tongue-clacking that up to now has defied transcription. In such languages, psychoanalysts would be likely to devote more attention to nonverbal sounds and noises which, after all, increase as the treatment progresses (patients feel freer to make more noises as analysis goes on). I have searched the literature for a psychoanalytic article on patients whispering and can find none, despite the fact that verbalizations during lovemaking are almost always whispered [p. 4].

Using a transcultural perspective, we can gain insight into the functions of the analyst as recorder or speaker. Freud's counsel that the analyst not write during sessions is glossed by the impatient rebuke of a Maya storyteller to a research anthropologist: "What I tell—did you *see* it or do you only write it?" (Zumthor, 1983, p. 235). It is as if the storyteller demands a full attention and internalization that would otherwise be diminished by scriptive mediation. The voice of the unseen analyst might at times be suggestively considered alongside the fascinating or terrifying role which occidental mythologies assign to a voice without body, such as the Hellenic Echo or the voices of revenants, earth, and clouds, which appear in French folklore. As if to subdue the voice, some cultures codify the link between it and posture; in one of the ethnic groups in Volta, for example, the reclining person manifests confidence whereas seated he speaks seriously, and standing he talks trivialities (Zumthor, 1983, p. 14).

I might briefly refer here to four other oral–aural subjects which have been neglected in psychoanalysis, for reasons of cultural or other limitations. First, it is quite germane that although the primal scene is mainly visual and auditory, we have no lexical auditive counterparts for voyeurism and exhibitionism. Next, analysts have yet to give systematic attention to that function of discourse called phatic (Jakobson, 1960), whereby the message chiefly serves to establish, prolong, or discontinue communication (hello . . . um-hum . . . that's that), to attract notice or confirm its continuation (wow . . . you got that?). Thirdly, we may duly reflect on the sensorial adjustments which psychoanalytic patients, who by and large are well-educated, must undergo. The therapeutic process involves rerouting such analysands, molded for years by the solitary visual experience of book culture, into an intense oral–aural interchange which they have never had before—designedly bringing them into contact with the endopsychic visual world of dreams, fantasies, and memories, which then must be verbalized and understood primarily within the verbalizable significance of the transference. Finally, the oral nature of psychoanalysis is also distinguished by the fact that during the clinical hour the analyst (of orthodox persuasion) hardly ever addresses the patient by name. No other personal, secret-sharing discourse of appreciable duration possesses this vocal peculiarity. Since one's name is intimately bound up with one's personality (Freud, 1913, p. 56), the analyst's hesitation to name causes a narcissistic privation which in turn helps to activate the most intimate memories and fantasies. In a future publication I hope to demonstrate, using Freud's case histories as specimens, how names reappear in a phonetically fragmented form as determinants in dreams and fantasies.

We may now turn our attention to Freud's complex sensitivity to sound, which, along with the historical vicissitudes of the sensorium, played an essential part in the origin and development of psychoanalysis. Let us note, first of all, that in view of Freud's open antipathy to music, it is fortunate that dreams are visual and verbal in nature rather than musical. Otherwise, the creative discovery of *The Interpretation of Dreams,* in reality so correspondent with Freud's personality, would have remained for another day. Less known than Freud's musical handicap is his stunted acoustic sensibility. As a matter of fact, this deficiency was so acute as to prevent him from understanding the treatment of tone relations in Lipps's *Grundtaschen des Seelenlebens.*[2]

Nevertheless, inner vocalized language was a significant characteristic of Freud's psychic life, as is shown in the following biographical passage from *On Aphasia* (1891) (a passage, by the way, not cited by either Jones [1955] or Schur [1972]!:

> I remember having twice been in danger of my life, and each time the awareness of the danger occurred to me quite suddenly. On both occasions I felt "This is the end," and while otherwise my inner language proceeds with only indistinct sound images and slight lip movements, in these situations of danger I heard these words as if somebody was shouting them into my ears, and at the same time I saw them as if they were printed on a piece of paper floating [p. 62].

In keeping with the phenomenon of his inner vocalization, Freud's hallucinations in Paris during 1885–1886 were of an auditive nature: "I often heard my name suddenly called by an unmistakable and beloved voice" (1901, p. 261).

We shall not be surprised to hear, then, that Freud's memory was exceptionally "phonographic." As he remarked, "Shortly before I entered the University I could write down almost verbatim popular lectures on scientific subjects directly after hearing them" (1901, p. 135). He also observed that as late as 1916 his "phonographic memory" was still powerful enough to enable him subsequently to record faithfully the improvised lectures he gave at the University of Vienna (1933, p. 5). In the light of the preceding, perhaps we should stress the sensorial import of the fact that Freud's decision to study natural science came upon hearing a public recitation of the essay "Ode of Nature." Wrongly attributed in the past to Goethe, this short three-page essay adulating Nature contains a sentence which may have particularly impressed the young Freud: "She has neither language nor speech, but she creates tongues and hearts through which she feels and speaks."[3]

Undoubtedly the oral nature of the Viennese milieu too had a decided influence on Freud. If different eras and cultures vary in their degree of taciturnity and prolixity and hence in a redistributed speech mass (Steiner, 1975), we may safely presume that 19th-century Vienna enjoyed a remarkable climate of verbalized expression, as one can judge from such interconnected phenomena as its literary resurgence on the one hand, and the intense social life of its famous cafes on the other. The extraordinary waves of Jewish immigrants coming to Vienna from diverse cultures also contributed to the atmosphere of vivid oral communication. More precisely, in 1855, the year before Freud was born, there were 6,000 Jews in Vienna, comprising one percent of the population; in 1870 there were 40,000, over six percent of the population; and by 1900, when *The Interpretation of Dreams* was published, Jews numbered nearly 147,000, or roughly nine percent of the population. Pertinently, most of these Jewish immigrants took up residence in Vienna's second city district, Leopoldstadt, where Freud lived for many years (see Klein, 1981, pp. 2, 9, 12). No wonder that one of Freud's books was based largely on his extensive collection of Jewish jokes—jokes, as Freud (1905) reminds us, being the most social of all discourses. But beyond the content of Jewish jokes, the whole manner of Jewish expression in Austria at the time benefited Freud. As the Germanist Heinz Politzer (1969) incisively remarked, "The manner of speaking of Austrian Jews before the turn of the century, their wit and their penchant for ambivalences and ambiguities of every kind, left traces in Freud's work" (p. 740).

If we pause momentarily before some of Freud's other works, we encounter other unexpected oral elements. For instance, given Freud's aesthetic sensitivity to oral communication, can it be an accident that his last great treatiese expressly dealt with the oral tradition of the Bible (1939, pp. 40, 43, 68–69, 94), the very text in which he was precociously immersed very soon after he learned to read? (see Freud, 1925, p. 8). Can it be sheer accident that his first major history of an allegedly completed case[4] concerned a patient whose immediate collapse was due to hearing a story told by a "cruel" captain? I refer, of course, to the Rat Man. It is quite to the point that Freud spoke about him five times at the meetings of the Vienna Psychoanalytic Society;[5] he never spoke there about Dora, and only once about the Wolf Man. And, again, was it mere chance that Freud chose to present a lecture on the Rat Man to the First International Congress of Psychoanalysis? Was it coincidental that that lecture, given without notes and lasting for nearly five hours (Jones, 1955, p. 42), was by far Freud's most memorable oral performance?

A clinical revelation about Freud's handling of the Rat Man is most apposite to our concerns. As opposed to the case reports of Dora and the Wolf Man, which were organized around visual dream events, the Rat Man text centers on obsessional acts and sayings; there are but three short references to dreams despite the wealth of dream material appearing in Freud's original case notes (see Freud, 1909, pp. 193, 200, 207n, 269–274, 276–280, 283, 285–286). What has been overlooked by psychoanalytic commentators is a particular verbal technique used by Freud when dealing with the obsessional ideation inherent in compulsive acts. Not only did he interpret the general meaning at various strata underlying those acts, but he also strove to coin orally marked, aphoristic formulae of which those acts were the *immediate* translation.[6] At one point in the Rat Man case, for example, Freud suggests: "Our present patient's obsessive fear, therefore, when restored to its original meaning, would run as follows: 'If I have this wish to see a woman naked, my father will be bound to die'" (1909, p. 63). For another compulsive instance, Freud proposes: "There formed in his mind some such answer as: 'Yes! I'll pay back the money to A. when my father and the lady have children!' or 'As sure as my father and the lady can have children, I'll pay back the money'" (p. 218). Compared with Freud, a typical modern clinician might report the compulsive act, bring in ancillary fantasy and mnemic material, and interpret only via elaborate verbal explanations. I further suggest that part of the contemporary unawareness of Freud's technique is reflected in Strachey's English rendering of one of the subheadings in the Rat Man case: "Some Obsessional Ideas and Their Explanation" (p. 186). In truth, "explanation" should be "translation," the English meaning of the German *Übersetzung* (*Gesammelte Werke,* Vol. 7, p. 409).

We might regard the foregoing remarks as a leisurely though essential preparation for an examination of the vital presence in Freud's postures as both speaker and writer. I can scarcely overrate this important observation, for it is not a matter of merely tracing in a superficial manner one of many determinants of Freud's prose. Rather, orality personalizes Freud's expression and renders it conso' nant with its lifelong subject, the human being. To convey the crucial implications of this claim, I shall venture into comparative statements between Freud's prose and what I feel to be the ill-fitting and quasi-denaturalizing prose of many analyst-writers.

Appropriately, Freud was faithful to the etymology of his first name, Si(e)g Mund, victorious mouth, and his style was ever at' tuned to the qualities distinctive of oral communication. Among the various reports of Freud's oral delivery by his contemporaries, we may single out Wittels's resonating contention that the persuasive impact of Freud's living voice far exceeded that of the cold print left for future generations. Let us now listen to Wittels's (1923) irre' placeable description of Freud talking to his Viennese associates:

> In this circle of intimates, Freud's method was far more audacious than it was in a public lecture. He would begin by enunciating his main contentions categorically, so that they were apt to repel; then he would provide such a wealth of argument in support of them that his hearers could hardly fail to be convinced of their truth. Those who know Freud only through the written word will be far more ready to differ from him than those who listened to the magic of his speech. Not that he is an orator, for he rarely raises his voice. . . . I find his later writings less admirable than I found the earlier ones. But I am perfectly willing to admit that they are no less excellent, and that the reason why they please me less is that I have to read

them in cold print, whereas before I used to learn from Freud's living speech [pp. 134–135].

We might, and I believe we should, question Wittels's emphasis in separating what Freud spoke from what he wrote. There are many evident similarities if one looks for them. Did not Freud dislike some of Mill's writing because it was not aphoristic, a virtual hallmark of oral style?[7] Indeed, Freud's own assimilation of proverbial lore and his ability to create oracular statements and enticingly quotable expressions (see Schönau, 1968, Chapters 4 and 5) set him apart from those many analysts who neglect the vital oral component and simply write in and for silent reflection.

Another oral element of Freud's style, and one typical of expressive discourse in general, is its tendency to some degree of inconsistency and illogical generalization: His "never" might become "sometimes," "possibly" might unexpectedly become "definitely," or vice versa (see Mahony, 1982, especially Chapter 4). Freud imported into print this characteristic of thinking aloud and of living speech. In this regard, we must not overlook the avowed influence of one of Freud's great teachers, Jean-Martin Charcot. Significantly enough, Freud so admired Charcot's lectures that he translated a number of them which had been gathered into a volume. Here is Freud (1892–1894) prefacing his translation of the *Tuesday Lectures,* referring approvingly to their quality of authorial improvisation and audience appeal:

> These lectures owe a peculiar charm to the fact that they are entirely, or for the most part, improvisations. . . . [Charcot] is obliged to behave before his audience as he ordinarily does in medical practice, with the exception that he thinks aloud and allows his audience to take part in the course of his conjectures and investigations [pp. 133–134].

The oral qualities of Freud's translation are manifest in his recurrent interruptions of Charcot's exposition, where he puts forward not only explanations and additional references but also "critical objections and glosses such as might occur to a member of the audience" (p. 136).

The improvised freedom which Freud admired in Charcot was also suggestive of certain aspects of his own vocal and written expression that were to gain widespread admiration. Surely a mechanical factor promoting "processiveness" and spontaneity was

Freud's unusual speed in handwriting,[8] which closed the frustrating temporal gap between his thinking and recording. With most people, handwriting is nearly one-tenth the rate of speech (Chafe, 1982, pp. 37–38); such cursive slowness favors a predilection for the premeditation evident in print culture. Freud, on the other hand, admittedly preferred to speak or write to find out where his thoughts would lead him, a practice in harmony with the oral sensitivity of his spontaneous expression.

Another oral element in Freud's prose is redundancy, which lends it a certain fluid ease. We may think of this consequential link in the following way:

> Since redundancy characterizes oral thought and speech, it is in a profound sense more natural to thought and speech than is sparse linearity. Sparsely linear or analytic thought and speech is an artificial creation, structured by the technology of writing. Eliminating redundancy on a significant scale demands a time-obviating technology, writing [Ong, 1982, p. 40].

We must not confuse the measured redundancy in Freud's prose, however, with the accidental feature of repetitiveness which he himself assigned to the oral tradition. That is to say, with the founding of the *Jahrbuch für psychoanalytische und psychopathologische Forschungen* in 1909, Freud felt that in psychoanalytic circles a written tradition emerged alongside the oral one. Relying on the typographic contribution to communication, Freud no longer had to repeat in every paper the fundamental psychoanalytic premises or refute elementary objections (see Freud to Jung, 17 October 1909, in McGuire, 1974, p. 254). As Freud put it to Jung in 1910: "In the meantime the printing press has been invented so to speak for our benefit, we are no longer dependent on the oral tradition" (2 January 1910, in McGuire, 1974, p. 282).

In order to forestall any possible misconceptions, a statement of caution is perhaps advisable: Freud's style is markedly oral though not exclusively so. But insofar as it is oral, Freud's manner of communicating is a far cry from the detached stance of those many analytic authors whose publications smack of the lifeless spatiality of print. To underscore this point, I will allude to the research of the ethnolinguist William Chafe (1982), who studied two maximally differentiated styles, the informal spoken and the formal written. Among other things, informal speakers refer more extensively to themselves and to their own mental processes and have greater involvement with their audience—making sure that the message is comprehensible, and so on. On the other hand, formal writers, using a detached kind of language, resort quite extensively to the passive voice and to nominalization (e.g., using *treatment* instead of *treat*). Such nominalization, Chafe continues, "suppresses involvement in action in favor of abstract reification" (p. 46). A little way along this path of thought leads us to conclude that many psychoanalytic articles are deadening to read precisely because they are plagued by impersonalism and drowned in the abstract reification of superabun-dant nominalizations.

We may readily see the far-reaching implications of written de-tached style if we turn closer to home. More precisely, I want to point to some analysts who studiously avoid the pronoun "I" in their writings and instead, rely on a grammatical expletive or dis-pensable filler, an impersonal "it" conjoined with the passive voice, e.g., "it was interpreted by the analyst to the patient that," or "it was repetitively observed that." In these same authors, a proposed ideal subtly emerges whereby the *it* or *das Es,* which vibrates throughout Freud's writings, gives way to a drive-less *it* which is highly subversive, silently referring to the privileged position, the impersonality, and the unerringness of mechanized calculations (Mahony, 1984).[9] The overdetermined "it" appears to be a con-cealed trace of nostalgia for the methodology of an "objective" psychology without the person-ness of transference and coun-tertransference. Orality and the pronominal trace of the living human voice seem alien to those who effectively make methodology its own end. One of my favorite quotations from Freud is right on target here: "Methodologists remind me of people who clean their glasses so thoroughly that they never have time to look through them" (in Sterba, 1982, p. 120).

A short step ahead brings us to a consideration of the orality in Freud's written prose in terms of two interconnected factors, name-ly, tone and the fictionality of the addressee. Even if Freud did not hesitate to use pronominal self-references, he still had to cope with the fictionality of his readership and with the baffling task of com-municating tone, the main carrier of affect in vocal discourse. The writer–reader relationship indeed has a significant element of fic-tionality—by the time this article is published, I or some of my intended readers may be dead or incapacitated, and, in any event, I cannot realistically conceive of the infinite variety of moods and settings in which my future readership will approach this text. Moreover, since finished texts are existentially in the past, they involve the reader with the past, present, and future in a fundamentally different way than a living voice of the present does—clearly "there is no visual equivalent of speech but only a set of visual patterns relatable to speech" (Ong, 1977, pp. 233, 267, 269; cf. his Chapter Two "The Writer's Audience Is Always a Fiction").

Offsetting that visual quiescence, Freud's processive style, with its frequent retrospections and anticipations, achieves an undercurrent of temporal flow. Collaterally, Freud the writer collapses the distance between himself and the unseen audience, a technical achievement which few if any analysts have equalled. As a public speaker, Freud was wont to have a double audience—the listeners at large and one or two he privately addressed. This procedure continues in his writing, where we are regularly drawn in to hear him speak to an interlocutor (expressly imagined or not),[10] and where we identify now with Freud, now with the interlocutor, and now with both. Concurrent with this compositional technique is another oral feature of Freud's writing, the semblance of tone. I stress *semblance,* because the use of tone in textual criticism is metaphorical; since tones are auditory in nature, their detection in writing comes from an inferential, not a direct sensorial process.

Let us finally shift our attention away from expressive virtuosity and ask why inhibitions about writing and public speaking affect many North American analysts. Perhaps some answers to this question may even alert us to other felicities in Freud's discourse. In fact, belletristic education has for the last several decades suffered from a disastrous turn of events in the history of teaching English on this continent. One crucial result of this turn, for present purposes, is that generations of future analysts were subject to high school and college courses in English suddenly stripped of integration with speech, logic, and rhetoric. The tale is as follows:

> In America departmentalization gave rise to the melodramatic walk-out of the speech and elocution members of English departments at the 1914 convention of the National Council of Teachers of English. These dissidents took rhetoric and debate with them to the now departments of speech. Henceforth in America at least, rhetoric was not a required course in the educational sequence. A similar direction

was taken at about the same time by logic, which went to the departments of philosophy or mathematics. These secessions made the English department, with its courses in literature and language (phi-
lology), the sole inheritor of the full liberal arts tradition.
Unfortunately, the teachers and scholars in the new departments of
English were not given any rhetorical training or any preparation in
systematic logic, either traditional or modern [Murphy, 1982, p. 23].

Beyond their subjection to a historically crippled linguistic education, cisatlantic medical analysts have additional reasons for being
reluctant to engage in descriptive writing. The medical and psychiatric models which they have interiorized for writing case reports
have the advantage of comprehensiveness, but do not favor fluent
articulation. The writer, perhaps following a kind of internalized
tick sheet of diagnostic categories and their established interre-
lationships, is apt to compose paratactically, piling sentences atop
one another, and avoiding subordination and connectives. And,
paradoxically, there may be an unexpected negative effect stemming
from oral discourse itself: Possibly due to the habit of giving
clinically isolated one-sentence spot interventions, certain analysts
may be inclined to compose their written reports by jamming together unconnected sentences into an unwieldy whole.

As I look back from this terminal vantage point on what I have
said, I am all too aware that I have travelled but a few of many
possible paths. I hope other voices will soon come to help us sound
the outlying area. Meanwhile, in closing, I can scarcely do better
than refer once more to the two citations that preface my presentation: *The mouth is the cradle of perception. The letter kills but the
breath gives life.* These adages, found in Spitz's (1965) classic work
and the Bible respectively, have a resounding timeliness. They serve
as reverberating oral reminders that forever after we may struggle
through the rites of passage.

Notes

1. To cite one dramatic example from ancient history: Eric Havelock (1963) has
shown that the final interiorization of the Greek alphabet influenced Plato to turn
against the orality of Homeric Greece and thus banish from his ideal republic the
race of poets who indeed were representatives of the old oral–aural world.

2. See the letter of 31 August 1898 to Fliess (in Bonaparte, A. Freud, and Kris, 1954, pp. 262–263).

3. This essay, along with some enlightening commentary, can be found in Kaufmann (1980, pp. 32ff.).

4. Of the other four major case histories, the eleven-week treatment of Dora was obviously incomplete for a number of reasons. Freud never treated Schreber and saw Little Hans but once. The treatment of the Wolf Man began later, in 1910.

5. Those meetings were on October 30, November 6, and November 20 of 1907, and January 22 and April 8 of 1908 (Nunberg and Federn, 1962, pp. 227–237, 246, 287, 370–371). The first two of the five meetings dealt exclusively with the Rat Man. We can hardly help noticing that in his case history Freud delivers the father's and mother's repeated narrative in a story book fashion: "The tale was as follows" (1909, p. 205). Freud quickly classifies the tale as "unimpeachable testimony" (p. 207n), which is somewhat attenuated 30 pages later as dealing with an event established "almost without question" (p. 237). Countless qualifications such as this one show us that composition for Freud was a "working through,"or better yet, a "writing through" his ideas.

6. My offhand impression is that Jones and Fenichel, more than Ferenczi, Abraham, or any of the earlier analysts, resemble Freud in his practice of formulaic translation. Since I noticed Freud's formulaic technique, I have used it clinically with some success with a pair of patients given to compulsive acts. Perhaps this success is due to a number of factors: rendering the unconscious meaning of the compulsive acts into a convenient citability and immediate recognizability, giving the patients a kind of verbal transitory object, etc. The danger is always that the formulaic translation, rather than promoting a resolution, would itself be adopted into the apotropaic strategy of the compulsive act; of course, timing and tact must moderate the temporary use of such formulaic translations, which otherwise would go from being incomplete interpretations to inexact ones (see Glover, 1931). My intention here is merely to put forward a technical procedure for eventual reconfirmation or rejection by the psychoanalytic community.

7. See Freud's letter of 15 November 1883 to his wife (E. Freud, 1960, p. 90).

8. Jones's (1957) remarks about the relationship between Freud's psychomotoricity and handwriting are worth quoting. Jones starts off referring to a letter in which Freud complains: "I find it very hard to substitute Latin characters for Gothic handwriting, as I am now doing. All fluency—inspiration one would say on a higher plane—at once leaves me." Here is Jone's gloss: "It is evident that the mere physical act of writing, which he performed at an unusually swift speed, had for Freud some special emotional significance" (p. 130).

9. Seemingly the neutral pronoun "it" enjoys an overdetermined suprasemantic status in "objective" psychology as wishfully represented in the devitalized, depersoned printed page of its scientific publications.

10. For further elaboration of this topic, see my *Freud as a Writer* (1982), especially Chapter 3.

References —————————————————————————

Anzieu, D. (1979), The sound image of the self. *Internat. Rev. Psycho-Anal.*, 3:253–258.

Bonaparte, M., Freud, A., & Kris, E., Eds. (1954), *The Origins of Psycho-Analysis: Letters to Wilhelm Fliess, Drafts and Notes: 1887–1902*, trans. E. Mosbacher & J. Strachey. New York: Basic Books.

Chafe, W. (1982), Integration and involvement in speaking, writing, and oral literature. In: *Spoken and Written Language: Exploring Orality and Literacy*, ed. D. Tannen. Norwood, N.J.: Ablex.

Freud, E. L., Ed. (1960), *Letters of Sigmund Freud*, trans. T. Stern & J. Stern. New York: Basic Books.

Freud, S. (1891), *On Aphasia*. London: Imago, 1953.

———— (1892–1894), Preface and footnotes to the translations of Charcot's *Tuesday Lectures. Standard Edition*, 1:133–136. London: Hogarth Press, 1966.

———— (1900), *The Interpretation of Dreams. Standard Edition*, 4 & 5. London: Hogarth Press, 1953.

———— (1901), *The Psychopathology of Everyday Life. Standard Edition*, 6. London: Hogarth Press, 1960.

———— (1905), *Jokes and Their Relation to the Unconscious. Standard Edition*, 8. London: Hogarth Press, 1960.

———— (1909), *Notes upon a Case of Obsessional Neurosis. Standard Edition*, 10:155–318. London: Hogarth Press, 1955. (*Gesammelte Werke*, 7:381–463. Frankfurt am Main: Fischer, 1941).

———— (1913), *Totem and Taboo. Standard Edition*, 13:1–161. London: Hogarth Press, 1961.

———— (1923), The ego and the id. *Standard Edition*, 19:12–66. London: Hogarth Press, 1961.

———— (1925) An autobiographical study. *Standard Edition*, 20:7–70. London: Hogarth Press, 1959.

———— (1933), *New Introductory Lectures on Psycho-Analysis. Standard Edition*, 22:5–182. London: Hogarth Press, 1964.

———— (1939), *Moses and Monotheism. Standard Edition*, 23:7–137. London: Hogarth Press, 1964.

Glover, E. (1931), The therapeutic effect of inexact interpretation. *Internat. J. Psycho-Anal.*, 12:397–341.

Havelock, E. (1963), *Preface to Plato*. Cambridge, Mass.: Belknap.

Isakower, O. (1939), On the exceptional position of the auditory sphere. *Internat. J. Psycho-Anal.*, 20:340–348.

Jakobson, R. (1960), Concluding statement: Linguistics and poetics. In: *Style in Language*, ed. T. Seboek. Cambridge, Mass.: M.I.T. Press.

Jones, E. (1955), *The Life and Work of Sigmund Freud*, Vol. 2. New York: Basic Books.

———— (1957), *The Life and Work of Sigmund Freud*, Vol. 3. New York: Basic Books.

Kaufmann, W. (1980), *Discovering the Mind: Freud versus Adler and Jung*, Vol. 3. New York: McGraw-Hill.

Klein, D. (1981), *Jewish Origins of the Psychoanalytic Movement*. New York: Praeger.

Mahony, P. (1979), The place of psychoanalytic treatment in the history of discourse. *Psychoanal. & Contemp. Thought*, 2:77–111.

———— (1982), *Freud as a Writer*. New York: International Universities Press.

———— (1984), Further reflections on Freud and writing. *J. Amer. Psychoanal. Assn.* 32:847–864.

McGuire, W., Ed. (1974), *The Freud/Jung Letters*, trans. R. Manheim & R. F. C. Hull. Princeton: Princeton University Press.

Mead, M. (1964), Vicissitudes of the study of the total communication process. In: *Approaches to Semiotics*, ed. T. Sebeck et al. The Hague: Mouton, pp. 277–287.

Murphy, J. (1982), Rhetorical history as a guide to the salvation of American reading and writing. In: *The Rhetorical Tradition and Modern Writing*, ed. J. Murphy. New York: Modern Language Association.

Nunberg, H., & Federn, E. (1962), *Minutes of the Vienna Psychoanalytic Society* Vol. 1:1906–1908. New York: International Universities Press.

Ong, W. (1967), *The Presence of the Word*. Ithaca, N.Y.: Cornell University Press.

———— (1977), *Interfaces of the Word*. Ithaca, N.Y.: Cornell University Press.

———— (1982), *Orality and Literacy*. London: Methuen.

Politzer, H. (1969), Review of *Sigmund Freuds Prosa*, by W. Schonau. *German Quarterly*, 42:739–741.

Schönau, W. (1968), *Sigmund Freuds Prosa*. Stuttgart: Metzlersche.

Schur, M. (1972), *Freud: Living and Dying*. New York: International Universities Press.

Spitz, R. (1965), *The First Year of Life*. New York: International Universities Press.

Steiner, G. (1975), *After Babel: Aspects of Translation and Language*. London: Oxford University Press.

Sterba, R. (1982), *Reminiscences of a Viennese Psychoanalyst*. Detroit: Wayne State University Press.

Wittels, F. (1923), *Sigmund Freud: His Personality, His Teaching, and His School*, trans. E. Paul & C. Paul. New York: Dodd, Mead, 1924.

Zumthor, P. (1983), *Introduction à la poésie orale*. Paris: Seuil.

Paul E. Stepansky ————————————————

Feuerbach and Jung as Religious Critics—
With a Note on Freud's Psychology of Religion

> *A squeamish concern that no harm must be done to the higher*
> *things in man is unworthy of an analyst.*
> —Freud to Pfister
> 27 July 1922

Ludwig Feuerbach casts his shadowy presence over much of Freud's psychology of religion. Freud's early familiarity with Feuer-bach, to which Rieff (1959, pp. 24, 314) first drew attention, has rated perfunctory mention in several recent reappraisals of psycho-analysis and religion (Meissner, 1978; Küng, 1979, Wallace, 1984).[1] But Frued's indebtedness to the radical young Hegelian critic has nowhere been taken as a touchstone of inquiry, a fundament out of which the psychoanalytic critique of religion evolves. Here I wish to address this issue, but I propose to do so in the roundabout way of a comparison of Feuerbach and C. G. Jung. Why have I chosen so indirect a route for framing this modest contribution to Freud stud-ies? I wish to argue that Jung, as a student of human religious experience, is in a very real sense Feuerbach's nemesis, his "shad-ow," and that it is by comparing Feuerbach with Jung that Freud stands revealed as the Feuerbachian that he is. This is to say that the comparison of Feuerbach with Jung is really a veiled comparison of Freud with Jung; I believe that a more focused comprehension of Freud the psychologist of religion grows out of the dialogue between

Feuerbach and Jung, but I leave it to the reader to decide how fruitful my oblique strategy actually is. At any rate, my concluding commentary on Freud is offered only as an addendum to recent assessments of Freud and religion (Rieff, 1959, 1966; Meissner, 1978; Küng, 1979; Rizzuto, 1979; Wallace, 1984); it does not purport to be coextensive with those accounts.

Why compare Ludwig Feuerbach and C. G. Jung? By what rationale does one bind the philosopher and young Hegelian critic of the early 19th century to the psychiatrist turned Freudian turned prophet of the early 20th? Feuerbach undertook religious criticism as a frustrated Hegelian, one who viewed Hegel's abstract categories of existence as disembodied figments of truths that are individually perceived and socially defined (see Hook, 1950, pp. 226–233, 260–264). Jung, by contrast, undertook his investigation of religion as a frustrated Freudian, a psychoanalyst who could not abide by the "reductive causalism" of Freud's outlook with its "almost complete disregard of the teleological directedness which is so characteristic of everything psychic" (Jung, 1952a, p. xxiii).[2] Feuerbach sought to defuse Hegel's metaphysics because it failed to do justice to the nature of common sensible experience; Jung sought to infuse Freud's empiricism with new spiritual content because it presumably did justice to nothing *but* the nature of common instinctual experience. Feuerbach ended his career a convinced atheist whose probing analysis of the fetishistic element of human religiosity fueled the demystifying social thought of Marx and Engels; Jung ended his career a prophetic visionary convinced that a lifetime of "empirical" psychological research subserved the irreducible "religious function" of the unconscious. Surely, the extraordinarily divergent intellectual traditions from which Feuerbach and Jung approached the phenomena of human religiosity render suspect any attempt at systematic comparison.

But there is reason to pursue such comparison nonetheless. Although the obvious contextual disparities make any attempt at historical comparison difficult, they do not render it altogether fruitless. Despite the radically different perspectives from which Feuerbach and Jung would reappraise the meaning of the traditional Christian message, the two men shared much in common. Both argued that the only "living" God from whom human values derive was the interior God within, and both bemoaned that dissipating religious projection that robbed humanity of its values, transforming inner ideals into remote objects of worship. Seeking to supplant the immortality provided by "mystified" Christianity with the immortality of a reactivated human spirit, both offered strategies for cultivating anew an inner apprehension of the God-image in man. Each man's divergent conception of what such inner apprehension would entail marks the point at which these two religious humanists part ways. For Feuerbach, the answer rested in tracing "mystical, perverted anthropology," i.e., theology, back to a "real anthropology" of human virtue (1841, p. 107). For Jung, it was a matter of engendering the "psychological culture" needed to develop an "inner correspondence" with the "outer God-image," a correspondence that could potentiate perception of the "sacred figures" in the unconscious (1944, pp. 12, 14).

As a critic of a Hegelian tradition intent on viewing religion as an essential "moment" in the realization of spirit, Feuerbach began by accusing Hegel of confusing the essential with the nonessential in his entire approach to human religiosity. For Hegel, the necessity of religion, as understood by philosophy, was the necessity of spirit's ineluctable ascent from preliminary "subjective" and "objective" modes to the realm of the Absolute. Religion, along with art and philosophy, signified the actualization of Absolute Spirit in the world of human experience; it accomplished "the universal destiny of spirit" (Hegel, 1831, p. 131). God himself was identified with Absolute Spirit and man's apprehension of God was but one form— the representational-feeling form—by which Absolute Spirit gained expression as pure self-consciousness (cf. Findlay, 1958, pp. 339ff.). For Feuerbach, on the other hand, God was the veritable antithesis of Absolute Spirit detached from man's "subjective" sensuous connection to the ordinary world. In fact, God was himself a sensuous being (or at least a "mediately" sensuous being), whereas religion itself was "sensuous and aesthetic" (1851, pp. 13, 104, 114). In making this claim, Feuerbach did no more than reiterate as a religious critic what he came to perceive as the first principle of philosophy in general: Not abstract spirit but the sensuous world was primary in the sense that it was self-subsisting and true. "Spirit," he wrote in his *Lectures on the Essence of Religion* (1851), "is nothing outside of and without sensibility, spirit is only the essence, the sense, the spirit of the senses" (pp. 86–87). God, from this philosophical standpoint, could only be an abstraction of the natural sensuous phenomena that constitute the objects of physical perception; he was in fact "nature in the abstract, that is, removed from physical perception, transformed into an object or concept of the intellect" (p. 104). Primitive nature religion, for Feuerbach, provided the most compelling testimony of the sensuous substrate of the Divinity because it issued from man's realization of his simultaneous dependence on, and obligation to live in harmony with, nature. In elevating nature to the first object of religious worship, pre-Christians did nothing but project onto a deity the feelings and impressions that nature aroused in them (p. 36). Correspondingly, the divine predicates of the God of nature religion were invariably abstracted from nature. God's power was "nothing other than the power of natural phenomena," his eternity expressed man's perception of the infinity of nature, whereas his wisdom embodied man's reverence for "the fabric of natural causes and effects." All in all, the divine predicates "objectify, represent, illustrate nothing other than the essence of nature, or nature pure and simple. The difference is only that God is an abstraction . . . while nature is concrete, that is, real" (p. 103).

At the same time as Feuerbach sought to demonstrate that God differentiated from man was nothing but abstracted nature, he simultaneously set out to prove that God differentiated from nature was nothing but man's own essence (1851, pp. 175–176). This contrasting perspective on divinity, in turn, underscores Feuerbach's interesting juxtaposition of primitive nature religion focusing on "the physical God, or God regarded solely as the cause of nature," with the later Christian preoccupation with God in his "moral and spiritual attributes." If, in the former case, God was indeed "the deified, personified essence of nature," in the latter he became "nothing other than the deified and objectified mind or spirit of man" (1851, p. 21). With the historical transition from nature religion to Christianity, Feuerbach's program of anti-Hegelian demystification underwent a corresponding change of direction. From the attempt to decipher God via the meaning of natural phenomena, to locate the "secret" of nature religion in physics and physiology, he proceeded to demystify the Christian God by appealing to man's own intellectual and emotional endowment: The "secret" of Christian theology became anthropology. It was this claim that underlay his major contribution to the philosophy of religion, The Essence of Christianity (1841).

Because Feuerbach's Christian "God" could not transcend the all-too-human "predicates" attributed to him, the interior relocation of God in man became a function not of psychological perception, but of pedestrian anthropological uncovering. The anthropological essence of religion, that is, was really no more than the summation of human potentialities that man treasured the most, and God himself was only the species-ideal as an individual, more specifically, a subjective human being "in his absolute freedom and unlimitedness." To distill the anthropological core of religion from externalized theology, it was only necessary to refract systematically the human constituents that jointly comprised divine omnipotence. In God's perfect understanding, Feuerbach found "nothing else than the nature of the understanding itself regarded as objective" (1841, p. 35). In his moral perfection, God was nothing but the "moral nature of man posited as the absolute being" (p. 46). As a loving God reconciling his moral perfection to sinning man, and as an incarnated God willing to renounce his divinity for man's sake, God embodied a human deification of love that took man as both its "essential content" and final object. In turn, the fact that man was an object of such immense divine love that God himself actually became a man expressed the true "worth of man." It was a human love capable of transcending the difference between the divine and human personality that represented man's real "saviour and Redeemer" (pp. 47–48, 50–57).

Just as the transcendent divinity of God readily decomposed into the ennobling human emotions that anthropology uncovered, so the alleged "mysteries" of God could be resolved by exposing the different human needs that God's illusory existence subserved. Christ's inexplicable suffering for men really meant that to suffer for others was divine, that feeling was "absolute, divine in its nature." The mystery of the Trinity expressed no more than man's "need of duality, of love, of community, of human self-consciousness" (pp. 60–63, 67). The mystery of the Logos and Divine Image reflected man's need for "Image Worship," whereas the mystery of Providence and Creation testified to man's belief in the "divine reality and significance" of his own creative capacity. The mystery of a "Faith" that enabled man to forego natural reason by appealing to God in prayer, and to embrace miracles as supernatural demonstrations of Divine Will, really signified the absence of limits or scientific obstacles to the power and scope of human feeling. Thus, "feeling is the God of man," and faith was the demonstration of human confidence in the supreme reality of "subjective" over natural rea- son (pp. 121, 126). The mystery of the miraculous conception was a human "wish fulfillment" subjectively integrating the "pleasing" idea of the pure virgin with that of the Mother; the mystery of Christ's resurrection was only the satisfied desire of man's quest for personal immortality (pp. 135–137). Self-evidently, these reductive anthropological verdicts make short shrift of any notion of the "holy."[3]

Jung began precisely where Feuerbach's critique of Christianity ultimately ended: with a projected God manufactured from the emo- tional stuff of human nature. For Jung, however, the realization was not a reassuring testimony to the potential of human virtue, but a horrifying tribute to the untamable unconscious. Feuerbach's de- mystification of Christianity was an intellectual *tour de force*, the brilliant extraction of an "esoteric psychology" from the mystified truth of the Hegelian dialectic (see Hook, 1950, pp. 259–260; Tucker, 1971, pp. 85–94). Jung's reappraisal dated back to his child- hood preoccupation with God and the fantastic products of his own youthful imagination. Whereas Feuerbach understood the Chris- tian God as a reified embodiment of human love and understanding, Jung at age 12 beheld a different kind of anthropomorphic vision of God, a "forbidden thought" he initially warded off with strained intensity but finally embraced as a "trial of human courage":

> I gathered all my courage, as though I were about to leap forthwith into hell-fire, and let the thought come. I saw before me the cathe- dral, the blue sky, God sits on His golden throne, high above the world—and from under the throne an enormous turd falls upon the sparkling new roof, shatters it, and breaks the walls of the cathedral asunder [1961, p. 39].

Although the conscious realization of this "forbidden thought" brought Jung "an enormous, and indescribable relief," it was imme- diately undercut by his "dim understanding" that a God capable of befouling his cathedral "could be something terrible." For Jung, this "terrible" insight undermined his tolerance for the empty, formal Christian theology of his father (a Protestant minister).[4] Recoiling from the supposition that "in the image of God" applied only to man, Jung henceforth apprehended God as a suprapersonal secret mystically perceived in another realm—that occupied by his "other," number two personality. "Esoteric matters" were henceforth felt to belong to "God's world," and could not be communicated to the schoolmates and adults of his everyday existence. Church, on the other hand, became a place of torment for Jung because it denied his intuited realization that God's will could be both terrible and terrifying. The emotional emptiness of his first communion shortly thereafter permanently shattered his sense of union with the church; his religious outlook "disintegrated" (1961, pp. 39–52, passim). God, he concluded, did not exist as an idea that could be philosophically (or religiously) engendered, but as "the most certain and immediate of experiences" (p. 62). Convinced by this time that Schopenhauer's "will" really signified God, Jung felt that man and the proper animals were only "bits of God that had become independent" (p. 67).

Because the anthropomorphic vision of the defecating God that had been revealed to him in childhood was both terrible and "inhuman," Jung could never rest content with the formalized anthropological uncovering operation that would preoccupy Feuerbach. Instead, he sought to locate in psychology the scientific tool that could decipher the collective sense in which man was really "a bit of God" become independent. The key to this process resided in the archetypes, the timeless symbolic forms through which collective psychic existence was enacted. In the symbolism spontaneously produced by his patients, Jung claimed to locate an archetypal "imprint" of God within the human psyche of the present age. In his 1937 Terry Lectures on psychology and religion, the archetypal imprint resided in the "quaternity," an age-old prehistorical symbol associated with the idea of a world-creating deity. In this symbol, Jung detected "a more or less direct representation of the God who is manifest in his creation," and in the continuing presence of this symbol in the dreams of modern people he saw evidence of "the God within." Modern man's "systematic blindness" to his own internally generated religious symbolism was "simply the effect of the prejudice that God is *outside* man" (1937, pp. 58, 61).

In the 1940s, this psychological perspective on divinity blossomed into Jung's mature Christology, a provocative attempt to reconstruct the meaning of both the historical Jesus and the symbols of Christianity from the standpoint of timeless archetypal themes that have reappeared throughout history. In pointed contrast to the 19th-century tradition of German Higher Criticism that, beginning

with D. F. Strauss's *Life of Jesus* (1835), had seized on the contradictory, unhistorical character of the Gospels to humanize Christ in
accord with liberal, communitarian values, Jung took the logical
incomprehensibility of Christian dogma as psychological evidence of
Christ's ahistorically archetypal character. Thus, the fact that the
real historical Christ almost immediately "vanished behind the emotions and projections that swarmed about him from far and near"
did not point to an accretion of "mystification" that required un-
raveling through historical (Strauss, Bruno Bauer), epistemological
(Max Stirner), or anthropological (Feuerbach) criticism. Instead, it
meant that Christ was immediately "absorbed into the surrounding
religious systems and moulded into their archetypal exponent. He
became the collective figure whom the unconscious of his contemporaries expected to appear, and for this reason it is pointless to ask
who he 'really' was" (1948, p. 154). From documentary reports
pointing to the "general projection and assimilation" of the Christ
figure as a historical presence, Jung proceeded to argue that Christ
elicited the cooperation of the collective unconscious for the very
reason that he himself, as an all-embracing totality encompassing the
mythological attributes of the perfect being, symbolized the archetypal idea of the self:

> It was this archetype of the self in the soul of every man that
> responded to the Christian message, with the result that the concrete
> Rabbi Jesus was rapidly assimilated by the constellated archetype. In
> this way Christ realized the idea of the self. But as one can never
> distinguish empirically between a symbol of the self and a God-image,
> the two ideas, however much we try to differentiate them, always
> appear blended together, so that the self appears synonymous with
> the inner Christ of the Johannine and Pauline writings, and Christ
> with God. . . [1948, p. 156].

Just as Christ embodied the archetype of the self, so the Trinity
symbol, for Jung, gave archetypal expression to the developmental
paradigm by which man arrived at his own self-realization or individuation: From a condition of passive, unreflecting dependency
(the Father), man's selfhood passed through an intermediate stage of
differentiated consciousness characterized by reflection and rationality (the Son), only to arrive at a higher level of Fatherhood
capable of integrating rational values with spiritual insight into the
higher directive authority of the collective unconscious (the Holy

Ghost) (1948, pp. 180–187). Jung's psychological analysis of the Trinity and his suggestive explanation of quaternity symbolism as the "missing fourth" of the Trinity formula (1948, pp. 164–180), in turn, paved the way for the conclusions reached in *Aion* (1951). In this late work, he carried the psychological internalization of God to its logical extreme. He argued that the quaternity or mandala sym-bols infiltrating the dreams of modern man represented a "unity of totality" that "stand[s] at the highest point on the scale of objective values because their symbols can no longer be distinguished from the *imago Dei*. Hence all statements about the God-image apply also to the empirical symbols of totality" (1951, pp. 31–32). The self, a "total personality" incorporating both conscious and unconscious contents, consequently became a "God-image, or at least cannot be distinguished from one" (p. 22).

In the original Christian conception of the *imago Dei* embodied in Christ, Jung posited as psychological meaning "an all-embracing totality that even includes the animal side of man." In the promised restoration of man through divine grace, he envisioned a religious integration equivalent to the psychological integration of the collec-tive unconscious through the process of individuation. Evaluating such correspondences as "psychological evidence for the existence of an archetypal content possessing all those qualities which are characteristic of the Christ image in its archaic and medieval forms," Jung finally submitted that Christ himself only embodied the myth of the divine Primordial Man. In reality, he exemplified the archetype of the self, embodying the "God-image in man" (1951, pp. 37–41, 67–68).

Although Feuerbach and Jung offered their reformulations of Christian doctrine as post-Hegelian philosopher of the spirit and post-Freudian psychologist of the unconscious, respectively, both offered strikingly similar rationales for the need to relocate God in man. For Feuerbach, God was an object "of the heart's necessity, not of the mind's freedom" (1841, p. 186), and the elaboration of the theological proofs seeking to isolate the divine existence from man was a deleterious enterprise fraught with contradictions that re-tarded man's intellectual and moral development.

Empirically, God's separate existence caused man to forgo the "scientific" presuppositions of common sense; the separate reality of God posited an empirical existence without empirical boundaries or limitations. Similarly, human perception of God was grounded in sensational consciousness but set aside the limits of sense. In espousing a Trinity that interpreted the three figures of the Christian Godhead as only one, theology cultivated a holy mystery that could only resolve itself into "delusions, phantasmes, contradictions, and sophisms" (1841, p. 235). By promulgating sacraments based on the alleged supernatural qualities of water, bread, and wine, theology denied "what objective reason affirms," and engendered "superstition and immorality" (pp. 236–246).

Morally, the theological detachment of God from man was still more unfortunate. In believing God to be the necessary condition of virtue, man had to believe "in the nothingness of virtue in itself" (p. 202). The belief in revelation similarly injured man's moral sense by evaluating moral behavior in terms of God's commandments instead of the intrinsic worldly quality of our deeds. Most devastating of all, however, was the consequence of "faith" in separating man from man: "Faith makes man partial and narrow; it deprives him of the freedom and ability to estimate duly what is different from himself. Faith is imprisoned within itself" (p. 249).

To escape the tragic contradictions of present-day theology, it was incumbent on man to recognize anew the human needs and values his externalized God had been made to represent. By embracing the religious nature of his own moral feelings, man could overcome alienation and realize a fully human identity:

> Only when we abandon a philosophy of religion, or a theology, which is distinct from psychology and anthropology, and recognize anthropology as itself theology, do we attain to a true, self-satisfying identity of the divine and human being, the identity of the human being with itself [1841, pp. 230–231].

In strikingly similar terms, Jung attempted to situate God in man in order to deify the human values that could alone promote man's inner development:

> The demand made by the *imitatio Christi*—that we should follow the ideal and seek to become like it—ought logically to have the result of developing and exalting the inner man. In actual fact, however, the ideal has been turned by superficial and formalistically minded believers into an external object of worship, and it is precisely this veneration for the object that prevents it from reaching down into the depths of the psyche and giving the latter a wholeness

in keeping with the ideal. Accordingly the divine mediator stands outside as an image, while man remains fragmentary and untouched in the deepest part of him [1944, p. 7].

To Feuerbach, man externalized God at his own expense: "To enrich God, man must become poor; that God may be all, man must be nothing. . . . The more empty life is, the fuller, the more concrete is God" (1841, pp. 26, 73). Jung's diagnosis of the present plight of Christianity expressed the same basic sentiment: "If the supreme value (Christ) and the supreme negation (sin) are outside, then the soul is void; its highest and lowest are missing" (1944, p. 8). To the increasing extent that modern man permitted Christian symbols to be "stiffened into mere objects of belief," he squandered his Christian heritage (1934, pp. 8, 15). This squandering, for Jung, was psychologically portentous: Juxtaposed with an "Eastern Attitude" that exalted the self beyond all bounds, "with Western man the value of the self sinks to zero" (1944, pp. 8–11).

If both Feuerbach and Jung felt impelled to reevaluate the status of God on behalf of an alienated and ethically depleted human race, the conclusions they reached remain distinct. Each saw the devastating consequences of formalistic externalization, yet each retained a different conception of what remained to be internalized. Feuerbach's philosophy of anthropomorphism, ever sensitive to the genetic roots of human culture, took sensible man as the measure of all things. The starting point of his psychology of religion—and the nexus of his critique of Hegel—revolved around the integrity of sense perception as man's basic instrumentality for deciphering the natural phenomena that account for divine transcendence. Although stressing the centrality of affective experience in obtaining knowledge, Feuerbach always understood human emotions in the pedestrian sense that such feeling states were accessible to reason and compatible with human sensory endowment. Thus, at the same time as Feuerbach prescribed the reactivation of moral sensibilities grown moribund through projection, he apprehended such sensibilities not as spiritual imponderables, but as the articles of what Sidney Hook rightly terms "a rather primitive empirical psychology" (1950, p. 236). Feuerbach not only traced religion back to human emotion, that is, but robbed human emotion of any mysterious spiritual content, concentrating instead on its humanizing import in the realm of social relations.

This is understandable, for as a radical young Hegelian committed to a secular interpretation of history, Feuerbach ultimately saw formal religion as a historically determined way station in the progressive development of spirit. Convinced that the content of Christianity was myth, he hoped to engender a philosophical humanism as the next progressive step of spirit above Christianity. In contrast to the right-wing Hegelians of his day who viewed Jesus as the paradigmatic culmination of Hegel's philosophy—the fusion of God and man in a historical figure—Feuerbach saw the unity of God and man as an emergent property of historical development occurring in all humanity. By espousing divine immanence, he was forced to deny that God was transcendent (see Brazill, 1970, pp. 13–61). Consequently, the keynote of *The Essence of Christianity* was that

> Man cannot get beyond his true nature. He may indeed by means of the imagination conceive individuals of another so-called higher kind, but he can never get loose from his species, his nature; the conditions of being, the positive predicates which he gives to these other individuals, are always determinations or qualities drawn from his own nature—qualities in which he in truth only images and projects himself [1841, p. 11].

The God (or Spirit) within man might subsequently emerge only when man accepted his humanity as the sole criterion of divinity. As the epitome of the revitalized human religiosity destined to issue from his critique, Feuerbach fixed on the emotion of love. Yet, in accord with the requirements of his empirical social psychology, he preached a humanistic religion of love not to deify a human emotion beyond the limits of empirical inquiry, but to promote the binding force that he viewed as the source of moral relations and the most effective agency of moral progress (see Hook, 1950, pp. 251–252).

If Feuerbach's mission was to humanize the predicates of divinity by interpreting them at the level of man's moral self-improvement, Jung's was rather to demonstrate the intrinsic "divinity" of the archetypal themes that radiated from man's collective unconscious. This seems to be the best way of conceptualizing Jung's repeated testimony to the significance of man's inborn "religious function." Jung believed the religious function, in the guise of the archetypal idea of God, was "an absolutely necessary psychological function" because the collective unconscious that was constitutive of human nature was itself "irrational," and thus able to gain expression only through a religious symbolism that transcended the categories of conscious mental experience. It stands to reason, then, that in tying man's "religious function" to his "empirical" psychological investi-gations, Jung hardly sought to demonstrate the empirical decomposi-tion of divine transcendence into mundane human attributes. In-stead, he sought to relocate the religious function in man because it was only in the human unconscious itself that positive indications of spiritual transcendence could be scientifically identified. As a therapist, moreover, Jung felt that to repress the religious function, or, in the manner of Feuerbach, to devalue it through demystifica-tion, was to court psychological disaster. Under such circumstances, man could not hope to integrate the expressive and prospective requirements of his collective unconscious with the claims of his conscious ego and, through this failure, the collective unconscious would be "prodigiously strengthened . . . and, through its archaic collective contents, [begin] to exercise a powerful influence on the conscious mind" (1917/1943, p. 94).

Jung, it should be stressed, was hardly hostile to the idea of a transcendent God existing outside man. Willing to concede that theology might readily take the psychological self as an allegory of Christ, he distinguished the archetypal "imprint" of God that psy-chology could demonstrate from the metaphysical derivation of the archetype:

> We simply do not know the ultimate derivation of the archetype any more than we know the origin of the psyche. The competence of psychology as an empirical science only goes so far as to establish, on the basis of comparative research, whether for instance the imprint found in the psyche can or cannot reasonably be termed a "god-image." Nothing positive or negative has thereby been asserted about the possible existence of God, any more than the archetype of the "hero" posits the actual existence of a hero [1944, p. 14; cf. 1937, pp. 5–6].

Again, in his important essay "On the Psychology of the Uncon-scious" (1917/1943), Jung reiterated his belief that the psychologi-cally necessary function supplied by the idea of God had

> nothing whatever to do with the question of God's existence. The human intellect can never answer this question, still less give any proof of God. Moreover such proof is superfluous, for the idea of an all-powerful divine Being is present everywhere, unconsciously if not consciously, because it is an archetype. . . . Our intellect has long

known that we can form no proper idea of God, much less picture to ourselves in what manner he really exists, if at all. The existence of God is once and for all an unanswerable question [p. 71].

By arguing that *mysterium magnum* was rooted in the human psyche, Jung believed he had located a verifiable psychological phe-nomenon that could heighten man's spiritual muscle tone apart from the "unknown and incomprehensible content" from which divine symbolism derived. As a psychologist of religion, then, Jung did not share Feuerbach's obsessive need to employ empirical psychology as a reductionist tool that could only decipher religious phenomena at the expense of God's transcendence. Instead, Jung maintained that questions involving God's separate existence and the truth or falsity of assertions of faith were "fundamentally sterile questions" im-mune to the rational criticism of the scientist. From this standpoint Jung's perspective on the advisability of a "belief" in a transcendent God became a pragmatic and psychological one. In the essay "On the Psychology of the Unconscious," he suggested, program-matically, that it is "wiser to acknowledge the idea of God con-sciously; for, if we do not, something else is made God, usually something quite inappropriate and stupid such as only an 'en-lightened' intellect could hatch forth" (1917/1943, p. 71). Yet, in the equally significant paper on "The Relations between the Ego and the Unconscious" (1928), he expressed concern lest patients who experienced the grandiosity of a "mana-personality" through conscious insight into their "anima"

concretize it as an extramundane 'Father in Heaven,' complete with the attribute of absoluteness—something that many people seem very prone to do. This would be tantamount to giving the uncon-scious a supremacy that was just as absolute . . . so that all value would flow over to that side. The logical result is that the only thing left behind here is a miserable, inferior, worthless, and sinful little heap of humanity. . . . On psychological grounds, therefore, I would recommend that no God be constructed out of the archetype of the mana-personality. In other words, he must not be concretized, for only thus can I avoid projecting my values and nonvalues into God and Devil, and only thus can I preserve my human dignity, my specific gravity, which I need so much if I am not to become the unresisting shuttlecock of unconscious forces [pp. 235, 236].

It is a typically Feuerbachian plaint, but one that incorporates a crucial reversal: For Jung, it was not a transcendent God but a reified collective unconscious that threatened to wreak havoc by depleting the conscious ego. By the same token, it was the archetyp' al imprint of God in man and not man's demystified emotional endowment that embodied "a living and ubiquitous psychic fact," and it was the potential for spiritual growth inherent in this psychic reality that was integral to the therapeutic aims of psychology. Be' lief in God might represent a valid therapeutic need, but a deepen' ing of the patient's endogenous religious function through integra' tion of the "divine" content of his collective unconscious with the ego remained the guiding therapeutic goal. The implications of Jung's pragmatic differentiation between God and his symbolic im' print in man became increasingly evident in his later writings. "One is then tempted," he wrote in *Aion,* "to attach greater importance to the immediate and living presence of the archetype than to the idea of the historical Christ" (1951, p. 68).

By the strength of this final value judgment making Christ a symbol of the self rather than the self a symbol of Christ, Jung ultimately ended up precisely where Feuerbach began: with a mysti' fied divinity rooted in the self, but still full of inexplicable contradic' tions. Feuerbach, ever the demystifier, provided a simple natu' ralistic explanation of God's "evil side" in his discussion of pre' Christian nature religion. Just as God's goodness abstracted those natural phenomena that were "useful, good, and helpful to man," so the evil God merely embodied the fact that "nature is also the cause of effects that are hostile and harmful to man" (1851, p. 111). It hardly mattered whether the evil side of nature was personified as a separate Devil or associated with the anger of the beneficent God. In either case, divine evil, like divine goodness, was decipherable and, as such, mundane. Jung, by contrast, took God's antinomies to heart precisely because he viewed them as profoundly suggestive of the problematic ethical dimension of man's own indwelling spir' ituality. Because Jung's psychological self is a transcendental con' cept expressing the totality of conscious and unconscious contents, it must be described in antinomical terms, incorporating the dark half of the human totality that Jung designated the "shadow." Inso' far as the Christ figure is a parallel to the psychic manifestation of the self, it too must represent an integration of Christ with the Anti' Christ, that "imitating spirit of evil who follows in Christ's footsteps like a shadow following the body" (1951, p. 42). Just as good and evil "being coexistent halves of a moral judgment, do not derive from one another but are always there together" (p. 47), so

Christ is the perfect man who is crucified, the composite representation of moral opposites paralleling the state of conflict operative in
the human self.

In his formal Christology, Jung invoked the principle of evil to
formulate the conception of divine "totality" that prefigured the
logical transformation of Trinitarian thinking into quaternity symbolism. For Jung, it was the positive substantiality of evil, as evi-
denced by the products of the collective unconscious, that belied the
Christian explanation of evil as a *privatio boni,* and mandated the
incorporation of the Devil into the Trinitarian formula:

> It is difficult to make out in what relation he stands to the Trinity.
> As the adversary of Christ, he would have to take up an equivalent
> counterposition and be, like him, a 'son of God.' But that would lead
> straight back to certain Gnostic views according to which the devil,
> as Satanaël, is God's first son, Christ being the second. A further
> logical inference would be the abolition of the Trinity formula and its
> replacement by a quaternity [1948, pp. 169–170].

This "counterposition" of Christ and Devil presupposed a "common life" uniting "not only the Father and the 'light' son, but the
Father and his *dark* emanation," and this commonality, in turn,
pointed to the "dual aspect" of God the Father (1948, p. 175).

In his *Answer to Job* (1952b) published a year after *Aion,* Jung
believed he had located in the saga of Job a veritable case study of
the Old Testament God's own "evil" side. In this "unvarnished
spectacle of divine savagery and ruthlessness," God emerged as a
natural phenomenon of unreflecting amorality venting his wrath on
a harmless but more self-reflective subject whose only crime is an
intuitive appreciation of God's own inner antinomy. "Job," Jung
wrote, "is no more than the outward occasion for an inward process
of dialectic in God" (pp. 366, 378), and he saw ample evidence of
the "dark side" of this dialectic not only in the misery of Job, but in
the human sacrifice of Christ needed to appease the "forgiving"
God of goodness and the imposition of an Anti-Christ on mankind
after the work of redemption had been done.

For Feuerbach, the contradictions of God's nature were the unhealthy offshoots of an artificial theology. Eliminate the faulty
"proofs" that separate God from man, he argued, and the contradictions would vanish. For Jung, however, the paradoxical nature of
God was unresolvable precisely because it was the reflection of a

telling psychological reality: the inner conflictedness of man himself. Insofar as God acted out of the unconscious, man was obliged to embrace the divine antinomy as psychological truth if he wished to be in a position to harmonize and unite the opposing influences to which his own mind was exposed. Like Feuerbach, he ended on a prescriptive note, but it was one without any trace of buoyant optimism. Man may indeed become himself, but not by simply re-trieving the human qualities he has unwittingly reified in God. Instead he must begin by accepting the unpalatable contradictions of God as his own, and then seek to resolve this antinomy with his own psychic resources. Since Apocalypse, Jung admonished in *Job*, we know that God is not only to be loved, but also to be feared:

> He fills us with evil as well as with good, otherwise he would not need to be feared; and because he wants to become man, the uniting of his antinomy must take place in man. This involves man in a new responsibility. He can no longer wriggle out of it on the plea of his littleness and nothingness, for the dark God has slipped the atom bomb and chemical weapons into his hands and given him the power to empty out the apocalyptic vials of wrath on his fellow creatures. Since he has been granted an almost godlike power, he can no longer remain blind and unconscious. He must know something of God's nature and of metaphysical processes if he is to understand himself and thereby achieve gnosis of the Divine [1952b, p. 461].

Jung too would have the religious truths of psychology be human-izing truths capable of draining the "apocalyptic vials of wrath." Unlike Feuerbach, however, he did not believe this could ever be a simple matter of deciphering the natural fetishism of human activity and extolling the "loving" human sentiments that remained once the operation was complete. For Jung, God's paradoxical two-side-ness can never be deciphered; it is the indecipherable rock bottom, the psychological primordium from which all attempts at self-over-coming must issue. This is hardly a cheery verdict, and it hardly betokens the "critical" attitude to religion embodied in the work of Feuerbach. As a psychologist preoccupied with the profound anti-nomies of the human unconscious, however, it was to be the logical resting place of Jung's mature religious thought.

"I should be very sorry if you, the student of law, would entirely neglect philosophy, while I, the godless, the empirically minded man of medicine, am attending two philosophy courses and, together

with Paneth, am reading Feuerbach." Thus mused the young Freud
to his Rumanian confidant Edward Silberstein in the fall of 1874 (8
November 1874, in Stanescu, 1971, pp. 199–200). Freud's interest
in Feuerbach, broached here in the context of his early philosophy
studies with Franz Brentano, was destined to outlive the phase of
his youthful liberal studies. Not incidentally, the portion of his
library that Freud transported to London in 1938—the selection of
titles that "is a product of Freud's judgment in his later years of
books he thought useful or worthy of preservation" (Trosman and
Simmons, 1973, p. 646)—included the sum of Feuerbach's mature
output: *The Essence of Christianity* (1841), *The Question of Immortality from the Standpoint of Anthropology* (1846), and *Lectures on
the Essence of Religion* (1851), along with the bible of all young
Hegelian criticism, Strauss's *Life of Jesus* (1835).

Predictably, Freud's forays into religious psychology bear the imprint of his early exposure to Feuerbachian criticism. Although
Feuerbach is not cited by Freud, the psychoanalytic critique of
religion is essentially a continuation of Feuerbach's anti-Hegelian
campaign, with psychoanalysis as a new and more potent vehicle of
demystification. Indeed, Freud's entire psychology of religion can be
read as an index of his continuing commitment to Feuerbach over
Jung, an opting for the demystification of consciously held religious
beliefs over the opposing campaign to sacralize unconscious contents. Freud, of course, strengthened Feuerbach's critique by invoking his own psychoanalytic anthropology to concretize the "feeling
of dependency" that Feuerbach had seen as the foundation of religion. Feuerbach, understandably, had envisioned his own conception of man's "sensuous" dependency on nature as a strengthened
reformulation of the vague feeling of dependency that his predecessor, the Christian apologist Schleiermacher (1799), had seen as the
basis of religious belief: "My feeling of dependency is not a theological, Schleiermacherian, nebulous, indeterminate, abstract feeling. My feeling of dependency has eyes and ears, hands and feet; it is
nothing other than the man who feels and sees himself to be dependent . . . And what man is dependent on, what he feels and knows
himself to be dependent on *is nature, an object of the senses*" (1851,
p. 44). For Freud, however, man is not simply a sensuous creature
who must animistically rationalize his connection to nature; he is
the perpetrator of the primal crime, and his "dependency" on re-

ligious beliefs is significantly constituted by the residue of "filial guilt" generated by this prehistorical human action. Pre-Christian man was dependent on his totemic systems of belief because they served to allay the "burning sense of guilt" associated with his "complicity in the common crime" (1913, pp. 144, 146). Correspondingly, Christian man became dependent on *his* system of beliefs because Christ represented a son-deity even better able to relieve the burden of complicity: "There was an alternative method of allaying their guilt and this was first adopted by Christ. He sacrificed his own life and so redeemed the company of brothers from original sin" (p. 153; cf. 1939, pp. 86ff.). When, at the end of his life, Freud sought to explain the Jewish people's resistance to the specifically Christian resolution to mankind's collective burden of guilt, he did so by appealing to a peculiarly Jewish vicissitude of religious history. The Jews were the putative murderers of Moses (1939, pp. 36–37, 47–50), the erstwhile liberator who was also the tyrannic promulgator of a monotheism hearkening back to the primal father. It was the Jews who committed the primal crime yet a second time:

> Fate had brought the great deed and misdeed of primaeval days, the killing of the father, closer to the Jewish people by causing them to repeat it on the person of Moses, an outstanding father-figure. It was a case of 'acting out' instead of remembering . . . To the suggestion that they should remember, which was made to them by the doctrine of Moses, they reacted, however, by disavowing their action; they remained halted at the recognition of the great father and thus blocked their access to the point from which Paul was later to start his continuation of the primal history. It is scarcely a matter of indifference or of chance that the violent killing of another great man became the starting-point of Paul's new religious creation as well [1939, pp. 88–89].

In both "The Future of an Illusion" (1927) and the last of his *New Introductory Lectures on Psycho-Analysis* (1933), Freud grafted psychoanalytic insight to more conventional Feuerbachian premises in order to gauge anew the strength of man's illusional dependency on his God. In these late works, he supplanted his original emphasis on the phylogenetic basis of the feeling of dependency with a more immediate infantile prototype: It was not merely the residue of the primal crime but the infant's ontogenetic helplessness before his parents—and especially his father—that induced man to transform the forces of nature into a transcendent Father that he termed God. By invoking psychological helplessness as a primary ontogenetic reason impelling man toward a system of religious projections, Freud expanded the explanatory range without really enhancing the explanatory depth of Feuerbach's original argument. The feeling of dependency to be dymystified by reason took on an added dimen‚ sion: God was not merely the projected representation of man's sensuous dependency on nature, but, specifically, the protective father who, alone, made good the helplessness each man experi‚ enced in childhood. Such helplessness, moreover, pertained not only to nature, but to the cruelty of fate and the privations imposed by civilized life (1927, pp. 17, 18; cf. 1933, pp. 163, 167–168).

When, bolstered by these ontogenetic insights, Freud indulged his phylogenetic preoccupations in his final religious commentary, *Moses and Monotheism* (1939), he showed how the "psychology of individual men" (p. 109) bequeathed by psychoanalysis could sub‚ serve Feuerbachian reconstructions about the course of religious history. This attempt to make the historical evolution of religion dovetail with the historical vicissitudes of dependency relationships is a Feuerbachian enterprise, however broadened by psychoanalytic categories. Appealing to the early "longing for the father" that subtends mankind's "powerful need for an authority who can be admired, before whom one bows down, by whom one is ruled and perhaps even ill‚treated," Freud opined that "all the characteristics, with which we equipped the great man are paternal characteristics, and [that] the essence of great men for which we vainly search lies in this conformity" (p. 109). And what of Moses, the prototypical great man of history? His efficacy on the historical stage, Freud observes, is reducible to his paternal stature; he is *a* primal father who hearkens back to *the* primal father. In his heroic paternal guise, Moses compels allegiance to a God who is made in *his* image. The Feuerbachian cast of Freud's cautious reconstruction is unmis‚ takable:

> It was probably not easy for them [the Jews] to distinguish the image of the man Moses from that of his God; and their feeling was right in this, for Moses may have introduced traits of his own personality into the character of his God—such as his wrathful temper and his relentlessness [p. 110].

Neither the ambitious historical design of *Moses and Monotheism* nor its meaning as a "novel of origins" (Robert, 1974, pp. 158ff.) nor its relationship to Freud's own "father complex" (Wallace, 1977) should obscure its status as a fundamentally Feuerbachian tract. By Freud's own admission, the psychological import of his "historical novel" (Freud to Zweig, 30 September 1934, in E. Freud, 1970, p. 91) parallels and extends that of *Totem and Taboo*. It "leads us to a conclusion which reduces religion to a neurosis of humanity and explains its enormous power in the same way as a neurotic compulsion in our individual patients" (1939, p. 55); it thereby reaffirmed his conviction that "religious phenomena are only to be understood on the pattern of the individual neurotic symptoms familiar to us" (1939, p. 58; cf. pp. 80, 85, 92). To this extent, then, *Moses and Monotheism* recalls, even as *Totem and Taboo* anticipates, the moralizing verdict of "The Future of an Illusion." It is the latter work that encapsulates Freud's Feuerbachian verdict on human religiosity. It is the work he "had been wanting to write for a long time" and could no longer put off because "the impulse became too strong" (Freud to Pfister, 16 October 1927, in Meng and E. Freud, 1963, p. 109). It is the work that constituted Freud's preamble to the ethical import of psychoanalytic knowledge, the work through which he sought to hand psychoanalysis over "to a profession which does not yet exist, a profession of *lay* curers of souls who need not be doctors and should not be priests" (Freud to Pfister, 25 November 1928, in Meng and E. Freud, 1963, p. 126). Little wonder, then, that Freud viewed "The Future of an Illusion," for all its reductive animus, as a capstone of his later creativity. "I shall probably not publish anything further unless I am definitely pressed to do so," he informed Arnold Zweig in the winter of 1929 (Freud to Zweig, 20 February 1929, in E. Freud, 1970, pp. 5–6).

And who is the looming presence that stands in the background of "The Future of an Illusion"? It is none other than Ludwig Feuerbach. Freud's belief that "infantilism is destined to be surmounted," his faith in the practicality of an "education to reality" that could nurture the rational operation of the intellect to the point of transcending religious illusions, his insistence that the soft voice of the intellect "does not rest till it has gained a hearing" (1927, pp. 48, 49, 53)—these eloquent protestations are all Feuerbachian at their core. They are strikingly reminiscent of the moving statement of intent that Feuerbach formulated early in his *Lectures on the Essence of Religion* (1851). It is a statement which, in its broad humanitarian sweep and unqualified faith in enlightenment, could easily serve as the motto of "The Future of an Illusion":

> My primary concern is and always has been to illumine the obscure essence of religion with the torch of reason, in order that man may at least cease to be the victim, the plaything, of all those hostile powers which from time immemorial have employed and are still employing the darkness of religion for the *oppression* of mankind. It was my purpose to demonstrate that the powers which man worships and fears in his religious life, which he seeks to propitiate even with bloody human sacrifices, are merely creatures of his own unfree, fearful mind and of his ignorant unformed intelligence; to demonstrate that the being which man, in religion and theology, sets up as a distinct being over against himself, is his own essence. It was my purpose to demonstrate this so that man, who is always unconsciously governed and determined by his own essence alone, may in future consciously take his own human essence as the law and determining ground, the aim and measure, of his ethical and political life. And this will inevitably come to pass. Whereas hitherto misunderstood religion, religious obscurantism, has been the supreme principle of politics and ethics, from now on, or at some future date, religion properly understood, religion seen in terms of man, will determine the destinies of mankind.
>
> It was this aim, and insight into religion that would promote human freedom, independence, love, and happiness, that determined the scope of my historical treatment of religion [1851, pp. 22–23].

Notes

1. Meissner (1978), discussing "The Future of an Illusion," observed that, in his assumption "that all religious behavior and belief is a form of obsessive-compulsive neurosis . . . Freud could not escape the heritage of Schleiermacher and Feuerbach" (p. 124). In his Yale Terry Lectures, the theologian Hans Küng termed Feuerbach the "grandfather" of Freudian atheism and made repeated mention of the "obvious" dependence of Freud's "illusion theory" on Feuerbach's "projection theory" (1979, pp. 3, 6–7, 44, 75–76). More recently, Wallace (1984) deems Nietzsche and Feuerbach the two figures whose work subtends Freud's equation of religion and psychopathology (p. 115); he is more specific still in pointing to Feuerbach as the writer to whom Freud was exposed and who "anticipated, in part, [Freud's] notion of religion as projection" (p. 116), as well as being a source of Freud's view of religion as infantile wish fulfillment (p. 124).

2. I have considered the grounds of Jung's discontent with Freud and psycho-analysis in some detail (Stepansky, 1976). Among more recent psychoanalytic commentaries on the Freud–Jung relationship following the publication of the Freud–Jung correspondence (McGuire, 1974), see Shengold (1976), Loewald (1977), Van Der Leeuw (1977), and, especially, the illuminating studies of Gedo (1983, Section IV).

3. Predictably, Rudolf Otto begins his inquiry into "the idea of the holy" by articulating the anti-Feuerbachian response to the notion that divine mysteries decompose into human emotions: "For so far are these 'rational' attributes from exhausting the idea of deity, that they in fact imply a non-rational or supra-rational Subject of which they are predicates. They are 'essential' (and not merely 'accidental') attributes of that subject, but they are also, it is important to notice, *synthetic* essential attributes. That is to say, we have to predicate them of a subject which they qualify, but which in its deeper essence is not, nor indeed can be, comprehended in them; which rather requires comprehension of a quite different kind" (1958, p. 2).

4. On Jung's early disenchantment with Protestantism, see the biographical material in Hannah (1976).

References

Brazill, W. (1970), *The Young Hegelians.* New Haven: Yale University Press.

Feuerbach, L. (1841), *The Essence of Christianity,* trans. G. Eliot. New York: Harper & Row, 1957.

—————— (1851), *Lectures on the Essence of Religion,* trans. R. Manheim. New York: Harper & Row, 1967.

Findlay, J. N. (1958), *The Philosophy of Hegel: An Introduction and Re-Examination.* New York: Macmillan.

Freud, E. L., Ed. (1970), *The Letters of Sigmund Freud and Arnold Zweig,* trans. E. Robson-Scott & R. W. Robson-Scott. New York: Harcourt, Brace & World.

Freud, S. (1913), *Totem and Taboo. Standard Edition,* 13:1–161. London: Hogarth Press, 1953.

—————— (1927), The future of an illusion. *Standard Edition,* 21:5–56. London: Hogarth Press, 1961.

—————— (1933), *New Introductory Lectures on Psycho-Analysis. Standard Edition,* 22:5–182. London: Hogarth Press, 1964.

—————— (1939), *Moses and Monotheism. Standard Edition,* 23:1–137. London: Hogarth Press, 1964.

Gedo, J. (1983), *Portraits of the Artist: Psychoanalysis of Creativity and Its Vicissitudes.* New York: Guilford.

Hannah, B. (1976), *Jung: Life and Work.* New York: Putnam.

Hegel, G. W. F. (1831), On religion. In: *On Art, Religion, Philosophy: Introductory Lectures to the Realm of Absolute Spirit,* ed. J. G. Gray. New York: Harper & Row, 1970.

Hook, S. (1950), *From Hegel to Marx.* Ann Arbor: University of Michigan Press.

Jung, C. G. (1917/1943), On the psychology of the unconscious. *Collected Works,* 7:3–119. New York: Pantheon, 1953.

_____ (1928), The relations between the ego and the unconscious. *Collected Works,* 7:123–241. New York: Pantheon, 1953.

_____ (1934), Archetypes of the collective unconscious. *Collected Works,* 9:3–42. Princeton: Princeton University Press, 1959.

_____ (1937), Psychology and religion. *Collected Works,* 11:3–105. Princeton: Princeton University Press, 1969.

_____ (1944), *Psychology and Alchemy. Collected Works,* 12. Princeton: Princeton University Press, 1953.

_____ (1948), A psychological approach to the dogma of the Trinity. *Collected Works,* 11:107–200. Princeton: Princeton University Press, 1969.

_____ (1951), *Aion. Collected Works,* 9(2). Princeton: Princeton University Press, 1959.

_____ (1952a), *Symbols of Transformation. Collected Works,* 5. Princeton: Princeton University Press, 1967.

_____ (1952b), *Answer to Job. Collected Works,* 11:355–470. Princeton: Princeton University Press, 1958.

_____ (1961), *Memories, Dreams, Reflections.* New York: Vintage.

Küng, H. (1979), *Freud and the Problem of God.* New Haven: Yale University Press.

Loewald, H. W. (1977), Transference and countertransference: The roots of psychoanalysis. *Psychoanal. Quart.,* 46:514–527.

McGuire, W., Ed. (1974), *The Freud/Jung Letters,* trans. R. Manheim & R. F. C. Hull. Princeton: Princeton University Press.

Meissner, W. W. (1978), Psychoanalytic aspects of religious experience. *The Annual of Psychoanalysis,* 6:103–141. New York: International Universities Press.

Meng, H., & Freud, E. L., Eds. (1963), *Psycho-Analysis and Faith: The Letters of Sigmund Freud and Oshar Pfister,* trans. E. Mosbacher. London: Hogarth Press.

Otto, R. (1958), *The Idea of the Holy: An Inquiry into the Non-Rational Factor in the Idea of the Divine and Its Relation to the Rational,* trans. J. W. Harvey. New York: Oxford University Press.

Rieff, P. (1959), *Freud: The Mind of the Moralist.* Garden City, N.Y.: Doubleday.

_____ (1966), *The Triumph of the Therapeutic: Uses of Faith after Freud.* New York: Harper & Row.

Rizzuto, A.-M. (1979), *The Birth of the Living God: A Psychoanalytic Study.* Chicago: University of Chicago Press.

Robert, M. (1974), *From Oedipus to Moses: Freud's Jewish Identity,* trans. R. Manheim. Garden City, N.Y.: Doubleday, 1976.

Schleiermacher, F. (1799), *On Religion: Speeches to Its Cultural Despisers,* trans. J. Oman. New York: Harper & Row, 1958.

Shengold, L. (1976), The Freud/Jung letters. *J. Amer. Psychoanal. Assn.,* 24:669–683.

Stanescu, H. (1971), Young Freud's letters to his Rumanian friend, Silberstein. *Israel Ann. Psychiat. & Rel. Disc.,* 9:195–207.

Stepansky, P. E. (1976), The empiricist as rebel: Jung, Freud, and the burdens of discipleship. *J. Hist. Behav. Sci.,* 12:216–239.

Trosman, H., & Simmons, R. D. (1973), The Freud library. *J. Amer. Psychoanal. Assn.,* 21:646–687.

Tucker, R. (1971), *Philosophy and Myth in Karl Marx.* Cambridge: Cambridge University Press.

Van Der Leeuw, P. J. (1977), The impact of the Freud–Jung correspondence on the history of ideas. *Internat. Rev. Psycho-Anal.,* 4:349–362.

Wallace, E. R. (1977), The psychodynamic determinants of *Moses and Monotheism. Psychiatry,* 40:79–87.

———— (1984), Freud and religion: A history and reappraisal. *The Psychoanalytic Study of Society,* 10:113–161. Hillsdale, N.J.: Analytic Press.

John E. Gedo ————————————————————————

On the Origins of the Theban Plague*:
Assessments of Sigmund Freud's Character

CHILDHOOD IN CORINTH

Not long ago, at one of our national meetings, I was asked to discuss an impressive paper (Abraham, 1982) dealing with the influence of Sigmund Freud's inner life on the intellectual history of psychoanalysis. Informed by the latest results of archival research, the author convincingly argued that Freud's personal difficulties were centered on the legacies of his troubled relationship in earliest childhood to his self-centered and volcanic young mother. The paper in question explored the possibility that Freud's clinical theories paid little attention to the pregenital era, and, *pari passu*, to maternal influences stemming from that period of development, because of his defensive need to deny the relevance of those emotional vicissitudes that he was unable personally to overcome. Only in his 1931 essay on "Female Sexuality" did Freud acknowledge the primal influence of the pregenital mother on human destiny.

One could scarcely dismiss the prima facie plausibility of this straightforward psychobiographical thesis. To be sure, its proponent

---

*In homage to Freud, I have chosen a title and headings that summarize my theses through allusion to the Oedipus myth. I have used foreign phrases throughout this essay in the same spirit.

seemingly overlooked the self-analytic insight Freud communicated to Fliess in 1897 (Bonaparte, A. Freud, and Kris, 1954, pp. 218–221) to the effect that the availability of a nursemaid during the second year of his life, when his next sibling had been born—and died—conferred lifesaving benefits on him. In other words, Freud was aware, before he constructed his initial psychoanalytic theory in 1900, that, in his own life experience, events decisive for character development went back to the preverbal era. Did he then repress this vital piece of insight for the next three decades?

Our answer to this question will depend on our assessment of Freud's character in adult life. As I understood her thesis, Abraham viewed the middle-aged Freud, in the process of erecting his psychoanalytic edifice, as a rather pathetic person, unable to obtain psychological assistance for the archaic problems besetting him. Thus she understood as an evasion Freud's statement of 1931 that a boy's ambivalence toward his mother is diminished during their oedipal love affair because of the opportunity to displace its negative component onto his male rivals. In her judgment, such an evolution of the child's relationship to his mother is primarily a defensive maneuver. To complete this picture, she implied that, in Freud's own case, developments of this kind would have lacked authenticity because the boy's father, far from being a threatening rival, was (in her view) a mild little man. Evaluations of the character of the protagonist may thus turn out to rely on dubious character diagnoses about other actors who have roles in the drama!

My own conception of the interplay between Freud's personality and his scientific contributions has changed little since I wrote my first piece of Freudiana almost 20 years ago (1968). In my opinion, Freud used introspective insights to validate and advance his clinical findings with neurotic patients; in other words, his attention was generally focused on the same issues in his own life that he was encountering as matters of central concern in his therapeutic activities. As Gardner (1983) has recently shown, analytic discoveries are unlikely to be made in any other way! And Freud himself was clearly testifying to this constraint when he informed Fliess (Bonaparte, A. Freud, and Kris, 1954, pp. 234–235) that self-analysis is basically the application to one's own instance of what one has learned from and about patients: Oedipus does not recapture memories of his infancy; he learns about it from witnesses.

In point of fact, whatever the subjective roots of his intellectual work may have been, Freud's delineation of the Oedipus complex in the late 1890s has stood the test of time. The psychoanalytic consensus today still views oedipal vicissitudes as nuclear for the neurotic conflicts of adults; if many of us are equally interested in studying a number of other psychological issues as they relate to personality organization, this expansion of concern to preoedipal transactions has been necessitated by the broadening scope of our investigations, beyond the boundaries of neurosis as such, to questions relating to character as well as creativity. Hence a significant *historical* inquiry must address itself to Freud's intellectual agenda around the turn of the century, instead of looking for reasons, in his subjective world or elsewhere, for a putative failure to tackle certain problems that interest us today.

During the period most relevant for the thesis we are considering, Freud was seeking a solution for the *general* problem of the psychological influence of the past on the present. We should recall that in *Studies on Hysteria* (Breuer and Freud, 1893–1895) only the pathogenic effects of traumatic events in *adult* life had been viewed as relevant aspects of the past. In the next decade, as Freud gained experience with nonhypnotic methods of exploratory therapy, the etiologically significant traumata he uncovered were invariably infantile-sexual. Consequently, he gradually came to realize that, in the neuroses, it is the shadow of the *childhood* past that falls upon the present. By 1900, he understood that his own neurotic conflicts, like those of his hysterical and obsessional patients, were centered on a nexus of repressed childhood fantasies that echo the manifest themes of Sophocles' *Oedipus Rex*. To gain understanding of these cardinal issues of psychoanalytic psychology—insights that were to insure him a unique place in the history of science—Freud did not need to investigate his troublesome preoedipal transactions with his mother (or with his nursemaid, or with his living and dead siblings, or with the members of his bewildering extended family).

To put the matter more briefly, I have begun my exposition by citing the cautionary tale of an author whose assessment of Freud's character miscarried because she failed to understand that the evolution of his scientific ideas was a logical outcome of certain historical necessities. To be precise, she imagined that Freud should have asked questions of maximal interest to contemporary psychoanalysts, such as the effects of transactions in the second year of life on the organization of the personality. But answers about such archaic issues are only now becoming available as a result of refine-ments in psychoanalytic technique that permit the management, without untoward consequences, of profound therapeutic regres-sions that involve largely nonverbal transference enactments (see Gedo, 1981, 1984). There was absolutely no way of arriving at valid insights about such matters before 1900, when Freud's therapeutic technique did not as yet make use of free associative material. To the contrary, Freud's genius showed itself in a very large measure in his uncanny ability to pick fruitful problems to investigate, i.e., problems for which heuristically useful answers could be proposed.

Perhaps, after all, I have merely stated the obvious in stressing that our psychological tools must be used with discretion in weav-ing the complex web of explanations necessary in historical studies. Yet I feel that it has not been generally appreciated that the rela-tionship between psychological conclusions and historical insights is fully reciprocal: We are just as likely to misdiagnose Freud's char-acter if we fail to understand the history of his ideas as we are prone to distort history through psychological reductionism (see Gay, 1976).

OEDIPUS REX

I last considered the problem of Freud's character about a decade ago, when I was compiling a collection of essays (Gedo and Pollock, 1976) intended to present a portrait of our great predecessor. That volume was entitled *Freud: The Fusion of Science and Humanism*—a phrase designed to sum up the man's complexity by means of synecdoche; I shall return to that characterization of Freud below. Despite his well-deserved reputation as a peer of Rousseau and Augustine in candid self-exposure, Freud was at the same time an intensely private man, and his family have guarded that privacy with a zeal that borders on secretiveness. Predictably, this policy has led to the very results it was intended to forestall: A spate of recent commentators (e.g., Swales, 1983a) have expressed dissatisfaction with the extent of Freud's public candor.

At any rate, on the basis of information in the public domain, it is scarcely possible to fathom the Freudian depths. Consequently, like many other Freud scholars, I have for some time confined my activities in the biographical realm to matters that do not call for intrusion into his private life (see Gedo, 1983, Chapter 11–13). I would note, however, that Pollock and I cap our 1976 volume of Freudiana with a specially commissioned essay about the difficulties inherent in writing about a genius of Freud's stature. The task was entrusted to Heinz Kohut, whose then recent clinical hypotheses about idealizing transferences (1971) seemed particularly germane to this theme. When Kohut undertook the assignment, the Freud biographies of prominence were the semi-official works of such worshipful Freud intimates as Ernest Jones (1953–1957) and Max Schur (1972). Consequently, Kohut (1976) rightly focused on the distorting influence of psychoanalytic training as such on the work of Freud biographers. He astutely pointed out that the process of steeping themselves in Freud's writings inevitably pulls psychoanalysts into an attitude of placing the "Founding Father" of their discipline in the position of an ideal object. Kohut also noted a tendency on the part of certain apostates to react to the temptation to overidealize Freud with compensatory efforts to debunk him. At the time he wrote his essay, Kohut had no major example of this genre to offer; the cogency of his formulation has been demonstrated only very recently in Masson's (1984) thesis that Freud's scientific views were shaped by their advantages or disadvantages for marketing his clinical services!

Be that as it may, the era of Freud studies undertaken only by psychoanalytic clinicians has come to an end. The author of the paper in which Freud was faulted for overlooking the significance of mother–child transactions (Abraham, 1982) is a young psychologist whose doctoral dissertation was a lengthier biographical study—of Sigmund Freud. Her ill-considered judgment about her subject is not likely to be a reaction against idealizing his person in the manner Kohut attributed to psychoanalysts, for she is not a student of psychoanalysis as such, but a trained psychologist-biographer whose interest in Freud appears to be a secondary result of a passionate commitment to women's issues. *Sic transit gloria patris!*

Although persons trained in disciplines other than psychoanalysis are not likely to have mastered the intellectual history of our disci-

pline—unless they happen to be intellectual historians with a spe-
cialization in psychoanalysis—the entry of a wide spectrum of individuals into the field of Freud studies may well prove to be salutary
for the very reasons that Kohut adduced in his pessimistic assessment of the capacity of analysts to avoid severe distortions in their
characterization of Freud. I do not mean to imply that nonanalysts
will necessarily be free of the need to idealize or debunk Freud; in
point of fact, however, to date most of them do not seem to have
fallen into these particular methodological errors. At the same time,
their work often fails explicitly to address the issue of Freud's personality, however germane questions about his character may be for
specific purposes of study.

Probably the most important effort that illustrates such an approach is Frank Sulloway's (1979) major attempt to demonstrate the
place of Freud's contribution in the biological thought of his time.
Sulloway is a historian of science, and his study is ostensibly confined to intellectual issues for which personality factors should have
little or no bearing. Yet his argument that Freud's development as a
psychological theorist is better understood in the context of Darwinian evoluationary biology than it is on the basis of the need to
order the data he collected in the course of his therapeutic work
(and his self-analysis) depends on an unstated assumption about the
psychology of Sulloway's subject: Whether a scientist's ideas are
more likely to emerge from the matrix of a preexisting theoretical
system, from fantasies stimulated by patterns perceived within his
observational field, or from one of a variety of ways to combine
inductive and deductive modes of inference is very much a matter of
character.

In my judgment, Sulloway's thesis presupposes that Freud was a
man for whom ideas were more important than personal experiences
of other kinds. To examine this view in the detail it deserves would
take me too far afield within the confines of this essay; suffice it to
say that, along with the vast majority of psychoanalytic readers, I
find Sulloway's assumption incredible. Needless to say, Sulloway
was entirely prepared for this reception; indeed, a lengthy chapter of
his book (pp. 445–495) is taken up with a discussion of the "myths"
psychoanalysts have, in his view, constructed about Freud and the
latter's scientific efforts, prominent among which (according to Sulloway) is their consensus that the decisive factor affecting Freud's
ideas was the outcome of his introspective self-inquiry. Here, I have

no wish to assert that Sulloway is mistaken whereas our fraternity has grasped the truth; I only wish to point out that these respective opinions are the all-but-inevitable consequences of commitments to intellectual history on Sulloway's part and to introspection on our own.[1]

The implications of the foregoing example are, I hope, transparent: Not only do biographers form transferences to Freud (see Baron and Pletsch, 1985); many of them choose to study him because he can serve as an externalized alter ego for some aspect of themselves. For Frank Sulloway, he is a fellow Darwinian; for John Gedo, he embodies a fusion of science and humanism. For the elderly Jones, he was the sage Methuselah; to the fortyish Masson, he looks like an ambitious careerist.

THE RIDDLE OF THE SPHINX

For me, the most intriguing, if least believable, Freud portrayal of the recent past is the one Peter Swales (1982a,b,c, 1983a,b,c) has communicated to a select readership in a series of private *feuilletons*. The media have relayed to the wider public one conclusion growing out of his investigations. Based on carefully researched circumstantial evidence, he argues that Freud impregnated his sister-in-law, Minna Bernays, and then arranged an abortion for her. This inference is only one of a number of similarly biographical inferences in which Swales portrays Freud, clearly on the basis of his overall conception of the latter's character, as an embodiment of hidden evil. In comparison, Masson's image of Freud as a "commercial Jew" with dubious ethics is almost endearing.[2]

Although I believe Swales to be grotesquely mistaken in his conception, I should like to note that, contrary to those of Freud's *detractors,* his view pays homage to his subject's greatness—as a Faustian figure. In light of the fact that Swales completely dismisses psychoanalysis, both as a psychology and as a method of treatment, it may be fruitful to ponder why he has chosen to devote a major portion of his own life to Freud studies. I suspect that his reasons for such a choice throw light on Freud's actual stature as one of the truly significant figures of the recent past. It is particularly striking that Freud is still seen as one of the crucial architects of our civilization, almost a century after he began to develop his central ideas.

For psychoanalysts, of course, this very fact gives him the aura of *vir heroicus sublimis;* Swales, in turn, characterizes him as a veritable Prince of Darkness. I suspect that Freud (1917) himself may have had such issues in mind when he bracketed his work with those of Copernicus and Darwin as decisive turning points in Western cosmology.

It is fruitless to engage in arguments about matters of faith and morals, and I do not discuss the fascinating work of Peter Swales in order to refute it. I cite him, instead, because his view exemplifies what I believe to be true of almost every Freud biographer: We all tend to experience our subject as a contemporaneous presence, rather than as a figure from a specific historical period no longer familiar to us. In a recent book, Bruno Bettelheim (1983) called attention to the pitfall of misreading Freud in modern English transʹ lation: His oeuvre is in fact encoded in a German no longer spoken by our contemporaries. Bettelheim's *caveat lector* is well taken, but the issue should not be construed narrowly as a matter of language: Much as we Freudians may dislike it, the West has gradually slipped into a postmodern era that is no longer the age of Freud (cf. Gedo, 1972).

There is some flavor of paradox, in fact, about the contemporary upsurge of interest in Freud's person, for his intellectual heritage finds less and less favor with the public in an age of mass culture (see Gedo, 1983, Epilogue; 1984, Chapter 12). Yet this apparent discrepancy between growing skepticism about a man's contribuʹ tion and interest in his person may well be one specific characʹ teristic of our era—witness the emergence of literary or artistic superstars whose main activities are confined to self-promotion. Hence awesome personalities of past centuries, like Michelangelo, elicit an unceasing stream of biographical attention, although nothʹ ing could be less congenial to the spirit of the late 20th century than Michelangelo's undeviating commitment to the human figure or his fervent religiosity. Pablo Picasso provides a more recent example of a genius who attracts more attention than his work; in contrast, his great peer and contemporary, Henri Matisse, enjoys the benefits of biographical neglect.

I have taken a roundabout way to say that Sigmund Freud, like Picasso and Michelangelo, seems to be one of those historical figures whose life is destined to become exemplary for a significant part of the public. These culture heroes are continually reinvented by new

devotees in the image the latter require; in order to make this process possible, the actual historical context of their activities must be
disavowed. An author like Swales, for example, dazzles his readers
with his detective work as an archivist and collector of testimonies,
but with this mass of material he creates a gestalt that impresses me
as brilliant science fiction—a portrait of Freud as if he were a member
of the contemporary drug scene electing to spend his life under the
yoke of clinical responsibility for the afflicted.[3]

THE LOVE OF JOCASTA

When, on the eve of the Second World War, Freud died, I was
11 years old; just ahead of *dies irae,* my family had left central
Europe. The decade of my adolescence, arguably the most cata-
strophic period in the history of the West, was spent (*fato profugis,*
as Freud would have said) on three other continents. When I began
my psychoanalytic apprenticeship at the age of 26, the discipline
had scarcely absorbed the shock of losing its founder. I believe I was
propelled into the field not only by the usual need to unravel the
tangles of my personal history, otherwise banal enough. Rather, my
interest in Freud's work was stimulated by a wish to sort out the
influence of a succession of civilizations on my inner world. If family
tradition turned me into a *médecin malgré lui,* I have been an ama-
teur historian from inner necessities even more pressing. To my
knowledge, this set of commitments is scarcely to be found anymore
in the psychoanalytic community.

I mention these personal matters only to underscore my own
emotional bias about the problem of Freud's character, not to lay
claim to professional credentials as a historian. For me, he stands for
the world of my grandfather—an exact contemporary who, like
Freud, was educated at the University of Vienna. I cannot assert
that such a perspective is more *cogent* than those of Sulloway, Swales, or Masson; only that it can illuminate certain aspects of Freud's
thought and his behavior that may appear to be based on personal
idiosyncrasies *if* we fail to distinguish the late 19th century from the
late 20th. Even the best educated segments of the American public
have been so caught up in the popular demand for current "rele-

vance" that their knowledge of Freud's early milieu is unlikely to go beyond the information contained in the provocative studies of Carl Schorske (1980) and Peter Gay (1978).

But works of this kind, excellent as they are, do not speak to the cultural context within which an *homme moyen cultivé*, such as the youthful Freud, operates; they are focused—and properly so—on the summits of civilized achievement, like Freud's mature oeuvre. Nor do we possess central European counterparts to the great 19th-century French, Russian, and English novels of manners to help us get our bearings in that archaic world, the *Kaiserliches und Königliches Reich* of Franz Josef. Freud did not emerge from the milieu of *Die Fledermaus* or *Der Rosenkavalier*—but neither are we likely to capture his spirit by falsely assigning him to the ambiance of the eastern European *shtetl*, even if his forebears did migrate to the Hapsburg Empire from the east.

How does the vantage point I espouse alter our perception of Freud's activities? Let us take, as an initial illustration, the current feminist critique of Freud, a good (and relatively muted) example of which is provided by the paper of Abraham with which I began this essay. It requires no expertise about central Europe or the 19th century to recognize that its author commits a solecism in expecting Freud to possess late-20th-century insights about the role of mothers in the emotional development of their children. But the critique of psychoanalysis (i.e., of the product of Freud's intellect) implicit in this and similar feminist statements accuses Freud of a contemptuous bias against women, presumably on the basis of the patriarchal nature of the "Victorian" bourgeoisie.

In my judgment, nothing could be further from the truth: Freud impresses me as a man whose admiration and respect for women was quite out of the ordinary, not only for the Victorian age, but in an absolute sense.[4] The evidence for this conclusion is ubiquitous; hence, I shall confine myself here to citing the fact that, as a result of Freud's attitude, women found a welcome within psychoanalysis on the basis of full equality earlier than in any other profession. I have long assumed that it may have been the unusual qualities of some of the early female recruits to his cause, such as Lou Andreas-Salomé, that helped Freud to do better than his contemporaries in this regard. If we can believe the report of Swales (1983a), however, it would seem that in the late 1890s Freud helped his patient Emma Eckstein to establish a "psychoanalytic" practice—in other words, even before the turn of the century, Freud promoted the talents and career of a woman who did not happen to be a Princess,[5] or the presumed inamorata of Nietzsche and Rilke, or the daughter of a Louis Tiffany or a Sigmund Freud . . .

All of which leads me to the conclusion that Freud's feminist critics confuse the central European bourgeoise of 1900 with her American great-granddaughters of today. They cannot even imagine how devastating are the effects of the actual oppression of women in a backward society. They do not seem to be familiar with the heroines of Chekhov, to cite a parallel from the same era, if not exactly the same milieu or social class. Girls raised in such circumstances are not simply victims (or transvestite rebels, as Isaac Bashevis Singer would impishly have us believe); they typically develop complex disturbances of character, like those of my grandmothers, or the protagonist of the *Seagull!* It is true that Freud believed this fate to be essentially unavoidable and therefore assigned universality to psychological developments that *can* be avoided by the happy few. But is this a valid reason for drawing inferences about *his* character, based on his alleged misogyny?

THE CRIMES OF LAIUS

Not to overburden this essay with examples, I shall take up only one other issue I deem to be incomprehensible without historical perspective: that of Freud's integrity, so insistently challenged by Swales and Masson. In this regard, I cannot here examine the very convoluted particulars of each specific charge leveled against Freud by such accusers—a task that would require a monograph following years of detailed study. I wish to focus, instead, on the very definition of "integrity," a concept I believe to be tightly culture-bound.

I would like to approach this problem by considering one of the matters Swales (1982b, 1983a) has stressed in his evolving indictment of Freud. I refer to the charge to which I have already alluded: that Freud had an affair with his sister-in-law. As I stated earlier, it is difficult for me to grasp why the possibility of such a course of action should be evaluated in moral terms.[6] Such moral judgments were hardly uncommon in the 19th century; Freud's well-known distaste for America was partly based on his opinion that our Puritan heritage would ensure the dominance of moralizing about sex-

uality for a long time to come. In the past generation, the old attitudes have largely disappeared from public view among us, but
they have made a startling reappearance in the writings of Swales.

But Freud's *integrity* in the sexual sphere should be evaluated in
accord with his own moral standards, rather than those of later
observers. In this regard, he is hardly likely to have been greatly
different from his peers: No central European gentleman was expected to be monogamous. I do not think it an exaggeration to
propose that the philandering heroes of Viennese operetta truly
represented a cultural *ideal*. The concept has reached our day in the
form of the celebrated joke about the courtesan and the Hussar:
When, the morning after, she gently reminds him about money, he
responds, his spurs clicking, "But Madam, a Hungarian officer never takes money!"[7]

Although I do not happen to think that Freud had the personal
freedom to console himself with his sister-in-law for the miseries of
his sour marriage, I also doubt that he was *semper fidelis*—only a
plaster saint would have been under the circumstances. The whole
matter is, of course, intimately connected with the oppression of
women and their hostility to males that inevitably followed. The
point was best made by Lampedusa, in his elegy for the *ancien
régime, The Leopard:* When his confessor reproves him for frequent-
ing prostitutes, the Prince angrily rejoins that the sin is on the head
of his wife who, in decades of marriage, had never permitted him to
view her navel! Bruno Bettelheim (personal communication) quotes
one of his uncles, who claimed to have gone to the brothels with
Sigmund Freud. *Honi soit qui mal y pense.*

Masson's charge that Freud changed his scientific views in accord with the desiderata of establishing a lucrative practice would,
if true, cast very serious doubts on Freud's integrity. Masson has put
the accusation badly, for the seduction theory that Freud abandoned would, on purely prudential grounds, have served him much
better than the theory of the Oedipus complex. But we should not
dismiss this challenge simply because it is maladroitly made; for
Freud's covetous attitude toward money was rather unusual in a
central European intellectual, as he himself recognized. The prevalent cultural mores demanded a prudish distaste for gold.

In his elementary instructions to psychoanalysts about setting
conditions for beginning treatment, Freud (1913) advocated maximally rational attitudes about these matters, but he often fell short

of that ideal. Thus in 1918 he took up a collection on behalf of his destitute ex-patient, the Wolf Man, largely because, prior to 1914, he had charged him extraordinary fees. During the postwar inflation, moreover, Freud did not hesitate to confine his practice to patients who could pay him in foreign currency (see Jones, 1953–1957, vol. 3, p. 29). In my judgment, these behaviors on Freud's part betray a conflict of some intensity about the possibility of exploiting (or being exploited) in terms of financial gain. The rules of thumb he recommended to his colleagues to avoid such difficulties with patients are effective; how extraordinary they must have seemed in the Vienna of the early 20th century may be gleaned from the fact that, until World War II, central European professionals often rendered their accounts of a *yearly* basis! *Pecunia olet.*

Freud's difficulties about money should not surprise us, for it is reasonably clear that during his childhood members of his family were engaged in seriously illegal "financial" activities. As Freud (1900, pp. 136–145) reported in *The Interpretation of Dreams*, his uncle "with the yellow beard" was sentenced to prison for such a crime. Maria Török (1979) has shown that this offense involved the passing of counterfeit (Russian) currency. Note the similarity to Freud's screen memory about his Czech nursemaid's petty thefts! Török (personal communication) has unearthed the records of the trial and discovered that the counterfeit rubles were produced in Manchester. She has inferred, quite plausibly, that Freud's half-brothers, who were Manchester residents, must have been implicated in the scheme.

Swales (1983a), who is apparently unaware of the foregoing information, reports that Freud's future wife and her mother came to Vienna from Hamburg in the early 1880s, that is, decades after the imprisonment of Freud's uncle, because his future wife's father, Herr Bernays, was then in prison—on a charge of counterfeiting! It begins to sound as if the secretiveness of the Freuds is designed to hide something truly shameful about Jacob, Sigmund's father.

The manner in which Jacob Freud earned a living in Vienna has been an unsolved mystery. If the criminal activities of other members of the family are any indication, we may soon be provided with an answer. Should Jacob be proven to be a party to the counterfeiting, as I fully expect, Freud's conflict about financial ethics would hardly be surprising. Nor would the patricidal wishes that gained expression in Freud's dreams, even following Jacob's death! Masson, reading the unconscious as if it determined every man's behavior in toto, looks upon Freud as the legendary *Galizianer*—a scoundrel. But it was Freud (1908) himself who first observed that every man unconsciously craves glory, gold, and the love of women. And if one actually wishes to be a mafioso, it is hardly necessary to make a detour through the laboratory of Ernst Brücke and the seminars of Franz Brentano.

I have taken a roundabout way to say that Freud, whose adolescent ideal was Don Quijote (see Gedo and Wolf, 1973) and who took the role of Shakespeare's Brutus in family theatricals at the age of 14 (see Freud, 1900, p. 483), was trying to *repudiate* a heritage of corruption. If occasionally an element of identification with his devalued father broke through, this fact in itself should serve to remind us that Freud achieved his stature in the face of great handicaps. And this is the point that brings me back to the historical dimension of my argument: Masson overlooks the emotional situation of the young genius whose father is a despised Jewish immigrant and probably a chronic scofflaw.

Why did Sigmund Freud become a *German* nationalist at the university? Why did he stress the probable origins of his family in the Rhineland of the Middle Ages? (see Freud, 1925). I believe these attitudes betrayed the insecurity of the second generation in the land of opportunity[8]—the effort to disavow origins perceived as unacceptable in many ways. If Freud's references to Jewishness were nonetheless generally positive, they invariably alluded to the higher values implicit in that culture. As for the stereotypes of Eastern Jewry, let me quote the earliest letters we have on the subject, written when Freud was 16 and 17: "Oh Emil," he wrote his friend Fluss on June 16, 1873, "why are you a prosaic Jew?" A year earlier (September 18, 1872) he had fulminated about a "Madame Jewess and family" whose behavior displeased him (Freud, 1969, p. 42; see also Gedo and Wolf, 1970).

OEDIPUS AT COLONUS

Was Freud the "commercial Jew" of Masson's imagination? Such an identification was probably the grain of sand around which the pearl of his genius formed. As I have discussed elsewhere (1984, Chapter 6), Freud was rendered incapable of dealing with patients who had problems of "integrity," advocating their exile to under-developed regions—a proposal not far removed from early Hitlerian schemes to resettle Jews in Africa. But the cultural issue is even more decisive, for the Freuds did not try to make good in contempo-rary America, where money suffices if one wishes to climb the social ladder. In the semi-feudal Hapsburg Empire, money was neither sufficient nor necessary for the purpose. *Only* aristocratic creden-tials would do, and the aim of every bourgeois was to obtain a patent of nobility. Hugo von Hoffmansthal, whose father had ob-tained the sought-after patent, immortalized these ambitions in the figure of his Sophie, bride of the Cavalier of the Rose.

One could become a baron if one made as much money as the Rothschilds, but scarcely by means of counterfeiting. The best way, of course, was to strive to enter the *noblesse de robe*, people who received their titles for accomplishments in professional spheres. The collapse of the Hapsburg Empire deprived Freud of the pleasure of becoming a *Freiherr*, but his daughter finally achieved equivalent status in the England of Elizabeth II.[9]

It is not in Manchester that Freud is commemorated with a monument, but in the aula of the University of Vienna and in "the place where three roads meet" near his Georgian mansion in Hampstead.

Notes

1. I have encountered an illuminating example of an identical divergence of opinion, one in which the subject of the biography gave unequivocal testimony about his own view in the matter. At a recent colloquium at the San Francisco Psychoanalytic Institute (partly reprinted in *Dialogue*, Fall 1981), some historians of art flatly contradicted Picasso's own statements about the *personal* meaning of his entire oeuvre. These highly intellectualized scholars asserted, with an extraordi-nary degree of certitude, that the artist's remarks were not to be taken at face value; allegedly, they were (deliberately) intended to conceal an elaborate program of (nonpsychological) intellectual messages encoded in Picasso's work. The psycho-analysts present found this thesis as unbelievable as that of Sulloway.

2. For my purposes here, the validity of the "charge" that Freud seduced Minna Bernays is not a matter of importance, for I cannot view the possibility of such an affair as a mark of evil. On the contrary, had Freud been capable of setting up such a *ménage à trois*, my estimation of his human qualities would be raised. It was Carl Jung, the earliest propagator of the sexual fantasy about Freud and Minna, who used this allegation as a rationale for his disillusionment with his mentor (Billinsky,

1969). As I have tried to show elsewhere (1983, Chapter 13), Jung never overcame a certain confusion between his own person and that of Freud; it was he who had more than once insisted on living in a *ménage à trois*. Hence I give *his* testimony little credence in this matter. Alas, I cannot believe that Freud was capable of seducing anyone; his lifelong inhibition vis-à-vis women stood in the way—as Abraham (1982) convincingly argues.

3. I suspect that no person can imagine how burdensome psychoanalytic work as Freud practiced it happens to be unless he or she has performed it on a continuous and full-time basis. If most American psychoanalysts devote less than a third of their professional time to the task, the explanation for this choice must lie, at least in large measure, in the fact that their alternative activities—research, teaching, administration, or even doing other forms of therapy—are experienced as much less difficult.

4. The psychological roots of this propensity are not strictly germane for my thesis, but they are easy to state: I believe they stemmed from Freud's hope to reestablish the qualities of his trusting relationship to his nursemaid before her dismissal for petty theft (see Jones, 1953–1957, Vol. 1, pp. 5–6). Hypotheses about Freud's relations with women which assume that these relations might repeat aspects of the disappointment with his mother overlook the efficient operation of characterological defenses against such potential calamities. Insofar as I can judge, Freud was threatened by setbacks of that kind only once or twice in his lifetime, when he fell into relationships characterized by aspects of an archaic transference.

As I have described elsewhere (1968), this conception best fits Freud's excessively trusting attitude toward Wilhelm Fliess. Masson (1984) has correctly pointed out that, on the occasion of the surgery Fliess performed on Freud's patient "Irma," this unwarranted confidence led Freud to condone an act of malpractice on the part of Fliess. Contrary to Masson, I do not understand this as evildoing; I see it, instead, as a repetition of Freud's childhood involvement with the criminality of his nursemaid. In his overly empathic response to Carl Jung's confession of a sexual involvement with the latter's patient Sabina Spielrein (see McGuire, 1974; Carotenuto, 1982; Gedo, 1983, Chapter 12), Freud may once again have repeated the same pattern. In neither case did the transference, if such it was, involve negative aspects of Freud's infantile relations with women.

5. In addition to Marie Bonaparte, Lou Salomé could also perhaps claim this title: Her husband, "Professor Andreas," is said to have been a member of the famous Georgian family of the Princes Bagration. I am unable to furnish a scholarly reference for this assertion; I found it some years ago in the memoirs of a Hungarian journalist, related to Ferenczi, who claimed she was a friend of the family (Dénes, 1970).

6. As a matter of fact, I have always believed that one of Freud's greatest (and probably most enduring) contributions to our civilization has been his persuasive recategorization of private behaviors, taking them out of the sphere of absolute morality and permitting their assessment in pragmatic terms, in accord with the moral principle of *nihil nocere*.

7. The aspect of the Sabina Spielrein–Carl Jung story that still has the power to shock is Jung's response to the protest of Spielrein's mother about the seduction of

her daughter, who was Jung's patient at the Burghölzli, a public institution (see Carotenuto, 1982, pp. 93–95). Jung apparently replied that the family would have grounds for complaint if he had continued (!) to receive payment for his profes-sional services. And he offered to break off the affair if the family resumed tipping him! By then, Switzerland had clearly suffered a great decline in public morality as a consequence of centuries of democratization.

8. In the 1870s, Germany had a greater claim to this title than any other country, and Freud was an advocate of the *Anschluss* that was to drive him from Austria in 1938!

9. For the most overt expression of these ambitions within the family, see the memoirs of Freud's son Martin (1957).

References ————————————————————

Abraham, R. (1982), Freud's mother conflict and the formulation of the oedipal father. *Psychoanal. Rev.*, 69:441–453.
Baron, S., & Pletsch, C., Eds. (1985), *Introspection in Biography: The Biographer's Quest for Self-Awareness.* Hillsdale, N.J.: Analytic Press.
Bettelheim, B. (1983), *Freud and Man's Soul.* New York: Random House.
Billinsky, J. (1969), Jung and Freud (the end of a romance). *Andover Newton Quarterly*, 10:39–43.
Bonaparte, M., Freud, A., & Kris, E., Eds. (1954), *The Origins of Psycho-Analysis: Letters to Wilhelm Fliess, Drafts and Notes: 1887–1902.* New York: Basic Books.
Breuer, J., & Freud, S. (1893–1895), *Studies on Hysteria. Standard Edition*, 2. London: Hogarth Press, 1955.
Carotenuto, A. (1982), *A Secret Symmetry: Sabina Spielrein between Jung and Freud.* New York: Pantheon.
Dénes, Z. (1970), *Szivárvány.* Budapest: Gondolat.
Freud, M. (1957), *Glory Reflected.* London: Hagus & Roberston.
Freud, S. (1900), *The Interpretation of Dreams. Standard Edition*, 4 & 5. London: Hogarth Press, 1953.
———— (1908), Creative writers and day-dreaming. *Standard Edition*, 9:141–156. London: Hogarth Press, 1959.
———— (1913), On beginning the treatment. *Standard Edition*, 12:121–144, Lon-don: Hogarth Press, 1958.
———— (1917), A difficulty in the path of psycho-analysis. *Standard Edition*, 17:135–144. London: Hogarth Press, 1955.
———— (1925), An autobiographical study. *Standard Edition*, 20:7–70. London: Hogarth Press, 1959.
———— (1931), Female sexuality. *Standard Edition*, 21:223–246. London: Hogarth Press, 1961.
———— (1969), Some early unpublished letters of Freud. *Internat. J. Psycho-Anal.*, 50:419–427.
Gardner, R. (1983), *Self Inquiry.* Boston: Atlantic Monthly Press.

Gay, P. (1976), *Art and Act: On Causes in History—Manet, Gropius, Mondrian.* New York: Harper & Row.

———— (1978), *Freud, Jews, and Other Germans.* New York: Oxford University Press.

Gedo, J. E. (1968), Freud's self-analysis and his scientific ideas. In: *Freud: The Fusion of Science and Humanism,* ed. J. E. Gedo & G. H. Pollock. [*Psychological Issues,* monogr. 34/35.] New York: International Universities Press, 1976, pp. 286–306.

———— (1972), The dream of reason produces monsters. *J. Amer. Psychoanal. Assn.,* 20:199–223.

———— (1981), *Advances in Clinical Psychoanalysis.* New York: International Universities Press.

———— (1983), *Portraits of the Artist: Psychoanalysis of Creativity and Its Vicissitudes.* New York: Guilford.

———— (1984), *Psychoanalysis and Its Discontents.* New York: Guilford.

———— & Pollock, G. H., Eds. (1976), *Freud: The Fusion of Science and Humanism.* [*Psychological Issues,* monogr. 34/35.] New York: International Universities Press.

———— & Wolf, E. (1970), The "Ich" letters. In: *Freud: The Fusion of Science and Humanism,* ed. J. E. Gedo & G. H. Pollock. [*Psychological Issues,* monogr. 34/35.] New York: International Universities Press, 1976, pp. 71–86.

———— & ———— (1973), Freud's *Novelas Ejemplares.* In: *Freud: The Fusion of Science and Humanism,* ed. J. E. Gedo & G. H. Pollock. [*Psychological Issues,* monogr. 34/35.] New York: International Universities Press, 1976, pp. 87–114.

Jones, E. (1953–1957), *The Life and Work of Sigmund Freud,* 3 vols. New York: Basic Books.

Kohut, H. (1971), *The Analysis of the Self.* New York: International Universities Press.

———— (1976), Creativeness, charisma, group psychology: Reflections on the self analysis of Freud. In: *Freud: The Fusion of Science and Humanism,* ed. J. E. Gedo & G. H. Pollock. [*Psychological Issues,* monogr. 34/35.] New York: International Universities Press, pp. 379–425.

Masson, J. (1984), *The Assault on Truth: Freud's Suppression of the Seduction Theory.* New York: Farrar, Straus & Giroux.

McGuire, W., Ed. (1974), *The Freud/Jung Letters,* trans. R. Manheim & R. F. C. Hall. Princeton: Princeton University Press.

Schorske, C. (1980), *Fin-de-Siècle Vienna.* New York: Knopf.

Schur, M. (1972), *Freud: Living and Dying.* New York: International Universities Press.

Sulloway, F. (1979), *Freud: Biologist of the Mind.* New York: Basic Books.

Swales, P. (1982a), Freud, Johann Weier, and the status of seduction: The role of the witch in the conception of fantasy. Privately printed.

———— (1982b), Freud, Minna Bernays, and the conquest of Rome. *New American Review* (spring/summer):1–23.

———— (1982c), Freud, Fliess, and fratricide: The role of Fliess in Freud's conception of paranoia. Privately printed.

———— (1983a), Freud, Martha Bernays, and the language of flowers: Masturbation, cocaine, and the inflation of fantasy. Privately printed.

———— (1983b), Freud, cocaine, and sexual chemistry: The role of cocaine in
Freud's conception of the libido. Privately printed.

———— (1983c), Freud, Krafft-Ebing, and the witches: The role of Krafft-Ebing in
Freud's flight into fantasy. Privately printed.

Török, M. (1979), L'os de la fin. Confrontation, 1:163–186.

Index